The Motif of Stranger in Calvin's
Old Testament Commentaries

Publicaties van het
Instituut voor Reformatieonderzoek

Publications of the
Institute for Reformation Research

Editors
Herman J. Selderhuis
William den Boer

PIRef 3

Instituut voor Reformatieonderzoek
Apeldoorn

The Motif of Stranger in Calvin's Old Testament Commentaries

Proefschrift

ter verkrijging van de graad van doctor
aan de Theologische Universiteit van de
Christelijke Gereformeerde Kerken in
Nederland te Apeldoorn
op gezag van de rector dr. H.J. Selderhuis,
hoogleraar in de kerkhistorische vakken,
volgens het besluit van het college van hoogleraren
in het openbaar te verdedigen
op D.V. vrijdag 29 oktober 2008
des namiddags om 15.00 uur
in de aula van de universiteit,
Wilhelminapark 4 te Apeldoorn

door

Gopalswamy Jacob

geboren 22 juni 1966

Instituut voor Reformatieonderzoek
Apeldoorn 2008

De examencommissie:
Prof. dr. H.J. Selderhuis, promotor
Prof. dr. J.W. Hofmeyr, copromotor
Dr. A.C. Neele, copromotor
Dr. W.A. den Boer
Prof. dr. H.G.L. Peels

© Instituut voor Reformatieonderzoek Apeldoorn 2008
(Theologische Universiteit Apeldoorn)

ISBN 978-90-79771-02-8
NUR 704
Omslagontwerp: Identifine Corporate Design, Apeldoorn
Druk: Drukkerij Verloop, Alblasserdam

Preface

There were two particular circumstances that motivated me to study the concept of stranger in Calvin's Old Testament commentaries. First, during my Master of Theology studies at United Theological College (Bangalore), I was asked to prepare and present a paper on 'The Israelite's Attitude Towards Strangers/Foreigners in Deuteronomy.' Although that study was limited to one of the book of the Torah, my interest in the topic was aroused, and I resolved not only to deepen myself in it, but also to broaden the perspective to other books of the Old Testament. The second motivation came from reading two articles of H.A. Oberman in *The Two Reformations*, namely 'The Recovery of the Historical Calvin' and 'The Cutting Edge: The Reformation of the Refugees'. Oberman points out the significance of Calvin's life as a stranger, serving also a congregation filled with strangers, for his theology and exegesis. These two factors kindled my interest in Calvin's understanding of the concept of stranger in his Old Testament commentaries. My goal was particularly to demonstrate how Calvin's biography played a role in his interpretation of 'stranger' in the Old Testament.

I must say that it has been a rare privilege to write a dissertation under the guidance and supervision of Professor Herman J. Selderhuis. More than that, he has been a model of patience, encouragement and grace throughout my studies. I found him a person of immense stimulus during a time when I faced extremely difficult personal circumstances. His never-give-up attitude really was the drive that enabled me to persevere in the academic journey.

I also wish to thank my co-promoters Prof. dr. J.W. Hofmeyr (University of Pretoria), and Dr. Adriaan C. Neele (Yale University), not only for their insights, but also for their understanding of my situation. Another person who deserves my gratitude is Prof. dr. H.G.L. Peels, who read my work and provided valuable comments.

Thanks are also in order to Dr. William den Boer and Mr. Albert Gootjes for the work they did in proofreading and editing the text. I wish to thank them for the care they took to help me express myself in a foreign language, and in particular for the patience with which they performed their task. I also owe a debt of gratitude to Dr. C.A. de Niet for the initial help he provided with the Latin language.

I wish to express my heartfelt thanks to Mr. Hubrecht Smits as he has been a great source of encouragement during my life and studies in the Netherlands. His family, as well as his staff members, were of no little importance for the completion of this study. Mr. Smits himself was always ready to provide assistance and support when needed.

The support and encouragement I received from the children, in-laws and grandchildren of the family Baan may not go unmentioned. It was in the relationship of love that they extended to me that I found the strength needed to overcome the difficulties that accompany life far away from home. In particular, I would like to recognize the great assistance and comfort I received from Mr. Jan Willem Baan.

I dedicate this work to Mr. and Mrs. Jan Baan. My gratitude goes beyond words; there are simply no words to express it. Their indefatigable inspiration, and their constant support, sustained me throughout these studies. In Mr. and Mrs. Baan, I experienced the grace and marvelous ways of our sovereign God in my own life.

Finally, I thank my wife Jackie, and our children, Gerrit and Calvin. This work would not have been possible without the constant encouragement with which they motivated me. Above all, I thank them for their willingness to allow their husband and father to go overseas in order to pursue further studies.

Soli Deo Gloria

G. Jacob

Contents

1. Introductory Matters

1.1. Purpose

This study intends to investigate John Calvin's (1509–1564) understanding of the Old Testament concept of 'stranger.' This will be done by examining how Calvin translates, exegetically interprets, theologically articulates, and contextually applies this concept.

The present study will also extend its focus to the exegetical principles and trajectories employed by Calvin in his Old Testament commentaries to highlight the historical, social and textual context of the גֵּר.

1.2. Motivation

All societies, both ancient (ancient Mediterranean, the Bedouin, the Egyptian, the Hebraic, the Assyrian, the Babylonian, the Persian, the Roman) and more modern (medieval, Enlightenment and post-Enlightenment, the current world), whether first- or third-world, urban or rural, civilized or uncivilized, literate or illiterate, must deal with the phenomenon of strangers. The reasons that leave people as strangers are common to all these types of societies: war, famine, family and tribal conflicts, blood shedding and so forth. The reasons can be political, social, economic and religious. Throughout all times and places, strangers live and have lived in similar precarious conditions and situations. Some societies include provisions for the treatment of strangers or aliens, while in others this is overlooked. All of this is a motivation to come to a better understanding of the concept of 'stranger' in general.

1.3. Historiography

Broadly speaking, it can be remarked that recent Calvin scholarship has tended to focus on one or another particular aspect of this magisterial Reformer. A general bibliographical survey will show that numerous volumes, books, articles and treatises have recently been published on Calvin's life, his theology, and his church political views. Further, much scholarly work has been done on Calvin's contribution to particular doctrines, such as election and predestination, as well as covenant. However, Calvin's scriptural exegesis has received much less attention, certainly compared to the aforementioned subjects. Studies on Calvin and Reformed theology that predate 1965 were marked by an approach that could be termed thematically dichotomous or dogmatic in nature[1] as they centered on the debates on themes such as that of 'Calvin against the Calvinists,'[2] his relation to humanism and scholasticism, and the question of piety versus dogma.[3] These lines of scholarship[4] have been challenged by the likes of Heiko Oberman[5] and David Steinmetz[6] since the early 1960s,[7] and since then by scholars including Susan Schreiner, Olivier Fatio, Richard A. Muller, Eef Dekker, Anton Vos, Carl Trueman, Martin Klauber and Lyle Bierma.[8]

To be more specific, throughout the last three decades scholarship has seen a shift from a synchronic approach more interested in giving a dogmatic/systematic evaluation of Calvin or his theology, towards a diachronic approach that offers descriptive, contextualized analyses of his theology.[9] In addition, this more recent, historically-oriented approach has tended to give less attention to the exegetical and interpretative aspect of Calvin's thought. Richard A. Muller has offered eleven new methodological presuppositions for Calvin studies, and in the sixth he makes the following suggestion: 'Continuities and discontinuities in the interpretive or exegetical tradition must be given at least equal weight with developments in scholastic method and philo-

---

1   TRUEMAN & CLARK, introduction to *Protestant Scholasticism*, xiii; MULLER, *After Calvin*, 1.
2   HALL, 'Calvin Against the Calvinists.'
3   MULLER, *After Calvin*, 3. Muller provides an extensive evaluation of the preceding thematically dichotomous approach, and explains the need for scholarly reappraisal of studies on Calvin, as well as Reformed theology in general, in the first nineteen pages of this work.
4   TRUEMAN & CLARK, introduction to *Protestant Scholasticism*, xviii.
5   OBERMAN, *The Harvest of Medieval Theology*; OBERMAN, *Forerunners of the Reformation*.
6   STEINMETZ, *Misericordia Dei*; STEINMETZ, *Reformers in the Wings*.
7   TRUEMAN & CLARK, introduction to *Protestant Scholasticism*, xiii.
8   MULLER, *After Calvin*, 64.
9   A thorough survey on the history of scholarship can be found in TRUEMAN & CLARK, *Protestant Scholasticism*; VAN ASSELT & DEKKER, *Reformation and Scholasticism*; GRAHAM, *Later Cavinism*; MULLER, *After Calvin*.

sophical usage.'[10] Muller's use of such phrases as 'at least equal weight,' highlights the fact that for too long scholarship has either overlooked, or not given enough attention to, the interpretive and exegetical aspect of Calvin and his theology. Even the works that did engage Calvin's exegesis have focused either on selected Scripture texts,[11] or on a comparison of Calvin's exegetical principles with those of other reformers.[12]

Some attention has been given to Calvin and the refugee[13], Calvin and the widow, and Calvin and the poor[14], yet these contributions have failed to recognize

---

10 MULLER, *After Calvin*, 71.
11 BLACKETER, 'Smooth Stones, Teachable Hearts: Calvin's Allegorical Interpretation of Deuteronomy 10:1–2,' *Calvin Theological Journal* 34, no. 1 (1999): 36–63; DE BOER, 'Calvin on the Visions of Ezekiel: Studies in His 'Sermons Inédits' With a Critical Edition of the Sermons on Ezekiel 36–48' (Geneva: University of Geneva – Faculté de théologie, 1999); FARMER, 'Changing Images of the Samaritan Woman in Early Reformed Commentaries on John,' *Church History* 65, no. 3 (1996): 365–75; KIM, 'Hermeneutics and the Law. A Study of Calvin's Commentary and Sermons on Psalm 119' (Th.M. thesis, Calvin Theological Seminary, 2000); MPINDI, 'Calvin's Hermeneutics of the Imprecations of the Psalter' (Ph.D. diss., Calvin Theological Seminary, 2004); MULLER, *'Scimus enim quod lex spiritualis est:* Melanchthon and Calvin on the Interpretation of Romans 7:14–23,' in *Philip Melanchthon (1497-1560) and the Commentary,* ed. WENGERT & GRAHAM (Sheffield: Sheffield Academic Press, 1997), 216–37; STEINMETZ, 'Calvin as Interpreter of Genesis,' in: *Calvinus Sincerioris Religionis Vindex: Calvin as Protector of the Purer Religion,* ed. NEUSER & ARMSTRONG, Sixteenth Century Essays & Studies 36 (Kirksville, MO: Sixteenth Century Journal Publishers, 1997), 53–66; THOMPSON, 'The Endangerment of Lot's Daughters in Sixteenth-Century Exegesis,' in *Writing the Wrongs: Women of the Old Testament Among Biblical Commentators from Philo Through the Reformation* 'Oxford: Oxford University Press, 2001), 214–17; THOMPSON, 'Hagar in the Sixteenth Century,' in *Writing the Wrongs: Women of the Old Testament Among Biblical Commentators from Philo Through the Refomation* (Oxford: Oxford University Press , 2001), 69–92; THOMPSON, 'Hagar, Victim or Villain? Three Sixteenth-Century Views,' *Catholic Biblical Quarterly* 59, no. 2 (1997): 213–33; THOMPSON, 'Jephthah's Daughter in the Era of the Reformation,' in: *Writing the Wrongs: Women of the Old Testament Among Biblical Commentators from Philo Through the Reformation* (Oxford: Oxford University Press, 2001), 154–69; THOMPSON, ''So Ridiculous a Sign': Men, Women, and the Lessons of Circumcision in Sixteenth-Century Exegesis,' *Archiv für Reformationgeschichte* 86 (1995): 236–56.
12 DYKSTRA, 'A Comparison of Exegesis: John Calvin and Thomas Aquinas,' *Protestant Reformed Theological Journal* 35, no. 2 (2002): 15–25; 36 no. 1 (2002): 12–23; 36 no. 2 (2003): 10–22; PARSONS, *Luther and Calvin on Old Testament Narratives: Reformation Thought and Narrative Text* (Lewiston: The Edwin Mellen Press, 2004); SCAER, 'Reformed Exegesis and Lutheran Sacraments: Worlds in Conflict,' *Concordia Theological Quarterly* 64, no. 1 (2000): 3–20; STEINMETZ, 'Luther and Calvin on the Banks of the Jabbok,' in: *Luther in Context* (Grand Rapids: Baker, 2002), 156–88.
13 BRACCESI, 'Religious Refugees From Lucca in the Sixteenth Century: Political Strategies and Religious Proselytism,' *Archiv fur Reformationsgeschichte* 88 (1997): 338–79; DOUGLAS, 'Pastor and Teacher of the Refugees,' in *Calvin in the Work of Heiko A. Oberman: Papers From the Symposium on His Seventieth Birthday* (Leiden: Brill, 2003), 51–65; GAMBLE, 'Sacramental Continuity Among Reformed Refugees: Peter Martyr Vermigli and John Calvin,' in *Peter Martyr Vermigli and the European Reformation,* ed. JAMES III (Leiden: Brill, 2004), 97–112; NEUSER, *Calvin and the Refugees* (Kital: Pretoria, 1990), 1–10; MONTER, 'The Refugee Colonies,' in *Calvin's Geneva* (New York: Robert E.

the importance of the concept of 'stranger' as understood by Calvin has for these areas. In short, virtually nothing has been done towards an exegetical study of Calvin's contribution to the Old Testament theme of 'stranger.'[15]

Heiko A. Oberman's articles 'The Cutting Edge: The Reformation of the Refugees,' and 'The Recovery of the Historical Calvin' came close to a treatment of the idea of stranger in Calvin's thought. Oberman's work showed how an understanding of being a stranger or refugee played a role in the formation of Calvin's theology. All of Calvin's major theological and doctrinal themes, including predestination, emerged out of his experience, for Calvin the experience of being a stranger. Oberman notes that the Calvinist doctrine of predestination is the mighty bulwark of the Christian believer against the fear that they will be unable to hold out under the pressure of persecution. The doctrine of election similarly served as Gospel of encouragement to those who suffered persecution. Although a landmark contribution in terms of highlighting a new direction, Oberman – like others – followed a dogmatic approach that was based on major doctrinal themes rather than exegesis.

All of the afore-mentioned scholarship, including Oberman's contribution, overlooked this underlining principle in what Calvin wrote about refugees, the

---

Krieger Publishing Company, 1975), 165–189. The present study will argue that the concept of 'stranger' forms the underlying principle to other concepts such as 'refugee,' 'poor' and 'widow' as understood by Calvin; cf. 3.1.3, 3.1.4 and 3.1.6 below.

14   SCHOLL, 'The Church and the Poor in the Reformed Tradition,' *Ecumenical Review* vol. 32 (1980): 236–56; SMITH, 'Calvinist Orthodoxy: Malthus and the Poor,' *Passive Obedience and Prophetic Protest* (New York: Peter Lang, 1987), 102–120. GAMBLE, *Mercy Ministry in European Cities during the reformation*, Urban Mission Vol. 6, September 1988, 27–31. TAIT, *Calvin's Ministry of Encouragement* Presbyterian: Covenant Seminary Review Vol. 11, 1985. 43–99. SPICER, *Reformations Old and New: Essays on the Socio-Economic Impact of Religious Change c 1470-1630* (Vermont: Scholar Press, 1996) 237–255; WOUDSTRA, 'John Calvin's concern for the Poor', *The Outlook*, vol. 33, Feb 1983, 8–10.

15   DOUGLASS, 'Pastor and Teacher of the Refugees: Calvin in the Work of Heiko A. Oberman', in: *The Work of Heiko A. Oberman* (Leiden: Brill, 2003) 51–65. GAMBLE, 'Mercy Ministries in European Cities during the Reformation' *Urban Mission* vol. 6, September 1988, 27–31. KINGDON, 'Calvinism and Social Welfare', *Calvin Theological Journal,* Vol. 17, 1982, 212–230. NORWOOD, *Refugees, Protestantism, and capitalism. The Reformation refugees as an economic force* (Chicago: American Society of Church History, 1942) 159–174. NORWOOD, 'The strangers' 'model churches' in sixteenth-century England', *Reformation studies: essays in honor of Roland H. Bainton* (Richmond: John Knox Press, 1962) 181–196. OBERMAN, 'Europa afflicta: The Reformation of the Refugees', *Archive for Reformation History*, vol. 83, 1992, 91–111. WOUDSTRA, 'John Calvin's concern for the poor', 8–10. Jeannine Olson and Elsie McKee have dealt with social concerns in Geneva: OLSON, 'Calvin and social welfare: deacons and the Bourse Francaise', (Selinsgrove, Pa.: Susquehanna University Press; London: Associated University Presses, 1988); McKEE, *Diakonia in the classical reformed tradition and today* (Grand Rapids: Eerdmans, 1989); McKEE, *John Calvin on the diaconate and liturgical almsgiving* (Geneve: Droz, 1984).

poor and widows. Therefore, the present study intends to contribute to the missing element: to illustrate Calvin's exegetical understanding of the concept of 'stranger,' and how that functions as the underlying principle to any study of the concepts of refugee, poor and widow.

Herman Selderhuis' article 'Calvin as an Asylum Seeker' deals directly with the notion of 'stranger' in Calvin's Psalms commentary. Pointing to the one-sidedness of previous Calvin scholarship, Selderhuis remarks that theology is not timeless and cannot be done in a historical vacuum. He further affirms that in order to be able to theologize well, the theologian should have a thorough knowledge of the cultural, social, political and religious situation, not only of biblical times, but also his own. This principle, the impact of time on theology, applies to Calvin as well. After positing the need for a historically-oriented theology, Selderhuis immediately illustrates – on the basis of Calvin's own confessions – how Calvin identified himself with David. Although with respect to the concept of 'stranger' Selderhuis' work was pioneering, it was still limited to Calvin's commentary on the Psalms. This gap in scholarship forms the point of departure for the present study, where the entire corpus of Calvin's Old Testament commentaries will be examined to ascertain what Calvin wrote about the stranger-motif.

It is very relevant to ask why scholarship has given little or no attention to Calvin's understanding of the concept of 'stranger.' One of two things must be true: either Calvin did not write anything on 'stranger,' or else all scholarship has overlooked the possibility of this underlying concept in Calvin's as he understood it exegetically and theologically. The first option cannot be true, as Calvin's writings contain significant discussions on the concept of גֵּר.[16] This realization implies that the second option must be valid, namely, that all preceding scholarship has viewed Calvin's study and use of the notion of 'stranger' as less significant. The present study will seek to address this gap in scholarship by looking at Calvin's interpretive and exegetical work on גֵּר.

1.4. Observations

1.4.1. Introduction

As was noted above, as biblical expositor Calvin devoted considerable attention to the concept of stranger in his writings. The Hebrew text (Biblia Hebraica

---

16 A total of 199 references can be found in the *corpus* of Calvin's works. The references in the Old Testament commentaries will be explored in the following chapters, but it should not be forgotten that Calvin also treated the 'stranger'-concept in his *Institutes*, sermons and letters.

Stuttgartensia) uses four terms to denote the very idea of non-belonging: גֵּר (stranger), תּוֹשָׁב (alien), נֵכָר (foreigner) and זָר (proselytes).[17] Calvin organizes these four terms into two major groups in terms of their position, relationship and position of liability over against the native-born.[18] The concept of 'stranger' forms an underlying principle in Calvin's exegetical work. Using the essence of the Old Testament concept of stranger, Calvin incorporates into it various types of lives people live, as well as different tragedies they may experience. This concept of stranger, as drawn from his exegetical works, is the focus of the present study.

1.4.2. Stranger: The Unknown Guest

When outlining the nature of hospitality, Calvin identifies the mysterious אֲנָשִׁים נִצָּבִים (three men) who visited Abraham at Mamre,[19] as well as the unknown שְׁנֵי הַמַּלְאָכִים (two messengers) who came to Lot's house, as guests and strangers.[20] It is further remarkable that in his exegesis, Calvin understands the concept of בְּנֵי־הָאֱלֹהִים ('Sons of god') in terms of 'strangers.'[21] Although the noun גֵּר does not appear in any of these three texts, Calvin's exegetical remarks demonstrate that these 'three unknown persons' in Abraham's tent, and the 'two unknown messengers' at Lot's house are strangers and guests. Similarly, Calvin understands the presence of Jacob and his sons in the house of Pharaoh, as well as the concept of 'sons of god,' in terms of the concept of 'stranger.' Interestingly, Calvin speaks of 'stranger' in the context of Joseph when he hides himself from his brothers.[22] Consequently, for Calvin any unknown person or guest who cannot or will not reciprocate what they receive could be classified as a גֵּר (stranger).

17　It is interesting to note that most current scholarship on the above-mentioned themes in the Old Testament, as well as some modern English Bible translations (e.g. NRSV), in spite of the advancements in Ancient Near Eastern studies and philology, nevertheless group the term 'alien' with other related concepts without drawing distinctions. Cf. VAN HOUTEN, *The Alien in Israelite Law*; KELLERMAN, 'גּוּר' in *TDOT*, 443; PETERSEN, 'Max Weber and the Sociological Study of Ancient Israel,' 117–50; MOORE, *Judaism in the First Centuries of the Christian Era*, 323–39; MEEK, *The Translation of Ger in the Hexateuchm*, 172–80; HORNER, 'Changing Concepts,' 49–53.

18　See ch. 4 below.

19　CALVIN, *Comm. in Gen.* 18,2 (CO 23,250).

20　CALVIN, *Comm. in Gen.* 19,1 (CO 23,267)

21　CALVIN, *Comm. in Gen.* 6,1 (CO 23,111–12).

22　CALVIN, *Comm. in Gen.* 42,23 (CO 23,534–35).

1.4.3. Stranger: The Faithful Servants

In his exegetical treatment of the event, Calvin speaks of Abraham's oldest servant entrusted with the responsibility of finding a wife for Isaac as a stranger. This servant of Abraham also prayed to the God of his master Abraham.[23] Calvin further describes both Jacob and Joseph as strangers when they were servant and slave in the house of Laban[24] and Potiphar[25] respectively. Also the alleged murderer of Saul, who as a military man gives David an account of Saul's death and describes himself as the son of an Amalekite, is referred to as a גר.[26] Thus in his exegesis, Calvin identifies a servant or slave who faithfully executes his responsibilities in an isolated environment or a strange land as a גר.

1.4.4. Stranger: The Refugee

In his exegesis of the account of Jacob and his children in Egypt, Calvin notes three important aspects concerning the condition of Jacob's family: they were guests in the house of Pharaoh; they were refugees who went to Egypt for their survival because of the severe famine; and because they were guests and refugees in a strange land, they were automatically placed in the class of the גר.[27] In his exegetical attempt to unify the concepts of stranger and refugee, Calvin skillfully correlates the story of Jacob and his children in Egypt with Jes 52,2–4.[28] Although the refugee laws in Dt 19,1–13 do not explicitly mention the גר, other texts such as Jos 20,9 and Nu 35,15 emphasize that the six cities chosen are to be regarded as cities for refuge for the גר. The exegetical rationale Calvin provides for the six cities of refuge for the strangers illustrates why the refugees are part of the stranger class.[29]

---

23 Cf. Gn 24,5.
24 CALVIN, *Comm. in Gen.* 29,14 (CO 23,401).
25 CALVIN, *Comm. in Gen.* 39,1 (CO 23,502).
26 Cf. 2 S 1,13.
27 CALVIN, *Comm. in Gen.* 47,5 (CO 23,567–68).
28 'Enlarge the place of your tent, And let them stretch out the curtains of your dwellings; Do not spare; Lengthen your cords, And strengthen your stakes. For you shall expand to the right and to the left, And your descendants will inherit the nations, And make the desolate cities inhabited. ' Do not fear, for you will not be ashamed; Neither be disgraced, for you will not be put to shame; For you will forget the shame of your youth, And will not remember the reproach of your widowhood anymore.'
29 Cf. note 13 above.

1.4.5. Stranger: The Poor

Yet another important observation for Calvin's view of 'strangers' centers on his combined exegetical explanation of Dt 26,12–15 and Dt 14,22.27–29, which speak about the tithe to be given every third year. According to the text, the recipients of the tithe are the לֵוִי (Levite), the גֵּר (stranger), the יָתוֹם (orphan/fatherless), and the אַלְמָנָה (widow). A similar arrangement is found in verses 12 and 13, as well as verse 29, of chapter 14. Calvin in his exegetical exposition on these texts not only lists similar nouns, but also inserts an additional category which the texts do not mention: the אֶבְי (poor). Calvin persistently refers to this category (poor brethren) in his exegesis to indicate that the poor are strangers too.[30] Elsewhere, Calvin even translates the term אֶבְיֹנִי (poor) as 'stranger' (Ex 23,10–11), where the text speaks about sabbathismus.[31] This study will have to consider carefully the differences between the various terms used to translate words related to 'stranger.'[32] A thorough exegetical study will be required to understand why Calvin includes the poor among the גֵּר.

1.4.6. Stranger: The Orphan

While various Bible translations of the Reformation era, including the Geneva Bible of 1599, translate יָתוֹם as 'fatherless,' Calvin consistently renders it as 'orphan' on the basis of his exegetical presuppositions. Why does Calvin translate the term differently from the other translators? On what did he base his rendering of this term? Is Calvin trying to link the physical condition of an orphan with that of stranger? For Calvin, the experience of being a stranger forms an underlying principle for most sufferings and struggles. Although there is no great difference between 'fatherless' and 'orphan' in Hebrew society, it must nevertheless be investigated why Calvin translated differently.

1.4.7. Stranger: The Widow

According to the prescriptions for priests as found in Lv 22,10–13, if the daughter of a priest marries a stranger, she automatically becomes a stranger as well, and is consequently prohibited from eating what is sacrificed (the 'holy things'). If her husband dies, she remains a stranger except if she is a youth, without child, and willing to return to her father's house. On the other hand, if she refuses to return, is older or has a child, she as widow remains in the wider

---

30 CALVIN, *Comm. in Mosis reliq. libr.*, Dt 14,28 (CO 24,482–83).
31 CALVIN, *Comm. in Mosis reliq. libr.*, Ex 23,10–11 (CO 24,585).
32 Cf. note 14 above.

category of 'stranger.' Interestingly, it is only in this context that Calvin translates the noun זר as 'alien.'[33] Furthermore, the text calls both Naomi and her daughter-in-law Ruth 'widows' and 'strangers' in Moab. Though widows as such form a separate category, they time and again come under the broader category of stranger.

1.4.8. The Triad

To build his argument even further, Calvin in his exegesis observes that in numerous places in the Old Testament the noun גר appears alongside יתום (orphan) and אלמנה (widow) to form a triad.[34] In Calvin's exegesis, the words 'oppressed' (חמוץ), 'poor' (עניי) and 'needy' (רלים) always appear as attributive adjectives to qualify this triad. Grammatically, this triad of גר, יתום and אלמנה forms a collective subject that denotes a particular condition, or refers to a particular action or need. For this reason, any study on the notions of 'orphan' and 'widow' in Calvin's Old Testament exegesis must be carried out from the basis of, or alongside of, the wider understanding of the 'stranger.' This leads the present author to conclude that any study on these concepts of 'widow' and 'orphan' in Calvin's thought cannot be carried out without in one way or another touching on the 'stranger.'

On the basis of the preceding survey of Calvin's understanding of גר, it is clear that Calvin unites the groups of unknown guests, refugees, poor, orphans, widows and faithful servants into one broader concept, so producing a complete and comprehensive idea of what a 'stranger' was according to the Old Testament.[35] Thus for Calvin 'all those who are destitute and deprived of earthly succor, are under the guardianship and protection of God, and preserved by His hand'[36] and could be identified as גר. It is more than evident that Calvin in his translation and interpretations on גור and גר crosses philological categories to depict the breadth of meaning contained in the terms גור, זר, תושב, and נכר. That very aspect of being a stranger accounts for the physical, emotional, soci-

---

33 CALVIN, *Comm. in Mosis reliq. libr.* Lv 22,10–13 (CO 24,458).

34 Ex 22,20f.; Dt 10,18; 1429; 16,11.14; 24,17.19.20.21; 26,12.13; 27,19; Ps 94,6; 146,9; Jer 7,6; 22,3; Ez 22,7; 22,29; 47,22ff.; Sach 7,10; Mal 3,5. It is surprising that the גר plays a very subordinate role in prophetic preaching. Amos, Hosea, Isaiah and Micah, although they all speak about the oppression of the weak and poor, did not often refer to the protected citizen (גר).

35 It is interesting to note that the Hebrew terms for terms 'guest', 'servant', 'widow', 'refugee', 'orphan' and 'poor' are not etymologically related to the terms גור ('sojourner'), גר ('stranger'), תושב ('alien'), and נכר ('foreigner'), but that Calvin in light of the textual context and the social condition of the guest, servant, widow, refugee, orphan and poor, understands them, and at times even translates them, as 'stranger.'

36 CALVIN, *Comm. in Mosis reliq. libr.*, Lv 19,33 (CO 24,673).

al and historical conditions of the person or persons involved. His exegesis related to various people of God brings out their precarious conditions: Abraham was a stranger who isolated himself from his earthly family[37]; Lot was a stranger in the midst of an inhospitable nation[38]; Isaac was a stranger due to famine[39]; Jacob was a stranger due to family conflict[40]; Joseph was a stranger due to the betrayal of his own brothers[41]; Moses became a stranger after shedding blood[42]; the prophet Elijah was a stranger because of starvation, as were David,[43] Amos,[44] the Levites in their own land[45] and so forth. Most importantly, the Israelites as nation were גרים in Egypt as slaves, who suffered under and were humiliated by the Egyptians. In all of the above situations, Calvin clearly and exhaustively draws out the domestic, sociological, and political circumstances that caused the persons concerned to be strangers. Calvin in his exegesis further places a lot of emphasis on the reasons for becoming a stranger,[46] as well as on the approach towards a stranger.[47]

1.5. Secondary Obervations

In building up such a comprehensive concept of what constitutes a 'stranger' in the Old Testament, Calvin time and again brings in evidence from the church fathers (Jerome, Ambrose, Augustine, Basil the Great, Gregory I, Origen) as well as various councils, both to support his own arguments and to undermine those of others. For example, Calvin states that election and predestination is the basic criterion for a stranger to become part of the holy gahal. Thomas Aquin-

---

37   CALVIN, *Comm. in Gen.* 12,10; 20,1 (CO 23,183,286).

38   CALVIN, *Comm. in Gen.* 19,9 (CO 23,270–71).

39   CALVIN, *Comm. in Gen.* 26,2.12 (CO 23,358.361–62).

40   CALVIN, *Comm. in Gen.* 32,4; 37,1 (CO 23,437.480).

41   CALVIN, *Comm. in Gen.* 47,3.9 (CO 23,566–67.569–70).

42   CALVIN, *Comm. in Ex.* 2,22 (CO 24,32). Cf. Hbr 11,27.

43   CALVIN, *Comm. in Ps.*16,4 (CO 31,152).

44   CALVIN, *Comm. in Amos* 2,4 (CO 43,19).

45   CALVIN, *Comm. in Mosis reliq. libr.*, Dt 18,6 (CO 24,487).

46   Reasons: (1) The most common reason for being a גר in a strange land is famine and starvation: Elimelech moved to Moab with his family due to famine in order he may be protected citizen (Ru 1,1); Elijah's stay at the house of the widow of Zarephath (1R 17,20); Isaac remains as a גר with Abimelech of Gerar (Gn 26,3) and Jacob sojourned with his children to Egypt due to a severe famine (Gn 47,4), and a similar situation applies to Abraham (Gn 12,3). (2) War: military confrontations played a big role in forcing the people to be גר: Jes 16,4 narrates that the outcasts of Moab seek refuge in Judah or Edom as protected citizens; it is also clear from 2S 4,3 that the original inhabitants of Beeroth had fled to Gittaim in order to live there as גרים; the Rechabites live as גרים in Judah in order to preserve the nomadic ideal (Jer 35,7). (3) Family conflict and bloodshed can cause a person to seek protection among foreigners as גר.

47   This is true not only for the commentaries, but also the sermons and lettres.

as, on the other hand, had argued that fulfillment of the Law (circumcision) was the key for a stranger to be included in the holy gahal. To strengthen his own argument, Calvin appeals to the writings of Augustine and Ambrose.[48] All the same, Calvin and Aquinas agree in what they write about the conditions of the stranger, and about what hospitality towards the stranger meant.

1.5.1. Calvin refers to Tertullian three times to support his argument on the religious obligations of the stranger.[49] Chrysostom is mentioned thirteen times, together with Jerome, Ambrose and Augustine. Twenty-four references to Augustine are found, as Calvin supported his exegesis on 'strangers' largely on his works. When Calvin includes strangers and poor in his list of beneficiaries of the tithe,[50] he takes Basil the Great, Gregory and Gelasius as his authorities. In his polemic against the papacy's inclination to acquire wealth for itself, Calvin once again appeals to Jerome,[51] as well as the decisions of some councils (Council of Aquileia, Council of Orleans, Council of Trullo), to defend his own conviction that the wealth should be distributed among the strangers. It further is not only Calvin who understands the mysterious אֲנָשִׁים נִצָּבִים ('three men') who came to the house of Abraham at Mamre in Genesis 18:2 as 'strangers,'[52] but also Eusebius Pamphilius in the fifth book of his Gospel proofs ('God appeared to Abraham by the Oak of Mamre') calls these three men 'strangers' and 'guests' at the tent of Abraham.[53]

1.5.2. Calvin also refers to Martin Luther and Desiderius Erasmus eleven times each in his exposition of the concept of strangers in the Old Testament.[54] Seven of the references to Luther are positive, while in four cases Calvin differs with Luther. With respect to Erasmus, Calvin is polemical in almost all instances.

1.5.3. For the question of Calvin's sources, there are certain practical limitations that must be taken into consideration. From Calvin's life it is clear that he did not have enough opportunity to reach libraries except during his Basel and Strasbourg periods, nor is there any indication that Calvin possessed many

---

48 CALVIN, *Institutes* III.22.8.
49 CALVIN, *Comm. in Gen.* 14,1–24 (CO 23,196–205); *Comm. in Mosis reliq. libr.* Lv 17,10–14 (CO 24,619–20); *Institutes* IV.2.
50 CALVIN, *Institutes* IV.4.7.
51 CALVIN, *Institutes*, IV.5.
52 CALVIN, *Comm. in Gen.* 18,2 (CO 23,250–51).
53 EUSEBIUS, *Demonstratio Evangelica*, Book V.
54 Eight times in the commentaries: CALVIN, *Comm.* ad locum: Gn 11,10–26 (CO 23,169); 13,14 (CO 23,193); Ex 3,18–22 (CO 24,47–50); Lv 22,17–25 / Dt 17,1 (CO 24,540–42); *Comm. in Jer.*, dedicatio; *Comm. in Dan.*, dedicatio.

books. He was also always pressured by time constraints, and after 1536 he certainly did not have the opportunity to devote himself full-time to scholarship any more.

1.5.4. On the other hand, Calvin knew how to get the maximum use out of minimum of available resources. He also borrowed quotations from others. He knew how to discuss texts without actually consulting them, and could cite extensively from memory.[55] The extent of Calvin's knowledge of his sources cannot therefore be limited to the authors he cites or refers to.

1.5.5. The references Calvin does provide are very helpful in identifying his sources, although these sources must always be treated critically. Calvin cites the Patristics primarily as witnesses to defend a viewpoint, as authorities to which to appeal.[56] The references to the church fathers in the Institutes will help us to identify some of Calvin's possible sources. However the identification is much more difficult when it comes to his medieval sources, as well as his contemporaries, as he did not mention them at all. One possible method would involve identifying parallels in thought and concepts. However, the problem is that once identified, the mere existence of these parallels and similarities does not prove dependence of one upon the other.[57]

1.5.6. Yet another way to determine Calvin's sources is to compare earlier commentaries with Calvin's. However, this would be a near-impossible task considering the great number of commentaries available. Also the results of a topical search for parallels and similarities between Calvin and earlier commentaries would be more luck rather than sound method. When Calvin makes certain references to other works, that reference could be the entry point for a source analysis. However, only a thorough analytical assessment will help one to get closer to Calvin's sources.

1.6. Statement of the Problem

1.6.1. The first problem the present study will deal with is descriptive in nature: what does Calvin say about the concept of 'strangers' in the Old Testament? From what has already been noted, it is clear that Calvin places great value on and devotes much space to the idea of the 'stranger' in his exegesis. Why did he give such an important position to this concept as found in the Old Testament

---

55 LANE, *Calvin Student of Church Fathers*, 6.
56 LANE, *Calvin Student of Church Fathers*, 3.
57 LANE, *Calvin Student of Church Fathers*, 7.

in his exegesis? Who are these strangers? What position did they hold within the community of Israel? How were they (to be) treated by the natives? How did Calvin view all these aspects in his exegesis? How did Calvin, as interpreter of Holy Scripture, translate and interpret the term גר in his exegetical writings? These are some of the questions that will guide our treatment of this first issue. In short, the core of the first issue will be a description of what Calvin says about the 'stranger' in his writings.

1.6.2. The second question to be addressed is analytic in nature: *what hermeneutics underlie Calvin's understanding of the concept of 'stranger'?* To this end, the sources of Calvin, as well as their hermeneutical and exegetical trajectories, will be analyzed for a historically-sensitive, theological understanding of Calvin's treatment of the 'stranger' in the Old Testament. What kind of hermeneutics guided Calvin so as to arrive at a broader and deeper insight on the stranger? In other words, what is the background for his concept? Was Calvin influenced by any of his predecessors, the church fathers, or patristic and medieval commentators? Is any particular scheme of thought involved in his construction of such a perception of the 'stranger'? What sources did Calvin use when commenting on this concept? Did Calvin's personal life experience play any role to deepen his understanding? If so, to what extent did he use these experiences when he wrote about 'strangers'?

1.7. Thesis Statement

Strangers are a phenomenon with which all societies, both ancient and modern, must deal. This is true no less for Calvin's time and the Reformation. As city, Geneva was filled with refugees. Calvin himself was for a short time a refugee. Calvin married a refugee widow. Calvin ministered to a refugee church. The political and social situation of Calvin's time meant that thousands of refugees moved from place to place, from country to country. The question can thus be asked whether the political and social situation of Calvin's time played any role in his understanding of גר and גרים It is hoped that this study will contribute towards a better historical, theological understanding of Calvin's exegesis on the concept of 'stranger' in the Old Testament.

1.8. Source Analysis

The present study is concerned with the lifespan of John Calvin (1509–1564), though it in fact concentrates on the period from 1531 to Calvin's death in 1564.

As to Calvin's sources in relation to the concept of 'stranger,' the present study will focus on a few selected works of Basil the Great (330–379), Ambrose (340–397), Augustine (354–430), and Gregory I (540–604), and from the early church. However, when necessary, also the works Tertullian, Aquinas and others will be treated.

Also selected works from the likes of Desiderius Erasmus (1466–1536), Martin Luther (1483–1546) and some other authors from the early Reformation era will be taken into consideration.

Calvin at times referred directly to these aforementioned works in his exegetical comments on the 'stranger'-concept as found in the Old Testament. He used them either to support his own argument, or else to refute their interpretations. In the context of his study of the 'stranger' in the Old Testament, Calvin referred to the church fathers and Reformers mentioned above more than anyone else. These explicit references have allowed the present researcher to select them for study.

1.9. Scope and Limitation

Although the idea of the 'stranger' is found spread throughout Calvin's *Institutes*, his sermons, letters and treatises, for a study of the present length the scope had to be limited to his Old Testament commentaries. In view of the many editions and translations of these commentaries, the references will be keyed to the appropriate Scripture passage on which Calvin comments.

1.10. Summary

Chapter one states the aim and reason for the present study. This chapter also outlines the problem which this study intends to resolve, as well as the methodological principles.

Chapter two deals with Calvin's exegesis, including the historical implications involved. How was the motif of 'stranger' as found in the Old Testament relevant to the historical developments during Calvin's life? How is Calvin reflecting on his own time?

Chapter three considers the major exegetical principles Calvin employed in his commentaries in order to uncover the meaning central to the stranger-motif in the Old Testament.

Chapter four deals with the exegetical trajectories of Calvin. This chapter gathers the exegetical comments of Calvin on the concept of the stranger in his Old Testament commentaries, and analyses how Calvin placed the theme in its textual, social, and cultural context.

Chapter five treats the exegetical conclusions. Some of the major themes which Calvin emphasized in his commentaries are listed. These include the relationship between stranger and native, the responsibility of the natives towards the strangers, and the regulatory laws concerning strangers in terms of the religious and legal setting.

Chapter six, as a concluding chapter, presents all the findings based upon the analyses of the preceding chapters.

2. Calvin's Old Testament Commentaries and the גר Concept in its Historical Setting

2.1 Introductory Matters

Calvin scholars generally agree that Calvin's commentaries were primarily intended for the benefit of the congregation.[58] It is also generally accepted that the members of his congregation were for the most part 'strangers' who had fled their native countries on account of religious persecution and took up refuge in Geneva. If these two principles hold, one can surmise that Calvin wrote his commentaries to edify and encourage the 'strangers' of his day.

A second remark concerns Calvin's approach to the Old Testament. Calvin was very sensitive to the historical setting of the Old Testament books, and this sensitivity affected his exegetical approach.[59] This same historical interest and sensitivity in connection with the Old Testament had other effects as well. For one, it led Hunnius to call Calvin a Judaizer,[60] but more positively, it set Calvin apart from the commentators of the preceding centuries[61] and even led Philip Schaff to name him the 'founder of modern historical-grammatical exegesis.'[62] Similarly, Joseph Haroutunian identifies Calvin as a 'historicist' because of his great concern for the historical developments in the era related to the Old Testament text, for the situation of the original author, his time, immediate audience, and so forth.[63] This raises the question as to the nature of Calvin's

---

58 HAROUTUNIAN, *Calvin: Commentaries*, 18.
59 PUCKETT, *John Calvin's Exegesis of the Old Testament*, 53.
60 PUCKETT, *John Calvin's Exegesis of the Old Testament*, 53.
61 SCHAFF, 'Calvin as a Commentator,' 466.
62 PUCKETT, *John Calvin's Exegesis of the Old Testament*, 56.
63 HAROUTUNIAN, *Calvin: Commentaries*, 29.

historical sensitivity to his own time. Did he attach a similar importance to the historical developments of his own time, to the immediate audience, and its situation when lecturing on the Old Testament, and working on his commentaries? This question forms the point of departure for the present chapter.

The third introductory remark concerns developments in scholarship concerning Calvin as person, or his humanity. Calvin scholarship has for very long looked at him merely through the lens of his Institutes, and on this basis constructed (or perpetuated) an image of a heartless Calvin, tough as nails. However, the accuracy of such an image has been questioned, and then discarded, by the likes of William Bouwsma[64], Heiko Oberman,[65] David Steinmetz[66] and Herman Selderhuis.[67] This has resulted in a much more balanced approach which, among other things, does more justice to Calvin's own description of himself: 'I

---

64 BOUWSMA, *John Calvin*.

65 In 'The Recovery of the Historical Calvin,' OBERMAN points to Calvin's inner personality and his deeply rooted feeling of being a 'stranger' outside his homeland. As he observes, 'Geneva has never been Calvin's foremost concern.' On being chased out of Geneva in 1538 after serving for two years as lector and as Farel's right hand man, he made up his mind never to return again. However, he changed his mind in 1541, thinking that Geneva was after all more geographically suited to spread the ideas of reform to the people in his beloved homeland. As Oberman also points out, Calvin did not receive Genevan citizenship until five years before his death in 1564. The fact that Geneva never occupied first place in Calvin's thoughts has, according to Oberman, not been given the attention it deserves by his biographers (OBERMAN, *The Two Reformations*, 114). With that, we see more clearly how much it would have meant for Calvin to have assumed the rights, duties and loyalties of citizenship in Geneva so as to make his exile from France official by giving up French citizenship. In 'The Cutting Edge: The Reformation of the Refugees,' OBERMAN also points out that nothing is abstract for Calvin, and all theological ideas are based on historical realities. Oberman agrees with Willem van 't Spijker that the doctrine of predestination is puzzling, and that it was born out of experience, but goes further than him by pointing specifically to Calvin's experience of being a stranger in exile as the basis for his doctrine of predestination.

66 STEINMETZ uses the first chapter of *Calvin in Context* to highlight some of the troubling realities of Calvin's life. Although Calvin had already lost his father earlier, Steinmetz thinks that the real trouble for Calvin, or his life of exile, began with All Saints' Day in 1533. From then on, Calvin continually experienced the painful realities of life: the affair of the Placards in 1534, being chased out of Geneva in 1538, the death of his wife and child, the slander, continuous illnesses, and so on. Steinmetz also confirms that Calvin never really wanted to return to Geneva, and that his heart was always in his homeland.

67 In his article 'Calvin as Asylum Seeker,' SELDERHUIS rejects the scholarship that considers Calvin only through his *Institutes* or through the lens of the Servetus affair. He highlights Calvin's self-consciousness as evident in his commentary on the Psalms, where Calvin identifies himself with David who also confessed that he was a stranger in the midst of his brothers, and children of his mother (cf. Ps 39,13). Selderhuis further also highlights some of the difficulties Calvin experienced: the death of his only child, the death of his wife after eight years of marriage, his continuous illnesses and fatigue, the attempts made on his life, the slander, incessant hard work, political entanglements, and – last but certainly not least – the constant pain of homesickness. This very homesickness made him feel like a stranger throughout his entire life.

have to admit that I am not courageous person by nature; I am shy, scared and weak.'[68] Calvin's own experience of living as a 'stranger' further made him sensitive to the plight of others, and led him to offer assistance to other fleeing refugees so that Geneva even became a center for all kinds of refugees and 'strangers.' The core of this chapter will trace how Calvin addressed, and responded to, these happenings in his exegetical work related to the 'stranger'-concept as found in the Old Testament.

Another salient feature of Calvin's exegetical work with respect to the notion of the 'stranger' comes from the dedication of his commentary on Jeremiah to Prince Frederick III, Elector Palatine. Here Calvin states that his exegetical works are adapted to the historical situation.[69] From Calvin's own words it can thus be proved that his Old Testament commentaries were directed specifically to his congregation. Given that the latter was largely composed of 'strangers,' this observation is of great significance for the present chapter. Calvin himself was a 'stranger' in exile in Geneva, he served a congregation that was full of other 'strangers,' and finally had to deal with and welcome yet another group of 'strangers,' composed of the refugees who passed through Geneva. In short, there was no part in Calvin's life where he would not have been confronted with estrangement, be it his own or else that of others. This chapter thus intends to place Calvin's Old Testament commentaries in their historical setting, so as to consider how Calvin's dual historical sensitivity – i.e. with respect to the biblical text, and to his own time – was of significance for his understanding of the concept of 'stranger.'[70]

T.H.L. Parker and Heiko Oberman have already pointed out that Calvin's own situation as a stranger, his pastoral ministry to strangers, and his involvement in aid for struggling strangers and refugees played a significant role in his life as exegete.[71] The present study therefore intends to determine to what degree Calvin related the historical situation of his own time with the stranger-motif as he encountered it in his exegesis of Old Testament passages. For each commentary below, a paragraph entitled 'Historical Setting' will be provided. The point of these is not to center on the history of Calvin's life during these times as such, but rather to highlight the difficulty of the situations he experienced during the writing of these commentaries, how he responded to these

68   CO 31,19.
69   CALVIN, Praelect. in Jer., dedicatio (CO 20,77).
70   Calvin did not write a commentary on every book of the Old Testament. Information on Calvin's Old Testament commentaries, and their year of publication, can be found in: OBERMAN, The Two Reformations, 121–22; PARKER, 'Calvin the Biblical Expositor,' 183–89; DE GREEF, The Writings of John Calvin, 105–09.'
71   PARKER, 'Calvin in His Age,' 102; OBERMAN, The Two Reformations, 116–18.

difficulties, and finally of what significance this was for his understanding of the stranger-motif.

2.2. Commentaries

2.2.1. Isaiah Commentary (1551)[72]

Historical Setting

The years 1547 to 1555 were among the most painful in Calvin's life. During these years, he and many other stranger-refugees were subjected to a growing hostility from the native Genevans. The resentment that had for some time remained internal eventually gave rise to various outbursts. Thus in January 1546, Claude, the wife of a certain Durbin, dryly remarked that the Frenchmen were already numerous, and questioned their need to flee to Geneva by suggesting that the Gospel was also everywhere in their own country.[73] In November 1546, Pierre Ameaux spoke out violently against Calvin: 'I see that you are French; you other Frenchmen come to make synagogues here after having driven out the honest men who told the truth; but before long you will be sent to make your synagogues elsewhere.'[74] In June 1547, the watchman François Mestrat concluded that the Frenchmen ought simply to be thrown into the Rhone. In 1548, Nicole Bromet would also have had the incoming French refugees destined for the Rhone, although he was willing to offer them the safety of a boat: he wished for nothing more than that the Genevans would 'take a boat and put all the Frenchmen and banished people in it to send them down the Rhone.'[75] That same year, Dame Grante, the mother of Ami Perrin, criticized Calvin and said that 'he came to Geneva to throw us into debates and wars, and that since he has been here there has been neither profit nor peace.'[76] To make things even worse, Calvin's sworn enemies came to power in the city when the Libertines won the elections in Geneva. This group, led once again by Ami Perrin, opposed the presence and new arrival of the huge numbers of foreigners in

---

72 Nicolas Des Gallars attended Calvin's lectures on Isaiah in 1549, took notes, prepared the commentary at home, gave it to Calvin to check, and finally printed it in 1551. Scholars are divided as to the exact date of the publication of this commentary: OBERMAN – 1552; MICKELSE – 1549; STEINMETZ and DE GREEF – 1550. All are agreed, however, that Isaiah was the first Old Testament book on which Calvin published a commentary.

73 CO 21,367.

74 CO 21,390.

75 CO 21,420.

76 CO 21,423.

Geneva, and on top of that, Calvin himself was forced to suffer for his attempts to make the Genevans adhere to a strict Christian lifestyle. Aside from all these political difficulties, Calvin in 1549 experienced the greatest loss of his life when his wife Idelette passed away.[77]

Historical Reflections

Observation 1: In the dedication to his Isaiah commentary addressed to Edward VI, king of England (December 15, 1550),[78] Calvin writes that it is appropriate to dedicate this commentary to a faithful Christian king, since Isaiah himself served as prophet in the royal courts of five of the Judean kings (cf. Jes 1,1). After this introductory remark, Calvin takes on a somewhat prophetic tone when he points to the twofold responsibility the king has: to look after the welfare of the church (as 'nursing-father'), and to provide care for the refugees.[79] It is quite likely that Calvin referred specifically to the refugees to direct the king of England away from the example of Henry II of France, who initiated aggressive persecutions of the faithful believers so that they were forced to flee as refu-

---

77   Calvin's grief can be seen in the letter he wrote to Pierre Viret: 'I have been bereaved of the best companion of my life, of one who, had it been so ordered, would not only have been the willing sharer of my indigence, but even of my death. During her life she was the faithful helper of my ministry. From her I never experienced the slightest hindrance [...] herself.' (CO 10b, 430–31)

78   CO 13,669–74. It was a common practice to mention the merits of the person to whom the work was being dedicated. In his dedication to the King of England, Calvin wrote: 'Though I acknowledge that this Commentary has been faithfully and skillfully compiled from my Lectures, yet, as it was drawn up by another person, I was at first afraid, most illustrious King, that if it should appear in public bearing your name on the Dedication, I might be thought not to have acted properly towards your Majesty. But this doubt was removed chiefly by one consideration, that as a Prophet who was of royal descent, and a most noble ambassador of Christ, the supreme King, is highly appropriate to your rank, so the labor which I had bestowed on the explanation of his Prophecies would be accepted and valued by your Majesty. His experience made him acquainted with five kings exceedingly unlike each other in their dispositions, to whom in uninterrupted succession he officiated as a teacher; and it is unnecessary to inform you.'

79   Calvin reminds of God's call to kings and princes to look after the church. He further refers to Jes 49,23, saying that the kings are the 'nursing-fathers of the church,' and reminds Edward VI of the following duty: 'In another passage Isaiah says, Prepare the way, prepare the way for my people. (Isaiah 62:10). It is well known how hopeless was the return of the captives to their native country. Nor did this event take place at that time; but the Prophet, beholding by the Spirit what posterity some time afterwards would actually enjoy, lest any of the godly should be disheartened by so sad a spectacle, meets them beforehand with the assurance that there would be no kind of obstructions so powerful and formidable that God would not break through them to deliver his Church. Not less do we need at this day to be cheered by consolation (Cf. Calvin's dedication to the first edition of his commentary on Isaiah. The commentary was dedicated to Edward the sixth, King of England).

gees and become strangers in other countries.[80] These circumstances, with which Calvin himself was all too familiar, may well have played a role in adding this request to care for the strangers in the dedication to his Isaiah commentary.

Observation 2: Calvin observes that when the people of Israel were in captivity in Babylon, they had a hope that they would one day be able to return to their country and to rebuild the temple. However, they were also afraid that they would not be able to realize this hope because they were in exile, poor, and few in number.[81] Calvin further considers the prophet's words in Is 60,10 ('the sons of strangers [בְּן־כֵנָר] shall build up thy walls, and their kings shall minister unto thee') to be his words of comfort to the exiles: the sons of strangers and their kings,[82] being under the direction of God, would serve them in rebuilding the temple. Impelled by God, they will supply all that is needed for its construction. Immediately following this exegetical note, Calvin turns his attention to the Papists and Anabaptists of his own day as counter-examples. Why would Calvin refer to the Papists and Anabaptists in the context of a discussion on the 'stranger'? Because the Papists refuse to submit to the yoke and direction of God, and claim that their authority is superior to that of kings.[83] The reference to the Anabaptists can be understood because of their rejection of any earthly kingship and its authority.[84] In any case, it is clear that Calvin sees similarities between the Babylonian captivity of the time of the biblical text, and the papal tyranny experienced in his own day. In both cases, God's people are in a place

---

80 In 1547, Henry II who succeeded Francis I as king of France established the *chambre ardente* to persecute all those who were not loyal to the Pope. Consequently, many French Reformed believers fled to Geneva as refugees, including Laurent de Normandie (August 1548), Theodore Beza (May 1549), Guillaume Bude's widow (June 1549) and Robert Estienne (1550). Cf. DE GREEF, *The Writings of John Calvin*, 66.

81 CALVIN, *Comm. in Isa.* 60:10 (CO 37,361).

82 Here Calvin refers to Cyrus as a 'stranger,' and a king who would come to the aid of the Israelites since he is under the direction of the Lord.

83 CALVIN, *Comm. in Isa.* 60,10 (CO 37,361): 'With aggravated wickedness, do the Papists pervert and corrupt this passage, by torturing it to uphold the tyranny of the Pope, whom they wish to possess supreme power over kings and princes. They speak impudent falsehood when they say that he is Christ's deputy; for Christ's "kingdom" is not of this world. The Pope rules barbarously and tyrannically, and claims the power of changing and disposing of kingdoms. But kings submit to Christ in such a manner that they do not cease to be kings, but exercise all their power for preserving the worship of God and administering righteous government.'

84 CALVIN, *Comm. in Isa.* 60,10 (CO 37,362): 'Hence, we see how much those persons are opposed to the kingdom of Christ who wish to snatch authority and power from kings, that they themselves may possess it. Hence also the Anabaptists may be refuted, who overturn political order so far as to imagine that kings cannot be Christians in any other way than by renouncing their own authority, since even in the royal rank God shows that he wishes to hold the highest place.'

where they are repressed, and from which they need to flee. And according to Calvin, those who decide to become strangers by fleeing elsewhere to seek out true worship of God are under his grace and direction.

2.2.2. Genesis Commentary (1554)

Historical Setting

Calvin lectured on Genesis in 1550, and published the commentary in 1554.[85] The historical setting for this commentary is thus situated between the years 1550 and 1554. In January 1550, Henry II, who succeeded Françis 1 as King of France, established the *chambre ardente* which led many prominent reform-minded believers to flee from France, and mostly to Geneva.[86] The Edict of Chateaubriant (1551) further deprived the Reformed who still remained in France of many privileges and opportunities.[87] Closer to home, there were other additional circumstances which affected Calvin. In 1552, his fervent opponent Ami Perrin was elected first syndic, and from this position he did his best to make life difficult for Calvin. By July 24, 1553, the situation had become so intolerable for Calvin that he submitted his resignation on that day. This request was refused, but life did not become any easier for Calvin. In fact, on September 3 of the same year, Calvin thought that Sunday could very well be his last time preaching in Geneva, and that he would to go into exile yet one more time. Again, this did not actually come to pass, but Calvin's words still attest to the immense pressure he was under as 'stranger' in Geneva. During this time, the conflict between the foreigners and the so-called 'Children of Geneva' had escalated such that the Perrinist (or 'Libertine') camp publicly humiliated the foreigners, slandered them, and at times even resorted to physical violence. These experiences with the natives may well have had a significant role in Calvin's exegesis on Gn 18 and 19 that speak about hospitality to the 'strangers.'

The fragility of Calvin's status as 'stranger' in Geneva is also evident in that the natives appear to have blamed him for virtually everything that went

---

85 In a letter to Guillaume Farel, Calvin states that the backlog at the printing press prevented him from publishing this commentary earlier (CO 13,623–55). Calvin dedicated this commentary to the three sons of Johann Friedrich, elector of Saxony, and the purpose of this dedication was to emphasize the unity of the church over against the Roman Catholics. On the advice of the Lutherans, however, the dedication was refused. Cf. LUPTON, 'Calvin's commentary on Genesis', 107–17.

86 CO 12,651.

87 CO 14,186–88.

wrong in their city. When the plague hit Geneva, a Dominican came from the Savoy to announce that the plague was the result of the devil's reign in Geneva. And that this devil was Calvin. The Libertines spread the rumor throughout the Swiss cantons, as well as neighboring France, that Calvin was dead. François Perrin spread gossip about Calvin's wife, Idelette, by which Calvin was traumatized. When Perrin was released from prison in 1547, he was given a hero's welcome that developed into a street-riot, in which Calvin, who happened to pass by, was beaten, kicked and pummeled before being rescued by friends.[88] After registering a complaint about these events before the Genevan council, he wrote to Viret: 'I am returning from the Senate, I said a great deal, but I might just as well have been talking to the deaf [...] I can not tolerate the manners of his people.'

On May 21, 1548, Calvin was accused of publicly degrading the Genevan magistrates and citizens.[89] In the council meeting at which Calvin was subsequently forced to appear, he was reprimanded 'to do his duty better another time.'[90] To add fuel to the fire, one of Calvin's letters in which he had spoken disparagingly of the Genevans had been made public several weeks earlier.[91] Calvin referred to these same internal struggles in his On Scandals, where he wrote: 'those who make war on us every day because they are angry that someone takes away their liberty to live according to their own will.' He added: 'these people are fornicators, debauched and dissolute' and are paid by the Pope.[92] The Perrins,[93] Favres,[94] Septs[95] and Bertheliers,[96] all families that originated from Geneva and enjoyed the highest reputation among its native inhabitants, united to form the core of the anti-foreigner party. They rather provocatively

---

88 BARTON, *Calvin and the Duchess*, 54.
89 Calvin was accused of making the statement that the 'magistrates permitted many insolences', and it was also falsely charged that Calvin exclaimed from the pulpit that the 'Children of Geneva wanted directly to cast down the Gospel and drive out the ministers.'
90 COTTRET, *Calvin*, 189.
91 COTTRET, *Calvin*, 197.
92 CALVIN, *Des scandales*, 193–94, as quoted in COTTRET, *Calvin*, 189.
93 Ami Perrin was condemned by Calvin for his luxurious lifestyle. He was elected as syndic between 1547 and 1555, and time and again wrote to the council to prevent the refugees from coming in, and even recommended that the foreigners be sent out of the city. He was the leader of a group that opposed not only Calvin, but also all the French ministers and refugees.
94 Françoise Favre, Perrin's mother-in-law, was condemned by Calvin for her repeated participation in social dances. She refused to appear before the consistory since it consisted of Frenchmen rather than native Genevans.
95 Septs led an adulterous life for which Calvin reproached him. Septs also wanted nothing to do with the ministers since they were French, while he himself was a vigorous opponent of France (cf. BARTON, *Calvin and the Duchess*, 53).
96 Philibert Berthelier was from among the Genevan nobility. Calvin refused him the Lord's Supper because of his immoral life, for which Berthelier in turn set himself against Calvin.

called themselves 'the children of Geneva.'[97] This struggle between natives and strangers would continue unabated until 1555, when the Libertines finally lost the elections.

In spite of the many internal struggles Calvin faced within Geneva itself, he did not hesitate to become involved for the plight of the Protestants persecuted throughout Europe. Calvin's letter to his close friend Viret (January 15, 1550) testifies clearly to his heartfelt concern for the refugees who were forced to flee after the establishment of the *chambre ardente*.[98] This *chambre ardente* caused many prominent personalities to flee France and to take refuge in various places, particularly Geneva.

Calvin notes that the proclamation of the Edict of Chateaubriant is malevolent against the believers,[99] and expresses his indignation on two accounts: first, that the edict is vindictive, and second, that it takes away from them the right of appeal to the highest court. The latter meant that any ordinary judge could reprimand them without any possibility of appeal. When Calvin learned of the situation of his fleeing brothers, he wrote to Bullinger (September 2, 1551) that the rights of appeal extended even to 'the prisoners, counterfeiters and highwaymen have been denied for the believers.' His motive for relating these things was the hope that Bullinger would be able to do something, also for the refugees who were now fleeing France. When Bern rejected Calvin's request for support, he again wrote to Bullinger, this time lamenting that 'while swords are being sharpened to murder us, we as brothers neglect to consult with each other.'[100] Yet Calvin would not let himself be impeded by Bern's cold response. When in 1552, the protestant Prince Maurice of Saxony formed an alliance with King Henry II of France against Emperor Charles V, the Germans in France benefited from this alliance. Calvin viewed this circumstance as an opening to help the reform-minded believers in France, and requested from the Genevan city council that he be allowed to make a journey to Germany in

---

97   There were three, clearly distinct groups of residents in Geneva during Calvin's time: citizens (required both birth in Geneva and baptism; the government offices were limited to this group), bourgeois (granted to certain strangers or newcomers on the fulfillment of certain conditions; Calvin received this status only a few years before his death), and foreigners (sons of foreigners who lived in Geneva) (COTTRET, *Calvin*, 162).

98   CO 12,651. Many prominent people like Laurent de Normandie (1548), Theodore Beza together with seven other Frenchmen (1549), the widow of Guillaume Bude (1549), the printer Robert Estienne (1550), Charles de Jonvillars, Laurent de Normandie, the Colladons, William Rabat, Galeazzo Caraciolo, the sons of Juan de Valdes, and other refugees fled to Geneva where they all became ardent supporters of Calvin (cf. COTTRET, *Calvin*, 57).

99   CO 17, 504, 'Whereby it is mandatory for every one to attend the mass failing, they were viciously killed, when they flee all the roads are blocked whereby they may not flee, and the properties of fugitives were confiscated by the king.'

100 CO 14,186–88.

order to plead the cause of the believers still under the Edict of Chateaubriant. On their way to Zurich, Calvin and Farel stopped at Bern to make one more petition for support. Here he was advised not to continue to Zurich since the time for such a request to the German prince was not yet ripe. Calvin reports on all these events in his letter to Bullinger from March 13, 1552. Although Calvin did not succeed in the original purpose of his journey, it was nevertheless not in vain. During his travels he met Caelso Martinengo, an Italian who had fled Brescia for religious reasons, and brought him to Geneva. This Martinengo would later become pastor to the Italian refugee-congregation in this city.

In 1553, Calvin also wrote letters to continue to encourage the five students who had been arrested and condemned to death in Lyon soon after their studies. He wrote:

> you know how the Scripture warns us to give us courage as we fight for the cause of the Son of God. Meditate on what you have seen and heard formerly, so that you may put it into practice. Everything that I can ever tell you will not help unless it is drawn from this well.[101]

Calvin also sent out Nicolas Colladon and Laurent de Normandie to various cities of the Swiss confederation in order to drum up support for these persecuted students. These efforts were in vain, however, as they were eventually burned at the stake.

While Calvin was occupied on many fronts with the plight of the Protestants outside of Geneva, he did not escape pressure from within the city. As Barton notes, when the Libertines' attacks on Calvin through John Trolliet failed,[102] they in 1553 somewhat changed their tactics and focused on stirring up nationalistic sentiments against all foreigners who were coming to Geneva, but in particular against the French. Bouwsma, too, points out that the foreigners were abused, robbed in the streets, pushed into the gutters, and all that while their appeals for justice were ignored.[103] Rumors were also spread against the ministers of French origin that they were actually involved in a conspiracy with the king of France. Any possibility to control the situation appeared to be lost as violence against the foreigners became rampant, and even the summons

---

101 CO 14,331–34.491–92.561–64.

102 John Trolliet was a monk from Burgundy who came to Geneva seeking an opportunity to preach. The council sent him to be examined by Calvin, who did not approve him for the ministry, but the council, largely composed of Libertines, appointed him as pastor anyway. Trolliet began to question Calvin's Institutes, stating like Bolsec that the Institutes make God the author of sin. Calvin wrote to Farel and Viret to ask for their support in the public debate on the issue. In the end, the council made a decision in favor of Calvin, and banned anyone who raised a voice against the Institutes. This incident led the Libertines to seek other ways to attack Calvin. Cf. BARTON, Calvin and the Duchess, 60.

103 BOUWSMA, John Calvin, 25–27.

to appear before the consistory were ignored by the 'Children of Geneva'. Even the city council could not curb the mounting lawlessness, and was not able to enforce its numerous edicts. Calvin felt he could no longer cope with the situation in these tense times, and so he wrote to Farel and Viret to come to Geneva to help him.[104] At the same time, Calvin attacked the Genevans with cold and harsh words.

Yet another shock in 1553 was Perrin's election as syndic, which resulted in all kinds of new difficulties for Calvin and his fellow 'strangers' who had taken refuge in Geneva. The pastors – who were 'strangers'! – were excluded from the General Council, and refugees who had not yet acquired the rights of citizenship were forbidden to walk outside bearing arms, as had always been the custom. In a letter to Bullinger, Calvin complained that he was encountered ill-will and opposition on every side: 'They suspect everything we say, if I simply said it was daytime at high noon, they would begin to doubt it.'[105] One of the reasons for the great tension between Calvin and the native inhabitants was that the latter were tired of the admonitions of the consistory.[106]

More Protestants fled to different countries as refugees upon the accession of Mary Tudor in England, also in 1553. When Calvin heard of the plight of John à Lasco and his English congregation, he wrote to the Swiss authorities to ask them to receive them with good care.[107] Throughout this time, the flow of foreigners into Geneva as refugees continued unabated.

In the city of Geneva itself, Calvin continued to do his best for the incoming 'strangers.' Calvin convinced the Seigneury to provide land for four hundred immigrant families, which was yet another mark against him in the view of the Libertines and nationalists. Monter and Bernard note statistically that, with the influx of refugees, the population of Geneva reached 13,000 in 1550, and climbed as high as 21,400 by 1560.[108] This increase coincided with, and was largely caused by, the massive exodus from France, England, Italy and Spain by those who were fleeing religious persecution. In Geneva, the massive influx resulted

---

104 Unlike Bouwsma and Barton who stress how difficult this time was for Calvin, Cottret suggests that he in fact found a refuge and asylum in Geneva's insularity (COTTRET, *Calvin*, 157).

105 CO 14,611.

106 The major reason for such an action to be taken on the part of the council was the dispute with Berthelier, who came from one of the most influential Genevan families. He was refused the Lord's Supper by the consistory because of his lifestyle, and Calvin was very firm that the bread and wine would not touch the impious man's lips.

107 Cf. BARTON, *Calvin and the Duchess*, 67–68: 'The congregation of John Laski sailed from London, but their ship was storm swept to Denmark, where Christian III's Lutheran Councilors prevailed upon him to forbid them sanctuary. Re-embarking in the teeth of another storm, they were repulsed at Hamburg and Rotterdam. They were welcomed by the Swiss whereby they joined the Italian and French refugees.'

108 MONTER, *Calvin's Geneva*, 166–74; COTTRET, *Calvin*, 169.

in a kind of xenophobia from which not even Calvin was spared, in spite of everything he did for the city.[109] Eventually, however, the tide turned as more and more of the foreigners obtained the status of 'bourgeois,' and this was finally also reflected in the outcome of the elections of February 1555. However, as Monter remarks, until then there was continual resistance against the granting of Genevan citizenship to the many foreigners.[110] Throughout this time, as the writings from Calvin and Perrin for and against the acceptance of foreigners into the city show, Calvin did his utmost to make room for the 'stranger' who, like himself, sought refuge in the city of Geneva.

Historical Reflections

Observation 3: Calvin's exegesis of Gn 13,6, where the concept of the 'stranger' appears, shows Calvin relating the situation of the biblical text with that of his own time. Calvin notes that Abram was a stranger on account of his condition, that he was hated by all, exposed to contempt and reproach, wandered without having a fixed abode, was driven here and there, suffered nakedness and poverty, and never enjoyed any repose. Yet he adds that, in spite of all these sufferings, Abram continued to hold firmly to the promises given to him by God. According to Calvin, Abram's life swung like a pendulum between the promises of God and the actual situation of his life. From there, Calvin makes a direct connection to his own time. The many refugees and strangers, he writes, should like Abram hold to the inheritance that has been promised to them.

Observation 4: In his exegesis of the narrative of the two strangers who came to visit Lot in Sodom, Calvin departs not only from the opinions of some of the earlier commentators, but also discards the LXX translation of the term ידע ('to know') in Gn 19,5. The LXX translates Ινα συγγενώμεθα αὐτοῖς ('so that we may have relations with them'), and other interpreters likewise understand ידע in a sexual sense. Calvin, however, argues that if this were indeed the correct translation, Lot – who already lived in Sodom as stranger for some time – could have known this fact and urged his guests to leave the city as soon as possible. Yet Lot in fact asked the strangers to stay longer in the city, and to spend the night in his house. On this basis Calvin argues that the verb ידע instead denotes the attitude of the men of Sodom towards strangers in general,

---

109 Note that Cottret has argued, against Bouwsma and Barton, that the xenophobia should not be exaggerated, as the huge number of refugees who came to Geneva proves that the city was still considered a home for strangers (COTTRET, *Calvin*).

110 MONTER, *Calvin's Geneva*, 169.

and that their question to Lot illustrates that attitude very clearly.[111] According to Calvin, the people of Sodom had a strong tendency to abuse all strangers.[112] This inhospitable attitude for Calvin also forms the reason for the destruction of the city. How bad things were is evident in that Lot comes under suspicion just for receiving strangers into his house.[113] The arrogance and haughtiness of the inhabitants of Sodom are clear from the fact that they shouted at Lot to 'stand back' (גֶּשׁ־הָלְאָה). According to Calvin, the people of Sodom violated Lot on three counts: first, simply in the fact that they were natives, and Lot a stranger, second, in that they did not give strangers any rights; and finally, in that they came out against Lot and his small family in large numbers. At this point, Calvin draws a direct comparison between the inhospitable pride of the Sodomites and that of the papists of his days.[114] Calvin calls those who do not extend hospitality to strangers 'wild beasts.'[115] It is the responsibility of every child of God to extend hospitality to strangers, even when it could be at the risk of one's life.[116] Calvin remarks that this quality was shown by Abraham when he welcomed the three unknown men,[117] by Abimelech who extended hospitality to Isaac,[118] and by Pharaoh in the way he received Jacob on his arrival in Egypt.[119] Why did Calvin place so much emphasis on showing hospitality to strangers?[120] Here the historical context of his lectures on Genesis (ca. 1550)

---

111 CALVIN, *Comm. in Gen.* 19,5 (CO 23,268): 'as if the men had said, "We wish to know whom thou bringest, as guests, into our city."'

112 CALVIN, *Comm. in Gen.* 19,5 (CO 23,268): 'They here imperiously expostulate with the holy man, for having dared to receive unknown persons into his house. Here, however, a question arises; for if the men of Sodom were in the habit of vexing strangers, of all kinds, in this manner, how shall we suppose they had acted towards others?'

113 CALVIN, *Comm. in Gen.* 19,4 (CO 23,268): 'as if Lot had been guilty of a fault in admitting unknown men into the city, wherein he himself was a stranger, they command these men to be brought out before them.'

114 CALVIN, *Comm. in Gen.* 19,9 (CO 23,270–71): 'Such is, at the present time, the boasting of the Papists against the pious ministers of God's word: they allege against us, as a disgrace, the paucity of our numbers, in contrast with their own great multitude. Then they pride themselves upon their long succession, and contend that it is intolerable for them to be reproved by *new* men. But contumaciously the wicked may strive, rather than submit to reason, let us know that they are exalted only to their own ruin.'

115 CALVIN, *Comm. in Gen.* 19,8 (CO 23,270).

116 CALVIN, *Comm. in Gen.* 19,6 (CO 23,269): 'It appears from the fact that Lot went out and exposed himself to danger, how faithfully he observed the sacred right of hospitality. It was truly a rare virtue, that he preferred the safety and honor of the guests whom he had once undertaken to protect, to his own life: yet this degree of magnanimity is required from the children of God, that where duty and fidelity are concerned, they should not spare themselves.'

117 CALVIN, *Comm. in Gen.* 18,2 (CO 23,250).

118 CALVIN, *Comm. in Gen.* 26,10 (CO 23,360–61).

119 CALVIN, *Comm. in Gen.* 47,7 (CO 23,568–69).

120 CALVIN, *Comm. in Gen.* 18,2 (CO 23,250–51): 'And certainly, the sense of nature itself dictates, that the strangers are to be especially assisted; unless blind self love rather impels us to mercenary

needs to be remembered, where large numbers of refugees were coming to Geneva from France. This was around the same time when Calvin's bitter opponent, Ami Perrin, who would later be elected as syndic, vehemently raised his voice against the incoming refugees.[121] His followers, the Perrinists assaulted, bullied and slandered the foreigners in the city. Calvin will most likely have had these situations in the forefront of his mind as he worked on his commentary on this episode in Genesis.

What is striking about Calvin's treatment of the Lot-episode is his departure from his regular exegetical approach. In general, Calvin would proceed verse-by-verse by giving a brief explanation on each. However, in this context, Calvin departs from his custom (and perhaps even his exegetical principles!) by making a lengthy excursus on the notion of hospitality to strangers and foreigners. In the *Calvini opera*, the explanation even covers seven entire pages! In addition, similar instances are found in Calvin's exegesis of Gn 26 (Abimelech and Isaac) and 47 (Pharaoh and Jacob).

Observation 5: In his treatment of Gn 21, Calvin identifies Ishmael's condition as that of a 'stranger.' He further notes that, although Ishmael was a wild man in the desert, he subjected himself to his mother's wish by marrying a girl she chose for him. At this point Calvin draws a direct line to the situation of his own day. For he points to the Pope and says that the latter is a prodigious monster, who not only overthrows the sacred rights of nature, but also refuses to listen to the preaching of a stranger or to subject himself to the yoke of the Lord.[122]

Observation 6: When Calvin narrates Isaac's blessing of Jacob as the older son (Gn 28), he asserts that Jacob would have to be a perpetual wanderer in order to inherit the blessings of his father.[123] For, immediately after blessing him, Isaac sends Jacob into the *terram peregrinationum*. There was a difference here with the Lord's command to Abram, however, in that Abram did not know where he was going, while Jacob had a definite destination for his exile.[124] It is

---

services. For none are more deserving of compassion and help than those whom we see deprived of friends, and of domestic comforts. And therefore the right of hospitality has been held most sacred among all people, and no disgrace was ever more detestable than to be called inhospitable. For it is a brutal cruelty, proudly to despise those who, being destitute of ordinary, have recourse to our assistance.'

121 In 1555, Perrin submitted an appeal to the city council to stop the refugees from entering Geneva, but this appeal was rejected. Perrin was elected as syndic until 1555.

122 CALVIN, *Comm. in Gen.* 21,20 (CO 23,306).

123 CALVIN, *Comm. in Gen.* 28,3–5 (CO 23,388).

124 CALVIN, *Comm. in Gen.* 28,3–5 (CO 23,387–88).

interesting to note that Calvin argues it was not Jacob, but Esau, who was the hypocrite. Calvin explains that Isaac was not pleased with the first two marriages of his son Esau, and that Esau hypocritically tried to please his parents by marrying a girl from the line of Ishmael, although his descendants had departed from the true worship of God. Once again, Calvin draws a comparison between the situation of the text and that of his own time, this time by linking Esau's attitude with that of the papacy:

> A remarkable proof of this is discernible at the present day, in the pretended and perfidious intermeddlers, who imagine they can admirably adjust religious differences by simply adorning their too gross corruptions with attractive colors. The actual state of things compels them to confess that the vile errors and abuses of Popery have so far prevailed as to render a Reformation absolutely necessary: but they are unwilling that the filth of this Camarine marsh be stirred; they only desire to conceal its impurities, and even that they do by compulsion.[125]

This leads to the question as to why Calvin may have compared Esau's hypocritical attempt to satisfy his father to obtain a blessing with the papal corruption he saw in his own time. Here it is pertinent to observe that the Roman Catholic church organized the Council of Trent (1545–1563) in order to tweak certain doctrinal aspects or formulations so as to appease the Protestants, and that the publication of the Genesis commentary fell well within the time of the Council.[126] Further, it is very clear that Calvin used this biblical narrative to encourage those believers who were forced into exile as strangers for religious reasons.[127] For Calvin, being a stranger is the first step towards inheriting God's protection and blessings.[128]

---

125 CALVIN, *Comm. in Gen.* 28,6 (CO 23,389).
126 CALVIN, *Comm. in Gen.* 29,4 (CO 24,109–10): 'The actual state of things compels them to confess that the vile errors and abuses of Popery have so far prevailed as to render a Reformation absolutely necessary: but they are unwilling that the filth of this Camarine marsh be stirred; they only desire to conceal its impurities, and even that they do by compulsion. For they had previously called their abominations the sacred worship of God; but since these are now dragged to light by the word of God, they therefore descend to novel artifices. They flatter themselves, however; in vain, seeing they are here condemned by Moses, in the person of Esau. Away, then, with their impure pretended reformation, which has nothing simple nor sincere.'
127 CALVIN, *Comm. in Gen.* 28,10 (CO 23,389–90): 'Meanwhile, let the reader diligently observe, that while he who was blessed by God is cast into exile; occasion of glorying was given to the reprobate Esau, who was left in the possession of everything, so that he might securely reign without a rival. Let us not, then, be disturbed, if at any time the wicked sound their triumphs, as having gained their wishes, while we are oppressed.'
128 CALVIN, *Comm. in Gen.* 15,12 (CO 23,217): 'And three things are, step by step, brought before them; first, that the sons of Abram must wander four hundred years, before they should attain the promised inheritance; secondly, that they should be slaves; thirdly that they were to be inhumanly and tyrannically treated. Wherefore the faith of Abram was admirable and singular, seeing that he acquiesced in an oracle so sorrowful, and felt assured, that God would be his Deliverer, after his miseries had proceeded to their greatest height.'

2.2.3 Psalms Commentary (1557)

Historical Setting

Calvin preached on the book of the Psalms every Sunday afternoon between November 1549 and January 1554. He also lectured on the Psalms to his students in 1552, and started writing a commentary in 1553. Calvin then continued his study on the Psalms during the weekly congrégation Bible studies (1555–1559), his commentary appearing in 1557.[129] Calvin thus delved deeply into the Psalms on numerous occasions.

As Selderhuis notes, the eight years between the first sermons on the Psalms and the publication of Calvin's commentary, were a period of transition in terms of the developments that took place in the political and ecclesiastical spheres. The political climate was marked by the state-sponsored persecution of believers in France and Italy, which resulted in them seeking refuge in Geneva. Selderhuis summarizes as follows:

> Historically speaking, very much was happening in Geneva during this period. Around 1550 Geneva had approximately 13,000 inhabitants, but mainly as a result of the immigration of protestant refugees from France and Italy particularly, the number of inhabitants amounted to more than 21,000 in 1560.[130]

Calvin thus preached to an audience that was largely composed of refugees or 'strangers' in Geneva, and in writing his commentary he kept the persecuted believers of France in mind.[131]

Calvin's continuous efforts also finally led the Genevan council to decide in January 1555 to introduce the church order of 1541. The victory of the Calvin-supporters in the elections of the following month gave them solid control of the city, and eventually caused the Perrinists to disappear from the political scene. Meanwhile, Calvin continued his efforts to seek help in various quarters for the fleeing brothers and sisters in France. He sent Jean Budé from Geneva, and requested Bern to send Beza along with Budé, to attend a conference of the

---

129 According to OBERMAN, *The Two Reformations*, 121; STEINMETZ, *Calvin in Context*, 18; PARKER, 'Calvin's Old Testament Commentaries,' 29–31; NAPHY, *Calvin and Consolidation*, 140; and SELDERHUIS, 'Calvin as an Asylum Seeker,' 285, Calvin published his commentary on the Psalms in Geneva on 1557. Between 1555 and August 1559, the Psalms were discussed at the weekly *congrégation* bible study. Calvin further also preached the Psalms in his Sunday afternoon sermons (72 sermons in November 1549, and 22 sermons on Psalm 119 in January 1553). See for a theological analysis of this commentary: SELDERHUIS, *Calvin's Theology of the Psalms*, Grand Rapids 2007.

130 SELDERHUIS, 'Calvin as an Asylum Seeker,' 285

131 Cf. SELDERHUIS, 'Calvin as an Asylum Seeker,' 285.

evangelical cause in German to try and persuade the evangelical princes there to stand up for the evangelical cause in France.[132]

During this time, Calvin wrote a letter of comfort to the women who had been put in prison, saying: 'put yourself in the hands of Him without whose providence nothing takes place, who holds the time and means in His hands.' On September 27, 1557, however, three of them were burned.[133]

On learning that Antoine de Bourbon, the king of Navarre, had come to embrace the Protestant faith, Calvin wrote him a letter to encourage him, and further asked him to take up the cause of the fleeing Protestants in France.[134]

When François d'Andelot, a French nobleman was arrested for holding to the evangelical doctrine of the Lord's Supper, Calvin wrote him several letters of encouragement in 1558.[135] When d'Andelot later participated in the mass, Calvin wrote to him once again and urged him to stand up for the true faith. If one stumbles one time, it does not mean that one has departed from the right path. Calvin called him to stand firm during this difficult situation, so that one day he could become one of the pillars of the Protestant community.[136]

While the Peace of Cateau-Cambresis (1559) between Spain and France ensured the release of some political prisoners, Henry II used the accord to intensify his persecution of the Protestants. Admiral Gaspard de Coligny was one of the prisoners who was released, and converted to the evangelical faith during his captivity in Ghent. He used his influence in the king's court to help the Protestant cause. Also to him did Calvin write a letter, so as to encourage him and his wife Charlotte to continue their good work (September 4, 1558).[137]

In 1560, Calvin wrote to Ambrosius Blauer in detail about the martyrdom of Anne Du Bourg at the hands of Henry II because of her support for the suffering Protestants in France.[138] Once again, this testifies to Calvin's deep involvement in the cause of the fleeing refugees, as does his letter of 1559 to the Protestants who remained behind in France and suffered severe persecution there.[139]

---

132 CO 16,747.

133 CO 16,632–34; cf. 15,346.

134 CO 16,730–34.

135 CO 17,192–94. François d'Andelot, brother of Gaspard de Coligny, was one of the first noblemen to join the Protestant faith. When Henry II asked him about his view on the Mass, his answer led to immediate imprisonment.

136 CO 17,251–53.

137 CO 17,319–20.321–22.

138 CO 18,13–16. Anne Du Bourg, as one of the presidents of the Parliament of Paris, objected to the king's strongly worded letter to all the courts to punish those who held to the Protestant faith forcefully. For this reason she was arrested and ultimately burned with Henry II's personal involvement.

139 CO 17,681–87.

When he learned of the congregation in Metz, which had served the Lord secretly for fifteen years, he wrote them in 1559 to come out openly for the evangelical faith.[140]

Calvin wrote numerous letters to Antoine de Bourbon, the king of Navarre, to stand up for the Protestant cause in France, and also requested him to help those fleeing his kingdom as refugees. When Henry II had passed away, and his son Charles IX was only nine years old, Calvin wrote to Antoine de Bourbon to use the opportunity to effect the release of Louis de Condé who had been judged involved in the conspiracy of Amboise. Calvin here uses his legal expertise to advise the king. He further wrote to de Bourbon that the Mass should not be made compulsory, so that everyone could have the freedom not to participate.[141] When Jeanne d'Albret, the wife of Antoine de Bourbon openly joined the evangelical faith, Calvin wrote her a letter in 1561: 'Thanks to God's great goodness, the seed that the Lord God had planted in her heart long ago had not been choked out.' Calvin further notes that those people who are in high positions generally do not come out openly and show that they belong to the flock of the great Shepherd.[142]

Also to Renée of France did Calvin write a letter of encouragement when her husband, the Duke Hercule d'Este, imprisoned her between 1553 and 1554 for her evangelical convictions,[143] though she later obtained her release by participating in the Mass. On his deathbed, her husband obtained her promise no longer to communicate with Calvin. After his death, d'Este's son gave her the choice to live in Ferrara as a Catholic, or else to leave France. She preferred the latter.

To de Falais, Calvin wrote the following: 'Since we seek Christ, we must be ready to find Him crucified wherever we go in the world.'[144] He further warns an unknown French nobleman not to have any illusions about leaving France for Geneva: 'If you follow Jesus Christ, be ready not to flinch from His cross. You will gain nothing from flight, for the cross will follow you regardless.'[145] What is interesting about Calvin's response to the situation of persecution is

---

140 CO 17,282–84.

141 CO 18,282–85.311–12 (January 16, 1561).

142 CO 18,313–14.

143 According to Barton, Renée was a great help for the fleeing refugees (BARTON, *Calvin and the Duchess*, 49). When Pope Paul III instituted the Roman inquisition in 1542, Ochino was required to appear at Rome for preaching justification by faith at Naples and at Venice. Renée enabled him to escape from Italy, and Calvin later welcomed him to Geneva and appointed him as pastor for the Italian congregation. Later also Celio Curione, a noted theologian who preached in Ferrara and other Italian cities, received help from Renée to escape from Italy, and was consequently welcomed by Calvin in Geneva.

144 CO 12,129.

145 CO 13,64.

that he advises the nobles to stay in spite of the difficulties they face, and to use their high positions in order to help their poor brothers and sisters. The ordinary, persecuted Protestants, on the other hand, Calvin advises to leave the country of France if they cannot worship God faithfully where they are.

Historical Reflection

Observation 7: In his exegesis of Ps 16,4, it is interesting and significant to note the way Calvin translates the term מָהַר.[146] While the LXX reads μετὰ ταῦτα ἐτάχυναν ('he who makes quick'), and the Geneva Bible translates 'other god,' Calvin renders the term as 'stranger' and that although not even in the Massorah do we find any word that might be behind this interpretation. So what led Calvin to translate מָהַר as 'stranger'? Calvin himself remarks that, when translating, he not only follows grammar, but also the principle of common language usage.[147] Calvin writes that the reason for the increase in sorrow is that sacrifices are being offered to false gods. The psalmist also condemns the ceremonies of the unbelievers that are actually external, adulterous acts because they carry them out without a real change of heart. He goes on to explain the connection between external religious ceremonies and superstitions. The reason for Calvin dwelling so extensively on the superstitious beliefs and practices is that in his own day he saw both the Nicodemites and the Papists following the outward ceremonies in order to exercise their superstitious beliefs. Thus Calvin once again condemns the external religious ceremonies of the Roman Catholics in the context of his treatment of the 'stranger'-concept in the Old Testament.

Observation 8: Another remarkable exegetical comment is found on Ps 120,5, where the psalmist says that he is a stranger who lives among the people who reciprocate war for peace, and that his heart longs for peace.[148] Calvin adds that David's condition here resembles that of some wretched individual who is compelled to live in the misery of exile until he grows old. But, if God is not

---

146 CALVIN, *Comm. in Ps.* 16,4 (CO 31,152).

147 CALVIN, *Comm. in Ps.* 16,4 (CO 31,152): 'I would, therefore, be much disposed to adopt this sense were it supported by the common usage of the language; but as grammarians observe that there is not to be found another similar passage in Scripture.'

148 Calvin's translation of Ps 120, 5–7 is as follows: 'Alas for me! that I have been a sojourner in Mesech, and have dwelt among the tents of Kedar. My soul hath long dwelt with him who hateth peace. I am for peace; and when I speak they are for war.' (CO 32,297). According to Calvin, the Mesechites and Kedarenes find their root in Japheth and Ishmael respectively: They hate peace, in fact, they reciprocate war for peace. David expresses his desire to move to a place where he can have peace. Cf. CALVIN, *Comm. in Ps.* 120,5–7 (CO 32,297–98).

hasty in his response to the mistreatment of the stranger, we need to endure the suffering.[149] In short, Calvin notes, David lives as a stranger among his own people. When Calvin wrote these comments, did he have his own situation in Geneva in mind? After all, he was looking for peace, but found war instead. Was he thinking of his own situation, where his enemies in Geneva tried to twist and misinterpret everything he said and wrote? After all, to Bullinger he once complained: 'They suspect everything we say, if I simply said it was daytime at high noon, they would begin to doubt it.'[150] Or is Calvin referring to the painful situation of the believers who live and suffer under papal dominion?[151] Whatever the case may have been, it is in any case clear that in his exegesis of Scripture, Calvin reflected on the historical developments of his time.

Observation 9: In his exegetical work on Ps 94,6, which refers to the triad stranger – widow – fatherless, Calvin brings up three kinds of actions directed to these people: persecuting the stranger, seizing the widow and robbing the fatherless. Calvin then identifies himself with the strangers, and says that one ought to pray to God that He may undertake their defense. From there, Calvin once again makes a direct connection to his own historical situation, pointing out that the Roman Catholic church treats the Protestants in a way similar to the way these people mentioned in this Psalm were oppressed. Though a law is in place, wickedness and corruption prevail. Calvin hopes that his comments may result in two things: first, a change of attitude in the Catholic church; secondly, he adds a warning to his own congregation in Geneva not to get carried away like the Roman Catholic church. By linking the sufferings of the stranger, widow and fatherless with the corruption of the Catholic church of his own day, Calvin is making a clear reference to the treatment of the faithful believers by the papists. Calvin could here not have been referring to any other papist corruption.

---

149 CALVIN, *Comm. in Ps.* 120,6 (CO 32,298): 'Let us, however, remember, that if God does not immediately stretch forth his hand in our behalf, it is our duty to bear the wearsomeness occasioned by delay, like David, whom we find in this Psalm giving thanks to God for his deliverance, while, at the same time, as if worn out with the weariness of waiting for it, he bewails the long oppression to which he had been subjected by his enemies.'
150 CO 14,611.
151 Cf. CALVIN, *Comm. in Ps.* 120,5 (CO 32,297): 'Now if the place where the uprightness of good men is overwhelmed by the criminations of lying lips is to the children of God converted into a region of miserable exile, how could they have pleasure, or rather, how could they fail to feel the bitterest sorrow, in abiding in a part of the world where the sacred name of God is shamefully profaned by horrible blasphemies, and his truth obscured by detestable lies?'

2.2.4 Minor Prophets Commentary (1559)

Historical setting

Calvin lectured on Hosea in 1556, and other minor prophets in 1558, from which his commentary would ultimately be published in 1560.[152] Nicolas Colladon notes that Calvin was unable to complete his commentary on Malachi since he was very ill,[153] and he in fact gave some of his lectures at home for the benefit of the printers.[154] The commentary was dedicated to King Gustavus Vasa on February 23, 1560. The year 1559 saw the very remarkable event of the establishment of the Genevan Academy. On his way to Frankfurt in 1556, Calvin visited Strasbourg in order to get some ideas from Jean Sturm who was the head of the academy there. Other events from roughly the same period include several visits Calvin made to Frankfurt beginning in 1555 in order to help the French church there grow stronger. In August 1557, tensions between Bern and the Genevans escalated on account of Ami Perrin, so that the Genevans were afraid to leave their territory.[155] Bern further asked Geneva to demand Ami Perrin to step down. Bern also forbade its ministers to speak about the thorny issue of predestination. On November 29, 1558, one of the city watchmen, Claude Pellisson, was attacked by Philibert Berthelier. The latter also slandered Calvin, calling him and all his supporters 'wicked men, traitors, and pests.' On December 15, members of the same group shot at one of the citizens of Geneva.[156]

Historical Reflection

Observation 10: Neither the Hebrew word for 'stranger,' nor the related words 'alien,' 'sojourner,' 'foreigner' and 'proselyte,' are found in the text of Jonah, but Calvin nevertheless brings this concept up in his exegesis, repeatedly noting that Jonah was a 'stranger' and of low condition.[157] Calvin further explains the fact that the King of Assyria, although a most powerful king and considered

---

152 OBERMAN, *The Two Reformations*, 122; DE GREEF, *The Writings of John Calvin*, 108–09.
153 CO 21,88.
154 DE GREEF, *The Writings of John Calvin*, 108.
155 CO 21,671–72.
156 COTTRET, *Calvin*, 256.
157 Calvin similarly notes that both Amos and Hosea were strangers of humble condition. This once again makes it clear that for Calvin, 'stranger' is not some philosophical concept, but points to the real life condition of living in a foreign land.

to be beyond reproach,[158] listened to Jonah by remarking: 'Jonah was a stranger and of humble condition, that he therefore so touched the heart of the king.' What does Calvin want to say here? Does he mean that a powerful king, above reproach and unwilling to listen even to equals, now yielded himself to a 'stranger' of low condition?[159] Why does Calvin ascribe such significance to the preaching of a stranger? Calvin focuses his argument on two points: first, the willingness to listen; and second, the king's response to what was preached. In connection with his first point,[160] it is interesting that Calvin here uses the personal pronoun 'we,' and explains that he has been engaged in 'continual preaching for twenty or thirty years'. Calvin thus seems to be placing himself in the shoes of Jonah the stranger, as he has by now been preaching as a stranger in Geneva for twenty or thirty years. As was noted before, Calvin gave his lectures on the Minor Prophets in 1558, and published the commentary in 1560. During this period, Calvin faced numerous attacks on his doctrine, especially from the likes of Pierre Caroli, Michael Servetus and Sebastian Castellio. In the context of this part of his commentary, therefore, Calvin does not refer to the papists. Rather, he is directing his words against the very people of Geneva who, unlike the papists, continually hear the true message of the Gospel, but are not willing to submit to it as even the King of Assyria did with Jonah. Calvin's second argument refers to the penitential ceremonies performed by the King of Assyria after listening to the preaching of Jonah the stranger. Calvin again immediately draws a connection to the papists of his day, remarking that they observe the outward ceremonies but do not show inward, genuine repen-

---

158 CALVIN, *Praelect. in Ion.* 3,6–8: 'It is worthy of being noticed, that the king of so splendid a city, nay, at that time the greatest monarch, should have rendered himself so submissive to the exhortation of Jonah: for we see how proud kings are; as they think themselves exempt from the common lot of men, so they carry themselves above all laws. Hence it comes, that they will have all things to be lawful for them; and while they give loose reins to their lusts they cannot bear to be admonished, even by their equals.'

159 CALVIN, *Praelect. in Ion.* 3,6–8 (CO 43,253): 'That the preaching of Jonah was severe, for he denounced destruction on a most powerful city; this might have instantly inflamed the king's mind with rage and fury; and that he was calmly humbled, was certainly a proof of no common change. We have then here a remarkable instance of penitence, – that the king should have so forgotten himself and his dignity, as to throw aside his splendid dress, to put on sackcloth, and to lie down on ashes.'

160 CALVIN, *Praelect. in Ion.* 3,6–8 (CO 43,257): 'But we must bear in mind that the king, as yet a novice, and hardly in a slight degree imbued with the elements of religion, through hearing what Jonah preached, gave orders to his people according to the measure of his faith and knowledge: but if he made such progress in so short a time, what excuse can we pretend, whose ears have been stunned by continual preaching for twenty or thirty years, if we yet come short of the novitiate of this king? These circumstances ought then to be carefully observed by us.'

tance.[161] Calvin suggests that the papists should learn from the heathen king who showed true penitence after hearing the preaching of a stranger.[162] As a side remark, Calvin notes also that it is through a stranger of humble condition that God works powerfully.[163] From the above, it is clear that Calvin applied the importance of the preaching of a stranger to his own historical situation.

Observation 11: In connection with Sach 7,10 ('And oppress not the widow, nor the fatherless, the Stranger, nor the poor; and let none of you imagine evil against his brother in your heart'), Calvin interprets the Hebrew אַל־תַּעֲשֹׁקוּ not only as a command against harming strangers, but also as a command to help those strangers who are oppressed. That is, if a person does not extend help to the strangers, he is by that fact actually oppressing the strangers. And conversely, by helping strangers, one does justice to them. Calvin continues in his exegesis by arguing that true service to or fear of God is not shown in the observation of rituals and ceremonies, but by extending help to the stranger.[164] His exegesis in connection with the 'stranger,' therefore, is meant to instruct the people of Geneva to show justice to the incoming refugees, since that is what true service of the Lord consists in.

Observation 12: Calvin understands the terms וּרְחוֹקִים in Sach 6,15 as 'stranger'[165]: the 'strangers' will come from far-away places to build the temple by contributing both labor and riches. He notes that the word 'stranger' here does not refer to Cyrus, since after Cyrus, no 'stranger' ever participated or contributed to the building of the temple. But to whom is the prophet referring then?

---

161 CALVIN, Praelect. in Ion. 3,6–8 (CO 43,257): 'The more shameful then is their dullness who seek to pacify God by frivolous devices, as the Papists do; for while they obtrude on God trifles, I know not what, they think that these are so many expiations, and they tenaciously contend for them. They need no other judge than this heathen king, who shows that true penitence is wholly different, that it then only takes place when men become changed in mind and heart, and wholly turn to a better course of life.'

162 CALVIN, Praelect. in Ion. 3,6–8 (CO 43,257): 'For the Papists, though they accumulate expiations, pass by charity; and in the whole course of life equity has hardly any place. Let them then learn, from the mouth of a heathen king, what God principally requires from men, and approves of in their life, even to abstain from plunder and from the doing of any injury. We now then perceive why rapacity was especially mentioned.'

163 CALVIN, Praelect. in Ion. 3,6–8 (CO 43,253): 'Jonah was a stranger and of a humble condition: that he therefore so touched the heart of the king, must be ascribed to the hidden power of God, which he puts forth through his word whenever he pleases.'

164 CALVIN, Praelect. in Zach. 7,1 (CO 44,226). Calvin calls strangers 'brethren,' and remarks that it one's duty to serve the. He adds that the fear of God is not proved by outward ceremonies, but by acting justly towards our brethren (cf. '[...] but discharges his duty as it were in the presence of God').

165 CALVIN, Praelect. in Zach. 6,15 (CO 44,215–16).

According to Calvin, the 'strangers' point to the building up of the church, not with stone and wood, but rather with the doctrine and gifts of the Holy Spirit.[166] But of whom does Calvin think in connection with the strangers who participate in the doctrine and gifts of the Holy Spirit? Does his interpretation reflect his Genevan context? The Genevan churches were for mainly pastored by refugee pastors who had fled France, and Calvin himself was a stranger pasturing a refugee church.

2.2.5 Daniel Commentary (1561)

Historical Setting

In connection with the historical context for Calvin's Daniel commentary, it can once again be noted that Calvin was quite sick, but nevertheless involved in numerous doctrinal, ecclesiastical and other personal matters. Writing to John Knox who had asked for advice on a number of ecclesiastical matters on November 7, 1559, Calvin expressed his disagreement with Farel's marriage in his old age with a very young woman. It is also clear that Calvin was aware of developments further away. When Elisabeth ascended to the throne of England, Calvin wrote to her that under her reign the pure gospel would be established. In France, the death of Henry II on July 10, 1559, and the accession of the young king Françis II, who was ruled by the Guise family, made the situation for the Protestants even more difficult than it had already been. The informers also multiplied the number of persons suspected of belonging to the Reformation, whom the *chambre ardente* handed over to the executioner. From August 1559 to March 1560, there was nothing but arrests and imprisonments, pillaging of houses, banishments, and massacres of the Reformed believers.[167]

---

166 CALVIN, *Praelect. in Zach*, 6,15 (CO 44,216): 'We then see that this prophecy cannot be otherwise referred than to the building of the spiritual temple, when Gentiles, formerly remote from God's people, joined them as friends, and brought their labor to the work of building the temple, not with stones or wood, or with other corruptible materials, but with the doctrine and the gifts of the Holy Spirit.'

167 In his 'Life of Calvin,' Beza describes these events vividly: 'we may say of this reign which lasted only seventeen months, what Jesus Christ says in St. Matthew, viz: "Except those days should be shortened there should no flesh by saved; but for the elect's sake those days shall be shortened." Not with-standing this, He who suffers not his own to be loaded beyond what they can bear, gave such assistance to his lambs, that were for the most part only newly born, and in like manner to the pastors who had just begun to arrange them in little flocks, that amid all those storms, they not only subsisted, but, what is more assumed a regular order, and increased their numbers in many parts of the kingdom. Disseminated from church to church, and multiplied by pious hands, the letters of the Reformer spread everywhere courage and self-denial.'

Historical Reflection

Observation 13: Calvin not only portrays Daniel as a stranger in Babylon, but also observes that because he was a stranger, he was ignored and despised by the king when the latter was overwhelmed with apprehension when the writing appeared on the wall.[168] Then when Daniel was given an opportunity to interpret the writing, he was bold enough to foretell the downfall of the king. Having made these remarks on the text, Calvin turns to his own historical situation and claims that people are hiding themselves behind ignorance, and willingly remained blind to the true Gospel.

2.2.6. Harmony of the Law Commentary (1563)[169]

Historical Setting

In 1561, Calvin writes a letter of warning to the king of Navarre to be careful as the Lutherans plan to introduce the Confession of Augsburg. In the year of the publication of the commentary on the Harmony of the Law, Balthasar Sept and Andre Philippe, together with Philibert Berthelier, organized a plot against Geneva, whereby the city was to have ended up under the control of Savoy, though their attempt was foiled on December 22, 1563.[170] A little earlier (July 2, 1563), Calvin wrote to Bullinger that his health was deteriorating rapidly. Finally, in 1560 some 1100 strangers were granted Genevan citizenship.

Historical Reflection

Observation 14: According to Calvin, the Lord as Defender of the 'stranger' takes vengeance on those who oppress them. What is the oppression of strangers? Calvin makes three interesting comments in this respect. The first comes

---

168 CALVIN, *Praelect. in Dan.* 5,7 (CO 40,702). King Belshazzar invited all the Chaldeans, magicians and astrologers to interpret the writing on the wall, but according to Calvin, the king should have invited Daniel first because he had already exhibited his wisdom in interpretation earlier to his grandfather Nebuchadnezzar. Daniel was despised because he was a stranger in that land; in Calvin's words, when the king invited the wise men to try and interpret the writing on the wall, he 'passed by' Daniel.

169 OBERMAN, *The Two Reformations*, 121–22; PARKER, 'Calvin the Biblical Expositor,' 73; DE GREEF, *The Writings of John Calvin*, 107, all correctly note that it was not Calvin's intention to improve on Moses when he followed a subject arrangement, rather than the chapters, in his exposition of the four books of Moses aside from Genesis. The aim of this content-based exposition was to make the readers understand the *torah* better and in a more simple fashion. It was published in 1563, a year before his death.

170 COTTRET, *Calvin*, 256.

even before he comments on the actual text, as Calvin introduces some remarks on equity. He notes that the Israelites think they discharge their duty perfectly when they maintain equity among the natives. However, Calvin demonstrates that to exercise equity fully, one ought to show it not just to other native inhabitants, but rather to all people, particularly to strangers, widows and orphans. Thus for Calvin, even withholding justice and equity from the stranger means vexing and oppressing them.[171] The second interesting remark is that according to Calvin, Israel's experience as strangers should make them ready to treat the strangers who are now in their own land with great kindness.[172] The final remark is that by practicing usury against the stranger, one vexes and oppresses him.[173] At the end, Calvin observes that the Lord will avenge the strangers who have been oppressed. Why does Calvin give such a long exposé on the oppression of strangers? It may well be in view of the historical circumstances, where Calvin expected fairness to be shown in Geneva also to the many foreigners and strangers who had come to the city.

Observation 15: According to Calvin, one of the main motives for the liberation of the people of Israel from Egypt can be found in Moses' appeal to Pharaoh: 'Let my people go, that they may hold a feast unto me in the wilderness' (Ex 5,1). This request was not deceitful, but a genuine attempt to gain from Pharaoh the freedom the people of Israel lacked to worship their own God. Later on in his exegesis on the same text, Calvin encourages his audience to go into exile voluntarily where the freedom to true worship no longer exists.[174] A second point concerns Calvin's exegetical comments on the phrase וְגַם־עֵרֶב רַב

---

171 Calvin translates Ex 22,21-24 as follows: 'Thou shalt neither vex a stranger, nor oppress him: for ye were strangers in the land of Egypt. Ye shalt not afflict any widow, or fatherless child. If thou afflict them in any wise, and the, and cry at all unto me, I will surely hear their cry: And my wrath shall wax hot, and I will kill you with the sword; and your wives shall be widows, and your children fatherless.' In his exegesis he remarks: 'No iniquity, indeed, will be left unavenged by God, but there is a special reason why He declares that strangers, widows, and orphans are taken under His care; inasmuch as the more flagrant the evil is, the greater need there is of an effectual remedy.' CALVIN, Comm. in Mosis reliq. libr. Ex 22,21-24 (CO 24,672-73)

172 CALVIN, Comm. in Mosis reliq. libr. Ex 22,21-24 (CO 24,673).

173 CALVIN, Comm. in Mosis reliq. libr. Ex 22,25 (CO 25,676).

174 CALVIN, Comm. in Mosis reliq. libr. Ex 5,1 (CO 24,69): 'We have said elsewhere that there was no deceit in the pretext that God called his people into the wilderness to hold a feast, although He does not reveal His counsel to the tyrant; for it was really His pleasure that a sacrifice of thanksgiving should be offered to Himself on Mount Sinai, and that they should be thus separated from the polluted nation with which they were mixed up; and, assuredly, He wished to arouse the tyrant's wrath, by ignominiously condemning the whole of Egypt, as not capable of pure worship.'

('mixed multitude'),[175] which refers to the heterogeneous group that left Egypt.[176] According to Calvin, when Jacob left for Egypt, he had no servants with him because he would have been unable to feed them due to the severe famine. However, when the Israelites left Egypt, they were called a mixed multitude, composed of the Israelites, their offspring, migrants from neighboring countries, and strangers. After this remark, Calvin immediately draws a connection to his own situation and to that of many of the members in the congregation: 'if any should think it absurd that ungodly men, with no better hope before them, would voluntarily forsake a rich and convenient habitation in order to seek a new home as wanderers and pilgrims.' Calvin then relates the oppression of the Egyptian bondage with the despotism and tyranny of the papacy.

Why did Calvin draw this connection between the mixed multitude that left Egypt and the many Protestant believers who fled the papal persecutions? Was he trying to draw a parallel between the attempt of the French king to remove all true believers from his country and that of Pharaoh to annihilate all the Israelite male children?[177] For Calvin, purity of divine worship was an absolute necessity, so that if this could not be achieved in France, one had to move elsewhere.[178] Thus in 1558, Calvin wrote to Madame de Rentigny to persuade her to go into exile, since she was in danger of ceding to the pressure of her Catholic surroundings.[179] He also wrote to an unknown French woman to flee from France,[180] and in 1543 he encouraged Seigneur de Falais to come to Geneva where he could enjoy true worship and preaching.

Does this interpretation reflect Calvin's personal experience as he was taking refuge, and moving from place to place between November 1, 1533 and July 1536 as 'stranger' from his native land to various different places,[181] until

---

175   The Vulgate and LXX use the derivative ערב to render the meaning 'to mix' or 'to intermingle' in order to denote those people who do not belong to the autochthonous population of a country. Here the term denotes descent, not specifically a social status. Philo says: 'children from marriages of Egyptian women with Hebrew, persons who had joined the Hebrew, impressed by their devoutness, person converted, affected as they were by the mounting catastrophes.' (VM I,347)

176   In Ex 12,38, Calvin translates this term as 'mixed multitude.'

177   Cf. CALVIN, Comm. in Mosis reliq. libr., Ex 1,22 (CO 24,20–21).

178   So OBERMAN, The Two Reformations, 122–123, NEUSER, 'Calvin and the Refugees,' 5.

179   CO 17,132: 'God has made manifest in you the fine marks of his election, so we have the right to hope that this good seed will also bring forth fruit.'

180   CO 12,453.

181   Calvin went from somewhere in the vicinity of Paris to Paris itself, then to the province of Saintonge in the south of France. In April 1534 he went to Nerac, then back again into the vicinity of Paris, to Poitiers, and to Orléans. When living in France became too dangerous, Calvin moved to Strasbourg via Basel, then to Italy, to Basel, and to France at which point he finally

he finally met Farel who convinced him to stay in Geneva?[182] The decision to stay in Geneva brought a certain amount of stability in his life from July 1536 to April 1538, since Calvin could live and serve there without being continually on the move.[183] However, Calvin was then forced to leave Geneva, from where he

---

left Paris for good. On his way to Strasbourg, Calvin passed through Geneva where he ended up staying.

182 The twenty-four year old Calvin had to go into exile as refugee when Nicolas Cop delivered a sermon on the relationship between the Law and the Gospel. Calvin came to the attention of the Parisian authorities with this sharply-worded sermon of Cop, which he gave November 1 (All Saints' Day) in the presence of professors of theology and other ecclesiastical dignitaries. It was believed that Calvin was involved in the preparation of the draft for this sermon. Fearing that they would be arrested, Calvin and Cop fled from Paris. (Cf. STEINMETZ, Calvin in Context, 9–10; DE GREEF, The Writings of John Calvin, 23–24). Though Calvin could come back to Paris twice after this incident, both returns were temporary. After making his way to the south of France, he for a short time found refuge in the house of the wealthy Louis du Tillet, where he had the opportunity to spend some quiet time studying various books. In the house of du Tillet, he worked on the first edition of the Institutes. Calvin and du Tillet then had to flee for Basel for a reason for which they were not responsible. Calvin returned to Paris once more, but this return was suddenly cut short when a placard against Catholic doctrine was posted in several important cities in France. Some of these placards were even found in the king's bedchamber. This incident coincided with a new treaty between the Pope and Francis I. As a mark of his gratitude towards the Pope, Francis I intensified his activities against the Protestants. Two hundred people were arrested, of whom twenty were executed. Once again Calvin, together with du Tillet, had to flee as refugees to Basel where Nicolas Cop had fled a year earlier. In Basel, Calvin had the opportunity to complete his first edition of the Institutes (1536). These experiences of being a stranger in exile were reflected in the dedicatory words of this first edition: 'For our hope in the living God, some of us are bound in chains. While others are beaten with rods and help up to scorn. Just as some are banished or subjected to horrible torture, so others, flee in secret.' (CO 1,13)
Later, these two scholarly refugees left Basel and took refuge in the house of Renée of France in Ferrara, where the princess offered Calvin a position as secretary. When members of Renée's entourage were arrested in April 1536 on charges of heresy, Calvin was forced to take refuge in another city. Later Calvin himself wrote: 'I only went to Italy that I might have pleasure of leaving it.' (CO 21,125) Once again, this turned out to be only a temporary refuge, and Calvin was forced to flee for a safer destination. Calvin went back to his hometown to sell the land he had inherited from his father, seeing that France was not going to be the place for him to live. This time, it was not Calvin alone, but his whole family who decided to relocate to Strasbourg (CO 31,28–31).

183 On his way to Strasbourg, Calvin stayed one night in Geneva (DE GREEF, The Writings of John Calvin, 28). However, Farel learned of Calvin's presence, rushed to the house where he had put up for the night, and forced him to stay in Geneva for its future reformation. Having spent the last three years in exile, Calvin yearned for an undisturbed life where he could spend his time in reading and writing. But as Calvin wrote in the preface to commentary on the Psalms, Farel did not request Calvin to stay in Geneva, but rather threatened him in the name of God should he not stay: 'Guillaume Farel detained me at Geneva, not so much by counsel and exhortation, as by a dreadful imprecation, which I felt to be as if God had from heaven laid his mighty hand upon me to arrest me. As the most direct road to Strasburg, to which I then intended to retire, was as shut up by the wars, I had resolved to pass quickly by Geneva, without staying longer

moved for a brief period to Basel. In September 1538, he moved from Basel to Strasbourg, where he served as pastor in the refugee congregation until September 1541.[184] At this point he moved one more time, now back to Geneva, where he involved himself in pastoral, literary and reformation activities until his death on May 17, 1564.[185]

---

than a single night in that city. A little before this, Popery had been driven from it by the exertions of the excellent person whom I have named, and Peter Viret; but matters were not yet brought to a settled state, and the city was divided into unholy and dangerous factions. Then an individual who now basely apostatized and returned to the Papists, discovered me and made me known to others. Upon this, Farel, who burned with an extraordinary zeal to advance the gospel, immediately strained every nerve to detain me. And after having learned that my heart was set upon devoting myself to private studies for which I wished to keep myself free from other pursuits, and finding that he gained nothing by entreaties, he proceeded to utter an imprecation that God would curse my retirement, and the tranquility of the studies which I sought, if I should withdraw and refuse to give assistance, when the necessity seas so urgent. By this imprecation I was so stricken with terror, that I desisted from the journey which I had undertaken; but sensible of my natural bashfulness and timidity, I would not bring myself under obligation to discharge any particular office.' (CALVIN, Comm. in Ps., praefatio [CO 31,23.24]). Later, in 1538, even Geneva turned out not to be a permanent place for Calvin when the Council of 200 ordered both him and Farel to leave the city in three days during the week of Easter. Calvin was deeply hurt when the council ordered him to leave. Accusations of all kinds were also made against them, such as being French government agents. They had been involved in theological disputes on topics like Communion, excommunication, the singing of Psalms in the worship-service, and above all, there was the bitter conflict that broke out when he refused to sign the Athanasian Creed and was accused of being an Arian. Saddened by these developments in Geneva, Calvin and Farel moved to Basel. Calvin considered his work in Geneva a failure, and his heart once again longed for nothing more than a quiet life of study by himself.

184 Against own desires, Calvin had to yield when both Martin Bucer and Wolfgang Capito seized the opportunity offered by Calvin's pitiable situation, and drew him to Strasbourg to become pastor for the refugee congregation of around 500 members. Calvin's first month in Strasbourg was marked by several tragedies that came to some people with whom he had been closely associated for quite some time. In Strasbourg, he came to know that his old friend du Tillet had left the evangelical faith and returned to the Catholic church. Later he heard about the death of Elie Coraud, who after his banishment from Geneva had become a minister in Orbe. He also learned of the death of his relative Olivetanus, who left him a number of books. In Strasbourg Calvin completed the second edition of his Institutes, which had by this time grown considerably. The most beautiful aspect of his life there is that he found a life partner in Idelette van Buren, a refugee widow who already had son and a daughter.

185 In March 1539, Cardinal Jacopo Sadoleto of Carpentras in Southern France sent a letter to Geneva to call the city back to the traditional faith of its ancestors. The letter was an eloquent appeal for reconciliation and reunion, which accused the protestant reformers of arrogantly introducing into the Christian faith heretical innovations that had no foundation in the Christian past. After having lengthy consultations with Bern, and being unable to persuade Viret to respond to Sadoleto, the council reluctantly decided to approach Calvin to answer on their behalf by sending Simon Sulzer. Impressed with Calvin's response to Sadoleto, the city council of Geneva acknowledged it had been a mistake to banish Calvin in 1538. The council therefore reversed its decision and invited Calvin back to Geneva for the same position he had held in 1538. On September 19, 1540, the council sent a letter through Ami Perrin to bring Calvin back to

Observation 16: It is interesting to note that in connection with the rejection of the Ammonites and Moabites (cf. Dt 23,3–8), Calvin states that the reason for it is their violation of the law of hospitality towards strangers.[186] Their inhospitality showed itself in two ways: in not being welcoming towards strangers,[187] and secondly in their cruelty in hiring a prophet to curse the strangers. Calvin comments that the Moabites, by hiring a prophet, thought they could overcome God and his plans for those who are strangers and in exile by magical formulas and incantations. He then goes on to connect the action of the Moabites with the attempts of the papists of his day to tarnish or stifle the true Gospel.[188] Why did Calvin make this connection? Perhaps, Calvin here had in mind the various attempts made by the Catholic party to convince the reform-minded believers to return to the 'mother church,' of which the letter of Cardinal Sadoleto to the council of Geneva (1539) is a classic example. Such occasions may well have led Calvin to reflect on the Catholic attempts to silence the Reformers and keep them from preaching the Gospel when he dealt with this passage concerning the Ammonites and Moabites.

Geneva. Calvin accepted the invitation, but he did not fail to express how he felt about the prospect of returning: 'I read that passage of your letter, certainly not without a smile, where you show so much concern about my health, and recommended Geneva on the ground! Why could you not have said at the cross? For it would have been far preferable to perish once for all than to be tormented again in that place of torture.' (CO 11,36) With the permission of Strasbourg, Calvin left for Geneva on September 13, 1541, on a six-month loan basis, but he would never return to Strasbourg again. Once back in Geneva, Calvin became pastor again to a city overwhelmed by the incoming refugees.

186   CALVIN, *Comm. in Mosis reliq. libr.* Dt 23,3 (CO 24,555). Calvin makes clear distinctions between the nations that are strangers to Israel in his exegetical comments on Dt 23,3–8. On the one hand, he advocates the complete annihilation of the Ammonites and Moabites from the congregation of the Lord. On the other hand, he advocates a responsive and reciprocal approach to the Edomites and Egyptians because the Israelites knew what it was to be strangers.

187   Calvin discusses their inhospitable nature in numerous other places. Calvin praises the hospitality both Abraham and Lot showed towards the unknown strangers (cf. Gn 18; 19). He also applauds Abimelech for his hospitality towards Isaac, and Pharaoh for his hospitality to Jacob. Similarly, Calvin finds the reason for the destruction of Sodom in its inhospitable nature shown towards strangers.

188   CALVIN, *Comm. in Mosis reliq. libr.*, Dt 23,4 (CO 24,556): 'Thus now-a-days no stone is left unturned by the defenders of the Papacy, whereby they may disturb the course of heavenly doctrine, nay, whereby they may altogether silence the Gospel if they could.' Further, Calvin observes: 'it appears how awful in the reprisal that anticipates all who of deliberate malice oppose God's Grace.'

2.2.7 Jeremiah and Lamentations Commentary (1563)

Historical Reflection

Observation 17: In his exegesis of Jer 22,1–3, Calvin translates the verbs ינה and חמס as 'do no wrong' and 'do no violence' respectively,[189] and states that this text points to the responsibilities of the kings not to do violence to the strangers, and to that of the judges to execute justice.[190] If they do not perform their responsibilities towards the strangers, they will suffer under the Lord's reproach since He is the Defender of the stranger. On establishing this historical point, Calvin immediately turns to his own day and to the papists who consider that they are under no reproach from God because they claim to be seated on the apostolic chair.[191] Why would Calvin draw this connection? Calvin was here making yet another appeal to the kings and princes to use their power to curtail papal aggression on true followers of the true Gospel, or the unwillingness of the papacy to listen to that true Gospel and submit their false doctrine to it.

Observation 18: Calvin's translation and exegetical comments on the term יתום are very significant for illustrating the importance this term had already from early on in his life as a wanderer. The word יתום occurs forty-seven times in the Hebrew text.[192] Both Luther and the Geneva Bible translate it in each instance as 'fatherless,' with the one exception of Thr 5,3.[193] The way Calvin treats this term, however, differs significantly. Out of the forty-seven occur-

---

189   The Vulgate and Targum translate the verb ינה as 'make not sad'; the LXX reads 'tyrannize not over'; and the Syraic reads 'wrong not.' Calvin interprets this verb as 'defraud not.' It is significant here to note that the next verb, חמס, is connected with a *waw*, in all of the above-mentioned versions, and all of them – with the exception of the Targum – translate the second force as 'to do no wrong by force or violence.' Calvin provides a similar translation.

190   Calvin considers that 'defraud not' refers to not doing justice to the strangers, and thus applies it to the judges. For him, the second verb means 'do no violence,' thus depriving strangers of their rights, and for that reason relates it to the kings and his officials.

191   It is interesting to see how Calvin relates the throne of David and the seat of Peter, and disparages the arrogant nature of the papists. Calvin ascribes the responsibility of not depriving the rights of stranger to the kings, and so for Calvin, the prophet refers to the throne of David. Calvin makes yet another interesting observation in this context when he remarks: 'Surely the throne of David was much more venerable than the chair of Peter? and yet the descendants of David who succeeded him, being types and representatives of Christ, were not on that account, as we here see, exempt from reproof.' CALVIN, *Comm. in Jer.* 22,1–3 (CO 38,374).

192   Ex 22,22.24; Dt 10,18; 14,29; 16,11.14; 24,17.19; 26,12f.; 27,19; Hi 6,27; 22,9; 24,3.9; 29,12; 31,17.21; Ps 10,14.18; 68,5; 82,3; 94,6; 109,9.12; 146,9; Prv 23,10; Jes 1,17.23; 9,17; 10,2; Jer 5,28; 7,6; 22,3; 49,11; Ez 22.7; Hos 14,3; Sach 7,10; Mal 3,5.

193   In Thr 5,3 the term יתום is translated as 'orphan,' thus allowing for the possibility of the phrase אין אב to be translated 'fatherless.' However, the grammatical feasibility of translating this phrase as such is questionable.

rences, Calvin translates יתום as 'fatherless' thirty-three times.[194] Remarkably, out of all these times, Calvin substantiates his translation only four times with an exegetical remark,[195] and on nine occasions he does not provide any exegetical notes at all.[196] For the remaining twenty occurrences where Calvin translates יתום as 'fatherless,'[197] his exegesis fully supports the idea of 'orphan.' For all of these twenty passages, Calvin gives a brief and at the same time clear explanation of this idea. However, in none of them does he mention the term 'fatherless,' even though he does there translate יתום as 'fatherless.'

Another interesting remark concerning Calvin's exegesis is that he time and again uses different translations. For example, Calvin translates Jer 49,11 as: 'Leave thy *fatherless children*, I will preserve them alive; and let thy widows trust in me.' However, in the exegetical comments that follow, he gives a slightly different translation: 'Leave thy *orphans* to me, I will nourish or sustain them, or I will be a father to them; and thy widows, let them hope or trust in me, or rest on me.' In seven other passages, Calvin similarly replaces his translation of 'fatherless' with the word 'orphan' in his exegetical comments.

The fourteen remaining occurrences of the term יתום[198] – i.e. where Calvin does not translate 'fatherless' – are always translated directly with the term 'orphan,' and the idea of 'orphan' in all of these cases also comes up explicitly in the exegetical comments. This indicates that the notion of 'orphan' overshadowed and dominated that of being 'fatherless' in Calvin's translation and exegesis.

One can observe the passion with which Calvin make his exegetical comments on Jer 5,28, where יתום was translated as 'fatherless,' but where the notes themselves betray Calvin's focus on the 'orphan'-concept instead. He writes:

> Pity towards young orphans is often found in those who are otherwise cruel; for that age, especially when deprived of all protection, touches our feelings in a peculiar manner. Since then young orphans were plundered with impunity, and found no defense from the judges, their dishonesty appeared most glaringly.[199]

---

194 CALVIN, *Comm. ad locum*: Ex 22,21–24.26–27; Lv 19,9–10.33–34; 23,22; Dt 10,17–19; 14,22.27.29; 16,11.14; 24,6–10.13.17.18.19–22; 26,12–13; 27,19; Ps 10,18; 68,1–6; 94,1–6; 109,9; 146,6–10; Jes 1,17.23; 9,1–21; Jer 5,8.28; 7,5–7; 22,3; 49,10–11; Hos 14,3; Sach 7,10; Mal 3,5.

195 Ps 94,6; 109,9; Jes 1,17; Hos 14,3.

196 Dt 10,17–19; 16,11.14; 26,12–13; 27,19; Ps.10:18; 68,6; 109:9; Jes 1,23; Jer 5,28.

197 Ex 22,21–24.26–27; Lv 19,9–10; 19,33–34; 23,22; Dt 14,22.27.29; 24,6–10.13.17.18; 24,19–22; Jes 9,1–21; Jer 5,8; 7,5–7; 22,3; 49,10–11; Ps 68,1–6; 94,1–6; 146,6–10; Sach 7,10; Mal 3,5.

198 CALVIN, *Comm. ad locum*: Ps 10,14; 82,3.4; 109,12; 146,9; Jes 1,17; 9,17; 10,2; Jer 7,6; 22,3; 49,11; Sach 3,5; 7,10. Calvin may here have based himself on the LXX (ὀρφανά) and Vulgate. Below we will explore the possible influences on Calvin's translation and exegesis of this word.

199 CALVIN, *Comm. in Jer.* 5,28 (CO 37,638).

But yet another interesting point can be noted in connection with the above interpretation of Jer 5,28. Two times did Calvin qualify the noun 'orphan' with 'young,' so that the emphasis falls on the fact that they are young. This might seem unimportant, except for the fact that neither the Hebrew text, nor any other translations or other commentators add this word in this context of the orphan. Does this not allow us to draw the conclusion that Calvin's 'early childhood experience of being orphan'[200] influenced his exegesis of this passage?

The notion of 'non-belonging' also played a significant role in Calvin's hermeneutic as shown in his translation and exegesis of Thr 5,3. The text reads יְתוֹמִים הָיִינוּ (אֵין) [וְאֵין] אָב אִמֹּתֵינוּ כְּאַלְמָנוֹת ('we became orphans and no father, our mothers are widows' [literal translation – JG]), but Calvin translates: 'We are orphans and fatherless, our mothers are as widows.'[201] Two points should be remarked on here. In the first place, Calvin here translates יְתוֹמִים as 'orphans,' even though on thirty-three other occasions he preferred the term 'fatherless.' The context appears to allow for either translation. The translation 'orphan' is acceptable because in the context of Hebrew the condition of the fatherless was similar to that of the parentless. In the second place, Calvin translated the word אֵין אָב as 'fatherless,' but did not make any exegetical note on the word. It rather appears as if Calvin based himself on the LXX's οὐχ

---

200 Calvin's mother died when he was a boy of four, and his father remarried shortly thereafter. Calvin left his father's house to receive his early school education at Montimor. Though Calvin had a good opportunity to study in the top schools of his time, he was not really under the care of his mother and father. Bouwsma says that Calvin had a kind of ambiguous feeling towards his father, and that feeling is clear in a letter he wrote to his friend Nicolas Duchemin when his father was on the point of death (May 14, 1528): 'I promised on leaving that I would return soon, and I have been on tenterhooks about this for some time. For when I was considering returning to you, my father's illness delayed me. When the doctors gave hope for his recovery, I only wanted you: and this longing, strong before, increased as the days passed. Meanwhile this drags on day after day until no hope of his survival remains; his death is certain. Whatever happens, I will see you again.' (CO 10b,8) Bouwsma's argument appears to be somewhat questionable, however, as Calvin was completely obedient to his father even to the extent that he changed his career plans to accommodate his father's wish. Calvin wrote about this incident in the preface to his commentary on the Psalms (July 22, 1557): 'When I was as yet a very little boy, my father had destined me for the study of theology. But afterwards when he considered that the legal profession commonly raised those who followed it to wealth this prospect induced him suddenly to change his purpose. Thus it came to pass, that I was withdrawn from the study of philosophy, and was put to the study of law. To this pursuit I endeavored faithfully to apply myself in obedience to the will of my father; but God, by the secret guidance of his providence, at length gave a different direction to my course.' (CALVIN, Comm. in Ps., praefatio [CO 31,21.22])

201 Calvin translates יְתוֹמִים as 'orphan' and אֵין אָב as 'fatherless.' Interestingly, in the exegetical notes on this verse in Lamentations, Calvin completely passed over the phrase אֵין אָב ('fatherless'), but gave a lengthy explanation of יתום ('orphan').

(ὑπάρχει) πατήρτο, and translated it as 'fatherless,' preferring to render ὀρφανά as 'orphan' so as to emphasize the condition of homelessness. Calvin further consciously included the term יְתוֹמִים in his exegetical note on the text. All of this illustrates that the idea of non-belonging – to put it another way, the idea of the גֵּר – played a significant role in Calvin's translation and exegetical work on the Old Testament.

Observation 19: In the dedication to his commentary on Jeremiah,[202] Calvin writes that if the prophet were still alive today, he would acknowledge his – Calvin's – work as having been done with honor and reverence. He further adds that his exegesis was done with his own historical circumstances in mind.[203] Immediately following this statement, Calvin pleads the cause of the strangers and refugees before the Prince to whom he had dedicated the commentary, asking that he might welcome them if they seek refuge in his dominion. For Calvin knew from personal experience the pain of being a miserable stranger, and described to the prince how he had been a stranger for more than thirty years.[204] The 'stranger'-experience was thus part and parcel of Calvin's very life. For that reason, argues Calvin, he has the responsibility to look after the strangers and refugees.[205] He further asks that the prince not let the ingratitude of the foreigner Françis Baldwin prevent his good heart from extending hospitality to the strangers.[206]

---

202 The commentary was dedicated to Prince Frederick III, the Elector Palatine, on July 23, 1563. After making an introductory remark, Calvin eulogizes the prince for his firmness in following and implementing the true Gospel in relation to the Lord's Supper in his dominion, in spite of the plots made on his life by the Germans. Calvin goes on to explain his position on the Lord's Supper, and to argue the falsity of the papist position as well as that of Luther. Calvin pleads the cause of the 'strangers' before the prince.

203 CALVIN, Praelect. in Jer., dedicatio (CO 29,77): 'and further, that they have been usefully accommodated to present circumstances.'

204 CALVIN, Praelect. in Jer., praefatio (CO 20,78): 'Thirty years have passed away since my voluntary exile from France, because thence were exiled the truth of the Gospel, pure Religion, and the true Worship of God. I am now become so inured to my peregrination, that I feel no desire to return to my country. I am indeed here so far a stranger, (though once banished, I was yet so recalled, that I never feel ashamed,) that they deem me no more a foreigner than if I could name my ancestors as the citizens of this place.'

205 CALVIN, Praelect. in Jer., praefatio (CO 20,78): 'The more kindly God has dealt with me, the greater concern ought I to feel for my brethren from France as well as from Flanders.'

206 CALVIN, Praelect. in Jer., praefatio (CO 38,78): 'Nor let it cause you any regret, Most Illustrious Prince, that you have been sometimes deceived in foreigners, and indeed in men of our language, but go on in your wonted course of benevolence.'

2.3 Summary

The above makes it clear that Calvin interprets the biblical text, strongly influenced by his historical context and even the events of his very own life. Calvin further uses the concept of the 'stranger' to make clear that, just as in the Bible the people – including kings, magistrates and other politicians – had to listen and submit to the Word brought by 'strangers,' so in his present day these same group would have to listen to Calvin who was just such a stranger. In short, Calvin identifies himself with the Old Testament 'strangers,' and this identification shaped both his exegesis as well as his understanding of his position in Geneva.

3. Exegetical Principles for the Interpretation of the Concept of גֵר

3.1. Introductory Matters

Calvin was a very prolific writer. To give an idea of the amount he wrote, a modern English edition of his commentaries alone fills twenty-two hefty volumes of approximately one thousand pages each. In spite of the mass of his exegetical works, Calvin did not leave behind a systematic account of his hermeneutical method, or his exegesis. Consequently, Calvin scholars are forced to determine his views by reading extensively from his works. The efforts that have already been undertaken have yielded a wide variety of opinions on Calvin's hermeneutics. In spite of these divergences, scholarship is agreed on one thing: the essential, if not unparalleled, impact of his work for modern hermeneutics. Bernard Ramm writes that Calvin was 'the first scientific interpreter in the history of the Christian exegetics.'[207] G.E. Wright concludes his survey of Calvin's commentaries with the following observation: 'the more one studies these commentaries, the more astonished he becomes at their scholarship, lucid profundity, and freshness of insight. Although Biblical studies moved a long way since the sixteenth century, there is still little which can be held being their equal.'[208] Already in the nineteenth century, the church historian

---

207 RAMM, *Protestant Biblical Interpretation*, 57.
208 WRIGHT, 'The Christian Interpreter,' 133. The nineteenth-century English translator of Calvin's commentary on the minor prophets wrote: 'The editor feels it to be his duty to say generally of Calvin's expositions, that the more maturely he considers them, after having compared them with those of others, both modern and ancient, the more satisfied he is with them, and the more he admires the acuteness and solid judgement they display. Perhaps no individual, pos-

Philip Schaff wrote that 'Calvin was the best theologian and exegete among the Reformers.'[209] Thomas Torrance is similarly positive on Calvin's contribution to exegesis, calling him the father of modern biblical exposition. For him, Calvin's concern for integrity in interpretation, and objectivity in exposition, made him much less a child of his age than most humanists or reformers of the sixteenth century. It paved the way for a systematic interpretation of the Holy Scriptures.[210] Finally, François Wendel argued that Calvin 'founded the modern science of exegesis.'[211]

The virtually universal appreciation of Calvin's exegetical works can perhaps best be illustrated by what Jacob Arminius could remark, even though he was fiercely opposed to Calvin on certain points of doctrine:

> Next to the study of Scriptures which I earnestly inculcate, I exhort my pupils to peruse Calvin's Commentaries: [...] for I affirm that he excels beyond comparison in the interpretation of Scripture and that his commentaries ought to be more highly valued than all that is handed down by the library of the fathers.[212]

If even Arminius had such a high regard for Calvin's exegetical skills, it is sad that for centuries, theologians, church historians, exegetes, and Calvin scholars have largely overlooked his exegetical works. Similarly, very little has been written about Calvin's place within the history of biblical hermeneutics. The paucity of studies led T.H.L Parker to remark in 1971 that the literature on Calvin's commentaries is meager and disappointing, comprising little more than 'paragraphs in the older writers, some articles in periodicals, a few unpublished dissertations from the nineteenth century, and one book which is predominantly concerned with the doctrine expressed in the commentaries and only incidentally with the form and method.'[213] Parker argues that attention ought to be given to the historical and contextual orientation of Calvin's exegesis, binding himself to the conditions of each respective author and his subject. In other words, according to Parker, Calvin used a contextual method to arrive at the inner meaning of the text.[214] However, Parker adds that, in additi-

---

sessing his high qualification, natural, acquired and spiritual has ever, either in ancient or modern times, exercised himself so much in the study of the Holy Scriptures, and produced comments so original and so valuable.' (OWEN, preface to John Calvin, *Commentaries on the Twelve Prophets*).

209 SCHAFF, *History of the Christian Church*, 7,32. Schaff continues: 'Calvin never abused reason, like Luther, but assigned it the office of an indispensable handmaid of revelation.'

210 TORRANCE, *The Hermeneutics of Calvin*, 61.72.

211 WENDELL, *Calvin: Origin and Development*, 31.

212 SCHAFF, *History of the Christian Church*, 8,280.

213 PARKER, *Calvin's Commentaries*, ix.

214 PARKER, *Calvin the Biblical Expositor* 65–73. Cf. among others, OBERMAN, *The Two Reformations*, 116–68; STEINMETZ, 'Calvin and the Patristic Exegesis of Paul,' 100–18; KRAUS, *Calvin's Exegetical Principles*, 2–12; GAMBLE, 'Brevitas et Facilitas,' 33–50; HAIRE, 'John Calvin as an Expositor,' 74–88;

on to the context of the individual author, Calvin also paid attention to the context of the entire biblical canon.[215]

Parker's work was a first step towards filling the gap in scholarship, but some ten years later (1982), David Steinmetz could still remark:

> We still lack a definite study of Calvin's hermeneutic [...] indeed, so little has been done on Calvin's exegesis that almost any kind of study will make some useful contribution to our knowledge. Still there is at the moment particular need for studies which will place Calvin's exegesis in the context of the history of Biblical Interpretation. How does Calvin's exegesis compare with Biblical interpretation of the ancient Christian Fathers, the Medieval Jewish and Christian commentators, the humanist, and, of course, Calvin's protestant and Roman Catholic contemporaries?[216]

To sum up Steinmetz' point, what we know about the sources of Calvin's exegesis remains little more than guesswork.

More recently, William J. Bouwsma (1988) has traced the many streams of thought, both medieval and modern, that made their way into Calvin's hermeneutic.[217] Bouwsma's main contribution to scholarship was his pioneering work on the psychological factors that shaped Calvin as an interpreter. However, because Bouwsma focused on the biographical aspect of Calvin, his study does not go deeper into Calvin's exegesis. Another pioneering work from around the same time was Thomas F. Torrance's *The Hermeneutics of John Calvin* (1988). In spite of its promising title, the study has a very narrow focus, certainly too narrow to qualify as a general study on Calvin's hermeneutics. Torrance placed Calvin's hermeneutical principles in the context of medieval theories of knowledge, and drew connections between Calvin and John Major, and indirectly to Duns Scotus as well. His main interest was in Calvin's hermeneutics as set forth in his biblical-theological work, the Institutes,[218] so that the content of Torrance's work does not do full justice to its title.

In the two decades that followed, however, a large number of scholars have attempted to make systematic studies of Calvin's hermeneutical principles.[219] Appreciation was expressed for Calvin's use of historical, grammatical and

---

FLOOR, 'The Hermeneutics of Calvin,' 163–73; MCKANE, 'Calvin as an Old Testament Commentator,' 250–60; MULLER, 'The Hermeneutic of Promise and Fulfillment in Calvin's Exegesis,' 68–82.

215 PARKER, *Calvin's Old Testament Commentaries*, 80.

216 STEINMETZ, 'The Theology of Calvin and Calvinism,' 217–18.

217 BOUWSMA, *John Calvin*.

218 TORRANCE, *The Hermeneutics of John Calvin*, 155

219 PARKER, 'Calvin the Exegete: Change and Development,' 33–46; STEINMETZ, *The Bible in the Sixteenth Century*; KRAUS, 'Calvin's Exegetical Principles,' 329–34; Muller, *The Unaccommodated Calvin*; GAMBLE, *'Brevitas et facilitas'*; MULLER & THOMPSON, *Biblical Interpretation in the Era of the Reformation*; OPITZ, 'Calvin as Bible Translator: From the Model of the Hebrew Psalter', in: SELDERHUIS, *Calvinus sacrarum literarum interpres*, Göttingen 2008, 9–26.

literal tools not only by historians,[220] but also by Old Testament scholars like B.S. Childs who observed that 'Calvin's work was characterized by its sober attempt to render the literal sense of the book' and he further claims that the sixteenth-century exegetical work of Calvin is relevant to that of modern scholars like von Rad.[221] C.E.B. Cranfield praised Calvin for not allowing his commentary to come between the text and the reader.[222] But the very first systematic presentation of Calvin's hermeneutics was presented by Kraus, who derived eight hermeneutical principles from Calvin's commentaries, and which he frequently quoted as typifying Calvin's exegetical method: 1. The principle of brevity and clarity; 2. The principle of determining the intention of the author; 3. The principle of investigating the historical, geographical, and institutional circumstances that are determinative for the author's situation; 4. The principle of setting forth the real meaning of a passage (also called the original, true, simple, or grammatical meaning); 5. The principle of investigating the context of a passage; 6. The principle of establishing standards concerning the extent to which exegesis can go beyond the literal biblical wording of a text; 7. The principle of recognizing metaphorical language; and 8. Finding Christ in the Old Testament.[223] In effect, Kraus went a step further than Parker in pointing out that Calvin not only looked at the context, but also the historical setting for the text, in contrast to Luther's non-historical approach. Richard A. Muller, added one more hermeneutical principle, namely that of 'promise and fulfillment.'[224] In pointing to this principle, Muller also indirectly maintained the 'tradition of continuity' in the trajectory of Calvin's hermeneutics.

But also different standpoints and nuances in the history of scholarship need to be noted. Some have argued that Calvin's hermeneutical approach basically Christianized the Old Testament, and Judaized the New Testament. He has also been criticized for viewing the Old Testament through the lens of the author of the letter to the Hebrews.[225] Alexandre Ganoczy and Stefan Scheld put Calvin's exegetical works in the background of the exegetical tradition of the Middle Ages, Renaissance, and Reformation. They studied Calvin's thought and practice, philological orientation, use of typology and rejection of allegory. They also worked on Calvin's historical references, and investigated some of his theological presuppositions. They concluded that Calvin was torn between biblical exegesis and systematic theology, thus positing that Calvin's method cannot be reduced to one principle, since it is a blend between historical and

---

220 PUCKETT, *John Calvin's Exegesis of the Old Testament*, 7.
221 CHILDS, *Old Testament Books*, 36.
222 CRANFIELD, *A Critical and Exegetical Commentary on [...] Romans* (ICC), 1,40.
223 KRAUS, 'Calvin's Exegetical Principles', 8–18.
224 MULLER, 'The Hermeneutic of Promise and Fulfillment in Calvin's Exegesis,' 68–82.
225 KRAELING, *The Old Testament Since the Reformation*, 32.

dogmatic exegesis.[226] Scholars like Edward J. Dowey looked at the inconsistencies between Calvin's historical exegesis and his doctrine of Scripture, and suggested that there were two Calvins: the theologian and the humanist scholar. Calvin was somewhere between traditional doctrine and the new approach to the text.[227] Kemper Fullerton and H. Jackson Forstman similarly identified a discontinuity between Calvin's doctrine of Scripture, and his exegetical method.[228]

The above survey illustrates the following. In the first place, lately a fair number of attempts have been made to study Calvin's hermeneutical principles. Secondly, these scholars may have had a similar focus (i.e. on Calvin's hermeneutics), but they had different approaches and, not surprisingly, also different conclusions. Third, virtually every single scholar ended his or her study with the note that the field was not yet exhausted, and on the contrary wide open for further investigation. Fourth, all of the above works concentrated on Calvin's hermeneutical principles in general. However, in order to have a focused study on a selected term or motif, we do not so much need the broader hermeneutical principles, but rather the specific exegetical method.[229] In

---

226 PUCKETT, *John Calvin's Exegesis of the Old Testament*, 9.

227 DOWEY Jr., *The Knowledge of God*, 104.

228 FULLERTON, *Prophecy and Authority*, 133; FORSTMAN, *Word and Spirit: Calvin's Doctorine of Biblical Authority*, 109.

229 In his biblical commentaries, Calvin used three different terms: hermeneutics, exegesis and exposition. Many scholars pay no attention to their usage, and assume that they refer to the same thing. A close reading allows us to distinguish clear patterns in the usage of these terms. *Hermeneutics* logically precedes the other two. Michael Armour notes that hermeneutics examines the suppositional skeleton of interpretation. It deals with the nature of the text, epistemological guides for exegesis, and the truth that could be claimed from the Scriptures. In short, hermeneutics establishes a broad philosophical construct and general framework of rules which guide the process of interpreting Biblical texts. Hermeneutics offers the scope for a general pattern of interpretation, not on the meaning of a particular passage. If hermeneutics is philosophical and theoretical in nature, then *exegesis* could be described as technical in nature. Exegesis deals with the meaning of specific texts, and in particular with the meaning intended by their author. Whereas hermeneutics looks at the broad sweep of Scripture, exegesis narrows the focus to an examination of an individual passage or motif like 'stranger.' To counterbalance the generalization associated with hermeneutics, exegesis focuses on analysis and detail. In exegesis, linguistic skills are extremely important. Vital, too, in modern theories of exegesis is the detailed knowledge of the historical and cultural setting in which the author worked. Finally, *exposition* is building on exegetical insights to bring out the pastoral or practical aspects of biblical interpretation. Exegesis stresses what the text meant when it was written, while exposition focuses on what it means in the present. For Calvin, exposition is extremely important. He was not a scholar who kept himself far from the world somewhere in a quiet corner of a remote monastery, pursuing scholarship for the sake of scholarship. He was a stranger and pastor for a congregation of strangers, and was actively involved in the lives of his people. Cf. Graham observes: 'For Calvin the real world was to be taken seriously, and for

order to achieve the goal of clarifying the concept of גֵר in Calvin's Old Testament commentaries, the present chapter will focus on his exegetical principles.

In what follow, the various exegetical principles Calvin used in order to bring out the idea of the 'stranger' in his Old Testament commentaries will be analyzed.

3.2. Exegetical Principles

It is interesting to note that in spite of the great volume of his exegetical work, Calvin did not write a systematic work on the subject of hermeneutics itself. All the same, some remarks on his exegetical method can be found in the dedication to his commentary on Romans. Calvin addressed the commentary to Simon Grynaeus, and reminds him of a discussion they had had some three years before on the best mode of expounding the Scriptures. Their conclusion had been that the chief virtue of an expositor is his lucid brevity (perspicua brevitas).[230] Calvin echoed a similar view on *brevitas* in his dedicatory remarks to the Psalms commentary.

> And so not only is a simple style of teaching maintained by me, bur for the purpose of being removed from all ostentation, I have abstained from refutation for the most part [...] Neither have I mentioned contrary opinion, unless there was a danger that silence would leave the readers in doubt or perplexity.[231]

The fact that both in Calvin's first commentary (Romans), and what is arguably the last commentary (Harmony of the Law), we find such similar remarks on exegetical method, illustrates that he remained consistent throughout his life in terms of method.

In his dedication to the Romans commentary, Calvin explains his opinion that the exegete has as 'almost his only work to lay open the mind of the writer whom he undertake to explain.' To achieve this goal, Calvin argues that the interpreter must use plain language as well as exercise brevity to avoid 'the evil of tiring his readers with prolixity.' He recognized that many interpreters would differ with him on this issue of simplicity and conciseness, but said he would urge tolerance for a variety of exegetical approaches, even if he himself wanted to avoid complex styles of exegesis:

---

him the real world involved shoe-makers, printers and clockmakers, as well as farmers, scholars, knights and clergymen.' GRAHAM, *The Constructive Revolutionary John Calvin*, 79.

230 CALVIN, *Comm. in Rom.*, dedicatio (CO 10b,402).

231 CALVIN, *Comm. in Ps.*, dedicatio (CO 31,33–35) : 'Itaque non modo simplex docendi ratio ubique a me servata est, sed quo longius abesset omnis ostentatio, a refutationibus ut plurimum abstinui [...]. Neque unquam contrarias sententias attigi, nisi ubi periculum erat ne tacendo dubios ac perplexos relinquerem lectores.' Cf. also the comments on *brevitas* in CALVIN, *Comm. in Mosis reliq. libr.*, dedicatio (CO 20,120–21).

We who approve of brevity will not reject nor despise the labours of those who are more copi-
ous and diffused in their explanation of Scripture. (And may it be) that they also in their turn
will bear with us, though they may think us too compressed and concise.[232]

A close reading of the passages where Calvin dealt with the idea of גֵר will lead
one to conclude that Calvin did indeed use a clear exegetical method while
dealing with the relevant passages from the Old Testament.

3.2.1. The Principle of Utility

According to Calvin, Christian exegetes should give themselves only to expositions which are useful. This principle of utility drives from Calvin's view of
God's design in Scripture: 'There is nothing vain and unprofitable contained in
the oracles of God, [...] and it is by the reading of the Scripture that we make
progress in piety and holiness of life.'[233] Since Scripture itself aims at utility,
the main task of the interpreter is to work with that goal of the Scriptures
themselves. 'The Lord, when he gave us Scripture, did not intend either to
gratify our curiosity, or to encourage ostentation, or to give occasion for chat-
ting and talking, but to do us good; and therefore the right use of Scripture
must always tend to what is profitable.'[234] Calvin wished also his own exegetical
work to be considered first of all according to the principle of utility: 'I do not
ask for people to agree with me, or my words, unless they have first of all reali-
zed that what I am teaching is useful.'[235] For Calvin, drawing on a passage from
Paul's letter to Titus, it is the teacher's duty to exhort to a holy life rather than
to occupy the minds of his audience with all kinds of useless questions.[236]

In a series of sermons on the letter to Timothy, Calvin strongly emphasized
the *principle of utility*:

Thus when I expound the Holy Scripture, I must be guided by this consideration, that those
who hear me may receive profit from the doctrine which I teach, that they may be edified for
salvation. If I have not that desire, and do not aim at the edification of those who hear me, I am
a sacrilegious person, profaning the Word of God. On the other hand, they who read the Scripture, or who come to the sermon to listen, if they are in search of some foolish speculation, if
they come here to take their amusement, are guilty of having profaned a thing so holy.[237]

---

232 CALVIN, *Comm. in Rom.*, dedicatio (CO 10b,403).
233 CALVIN, *Comm. in Rom.* 15,4 (CO 49,271).
234 CALVIN, *Comm. in 2 Tim.* 3,16.
235 CALVIN, *Contre les libertins spirituels* (COR 4/1,170).
236 CALVIN, *Comm. in Tit.* 2,11.
237 CALVIN, *Sermons de Jean Calvin sur les deux Epistres de Saint Paul a Timothee, recueilles par l'escrivain
     ordinaire pour le bien at l'edification de l'eglise du Seigneur*, as cited in CALVIN, *Commentary on the
     Epistles to Timothy, Titus, and Philemon*, Calvin Translation Society, 250 n 1. The translator, Wil-
     liam PRINGLE, only identifies it as coming from 'a rare work.'

Calvin's concern for 'useful interpretation' also seems to have been behind his definition of prophecy. For him, prophecy is not the gift of foretelling the future, but 'the science of interpreting the Scripture,' or more specifically, it aims at edification, exhortation and consolation. Hence, Prophecy is an 'interpretation made suitable for present use.'[238]

It is this same principle of utility that guides Calvin in his exegesis when he decided to treat, or else omit, certain controversies in connection with the concept of the גר. One clear example can be found in his treatment of the superscriptions that are found with Ps 12. Although there were different opinions surrounding them, Calvin dismissed the entire issue by saying, 'as it is of no great importance which of these opinion is adopted, I do not trouble myself much about this matter.'[239] But how did Calvin let himself be guided in his exegesis by this principle of utility? Two factors can be identified, which may have played a significant role in Calvin's thought while dealing with the stranger-motif. In the first place, as particularly the examples taken from his treatment of the letters to Timothy and Titus show, Calvin drew his principle of utility from the Scriptures themselves. Secondly, one could point to Calvin's humanism. As Bouwsma points out, his humanist background shaped Calvin as it was 'a self-conscious reform movement, concerned to reform not all times but its own time [...] It did so with the sense of urgency that was a major element in its rejection of speculative system building, which seemed a kind of luxury that the times could ill afford.'[240] Bouwsma also argued that since Calvin 'felt keenly the urgency of the times,' the 'central motive force of Calvin's life was not to set forth a true theology for the ages but to remedy the particular evils of his own age. He aimed [...] to galvanize other human beings to appropriate action, to induce activity, to obtain results.'[241] If Bouwsma's view holds, it would prove all the more that the principle of utility really was one of the most basic ones in his entire exegetical method.

3.2.2. The Principle of Edification

There is a close connection in Calvin's thought between the principle of utility and the principle of edification. He once warned: 'do not covet new things and have tingling ears that carry you away with curiosity, but seek what is profitable and edifying.'[242] If a particular doctrine or exegesis does not edify, it is also

---

238 CALVIN, *Comm. 1 Thess.* 5,20 (CO 54,176); cf. *Comm. in 1 Cor.* 12,28 (CO 49,507).
239 CALVIN, *Comm. in Ps.* 12,1 (CO 31,126).
240 BOUWSMA, 'Calvinism as Renaissance Artifact,' 35.
241 BOUWSMA, 'Calvinism as Renaissance Artifact,' 35.
242 CALVIN, *Contre les libertins spirituels* (COR 4/1,170).

not genuinely profitable. Calvin thus made the broad statement that 'all doctrine must be tried by this rule, that those which contribute to edification may be approved and that those which give ground for unprofitable disputes may be rejected as unworthy of the Church of God.'[243] But what did Calvin mean by 'edification'? For him, it means the promotion of a proper regard for God in the heart of the believer. A true exegete is thus one 'who edifies consciences in the fear of God.'[244]

In light of the above, it should also not be surprising that Calvin's fundamental criticism of the scholastics is centered on what he judged to be their shortcomings in terms of edification. For him there were two basic things in which the scholastics were misguided: first, in their failure to respect the limits of human knowledge, which resulted in their fascination with frivolous questions; and second, 'neglecting all together or testing but slightly, and carelessly, doctrine that tends to edification.'[245] He thus charged that scholastic theology 'contains contentions or ideal speculation, from which no advantage is derived.'[246] As to his own practice, Calvin limited himself in his exegetical work to issues that passed the principle of edification.

3.2.3. The Principle of Simplicity

If the principle of edification is an umbrella concern in Calvin's exegesis, then simplicity became the central concern of his interpretation.[247] At one time, Calvin writes that his sole intention in what he was about to write was to help the faithful poor, who are uncultured and illiterate, to avoid poisonous doctrines.[248] At the end of the same treatise he emphasizes once more that he had written for common Christians, and not for scholars: 'I have sought insofar as possible, to accommodate myself to the rudeness of the simple, for whom I primarily labour.' For that reason, he said: 'I have used as popular and simple a means I know how.'[249] This care for simplicity in his exegetical works led to the exceptional clarity of Calvin's writings. Thus François Higman, who has devoted several monographs to Calvin's writing style, observes that the first and most

---

243 CALVIN, *Comm. in 1 Tim.* 1,4.
244 CALVIN, *Comm. in Tit.* 1,1.
245 CALVIN, *Comm. in 2 Cor.* 12,4 (CO 50,138; COR 2/15,195).
246 CALVIN, *Comm. in 1 Tim.* 1,4.
247 One specialist on Calvin's humanist background notes that 'Calvin writes for the common man of general education, and that he expressly avoids subject matters which require special training.' See BREEN, 'John Calvin and the Rhetorical Tradition,' 11.
248 CALVIN, *Contre les Anabaptistes* (COR 4/2,36).
249 CALVIN, *Contre les Anabaptistes* (COR 4/2,140).

obvious quality of Calvin's writing is the clarity of organization.[250] Higman also notes that this simplicity and clarity are not limited to the organization of the materials, but also come out in his syntax and vocabulary.[251]

Calvin's simplicity in style went hand-in-hand with an exegetical methodology which gave preference to simplicity. When a passage could be understood to have a variety of different meanings, Calvin tended to accept the simplest option, even when the weight of respected authorities pointed in the other direction. When it comes to the concept of the גר, we note the presence of such statements in Calvin's exegesis such as, 'I should prefer to understand the expression in a more simple way, agreeably to the common usage of Scripture.'[252] Similarly, Calvin makes remarks along the lines of 'I do not much object to it [...] however, it is more simple [...]'[253] when he disagrees with, but does not outright reject, the interpretations suggested by others.

In connection with his exegesis of the גר notion as it appears in Lv 13,58, Calvin clearly states that it is not his intention or purpose to perform the duties of a grammarian.[254] On seven occasions does Calvin use simple grammatical and syntactical aids to translate, and make exegetical remarks on, the concept of 'stranger' in a sense that differed with the tradition of translation and exegesis. In Gn 50,16, Calvin gives a translation, on which his exegesis is later also based, of the phrase וַיְצַוּוּ אֶל־יוֹסֵף לֵאמֹר. Although the word גר is not found in the text, Calvin infers the presence of an 'unknown messenger,' whom he also identifies as a 'stranger,' whereas no such inferences are found in the LXX, in Luther, or in the Geneva Bible.[255] In connection with Jes 14,32, he calls the futu-

---

250 HIGMAN, *Jean Calvin: Three French Treaties*, 26.

251 HIGMAN, *Jean Calvin: Three French Treaties*, 28–29.

252 CALVIN, *Comm. in 1 Cor.* 2,8 (CO 49,338).

253 CALVIN, *Comm. in 2 Cor.* 1,15 (CO 50,20; COR 2/15,25).

254 CALVIN, *Comm. in Mosis reliq. libr.*, Lv 13,58 (CO 24,321–22): 'It has appeared to me sufficient to touch upon the sum of the matter, because it would be almost superfluous labor to insist upon the words, although I should be unwilling to condemn the diligence of those who examine these points also; but it is not my purpose to perform the office of the grammarian.' However, Parker observes that Calvin in his commentary analyzes Hebrew words, grammar and syntax to bring out the inner meaning of the text (PARKER, *Exposition and Method in Calvin*, 65–66.). Further, Pucket observes that Calvin's interest in philology as a tool for understanding the Biblical text, and his resulting deviation from the opinions of earlier Christian exegetes, may be rooted in his training as a humanist (PUCKET, *John Calvin's Exegesis of the Old Testament*, 60).

255 In Gn 50,16, the brothers of Joseph were trying to reconcile themselves with him after the crime they had committed against him years before. The text reads וַיְצַוּוּ אֶל־יוֹסֵף לֵאמֹר. The LXX translates as, 'They came to Joseph,' while Luther and the Geneva Bible read, 'They sent unto Joseph to say.' Calvin, however, takes his starting point in the basic meaning of the root צוה in piel form ('to lay upon, lay charge upon, command to') to translate, 'they lay charge upon.' Calvin further goes on to connect the other verb לֵאמֹר (qal) to translate the verb as 'to say.' The combination of צוה and אמר thus leads Calvin to translate the text as follows: 'They sent a messenger unto Joseph to say.' For one who is commanded to bring a mes-

re messengers 'strangers,'[256] and a similar jump is made with respect to the
מָגוֹר in Gn 28,4.[257] Thus the עַם־קְרֹבוֹ in Ps 148,14 are identified as 'strangers,'[258] and the same is true for the noun וּרְחוֹקִים in Sach 6,15[259] and מַמְזֵר in
Sach 9,6.[260] In all of these instances, Calvin differed from other translations and
exegetes, including the LXX, Luther, the Geneva Bible, and on several occasions
also Sebastian Munster's Latin Vulgate.

Calvin feared that if simplicity was abandoned, exposition would become
complicated and indirect, and thus invite disdain from the non-believers. This
principle can be illustrated from Calvin's work on Ps 16,4-10. Most of the Greek
and Latin fathers interpret 'strangers' as those who follow the false gods. [261]
Calvin, however, understands the text to refer, not to those who *follow* false
gods, but to the false gods *themselves*. What is significant in this respect is the
way Calvin defends his choice of translation, for he remarks: 'but it is better to
adhere to the natural simplicity of the interpretation which I have given, that

---

sage must be a messenger. Calvin also went beyond the simple grammatical sense, laying out
the circumstances in which the events of this text took place. For after the death of Jacob, Joseph's brothers who still live in a foreign land, send an unknown person to effect their work of
reconciliation. In his exegetical notes, Calvin calls this unknown messenger a 'stranger.' He
later expands even more on this deduction when he notes the danger that the brothers ran in
revealing to him the crime they had committed against Joseph, since it would lower their reputation.

256 Similarly, Calvin in his translation of Jes 14,32 renders the noun מַלְאָךְ as 'messenger' on
strictly grammatical grounds, but in his exegetical comments he prefers the term 'stranger.'
See CALVIN, *Comm. in Isa.* 14,32 (CO 36,272.293).

257 Another remarkable aspect in Calvin's use of the grammatical sense can be found in his discussion of Gn 28,4, where the text reads אֶת־אֶרֶץ מְגֻרֶיךָ. The LXX translates 'land of thy sojourning,' and the Geneva Bible 'the land where thou art a stranger.' In Calvin's estimation, however, both translations overlook the importance of the plural form of the noun מָגוֹר, which led
Calvin to translate 'Terram peregrinationum,' and which he considers to express the multiple
exiles suffered by the stranger. Although Calvin acknowledges that the use of a plural form in
Hebrew is not always this significant, in this context he maintains that it is.

258 Calvin compares this passage with various other passages where the 'children of God' are
placed on the same level as the 'strangers,' so that the latter receive various blessings and protection provided for under the Law. Using this contextual clue, Calvin here understands the בוֹ
עַם־קְרֹ (literally: 'people near unto him') in Ps 148,14 as 'strangers' who are circumcised and
grafted into the congregation of the Lord.

259 Calvin relates the term וּרְחוֹ קִים (literally 'they that are far') in Sach 6,15 with the term נֵכָר־
בְּנֵי ('sons of stranger') because in the both situations the thrust of the texts is that the strangers from far off would come and build the temple for the people of God. Although there are
similarities, in Sach 6,15 the subject of the verb is not specified as it is in Jes 60,10. Calvin understands the subject to be 'stranger,' and on the basis of the following phrase וּרְחוֹ קִים, he
concludes that the stranger would come from a far-off country and rebuild the temple.

260 Calvin once again appeals to grammar to arrive at a better understanding of the text. The LXX
and Targum translate the noun מַמְזֵר (Sach 9,6) as 'strange people.' However, Calvin thinks
that the noun rzmm derives from the root זור (double m), and thus translates as 'extraneous.'

261 Ps. 16,4-6.

we may not make ourselves objects of ridicule to the Jews; and fathers, that one subtlety, by engendering many others, may not involve us in a labyrinth.'[262]

In essence, Calvin thus followed a hermeneutical principle not unlike Ockham's razor. He thought that no interpretation should be more complex than the context itself demanded. Calvin rejected any approach to exegesis that was so heavy that an average listener could not follow the line of the expositor's argument. Thus it is not surprising to learn that Calvin scholarship is virtually unanimous in identifying the intended audience of the commentaries of Calvin as his congregation, which in his case was further largely composed of refugees and strangers. Yet the simplicity in exegetical work, however, does not restrict the theologian or teacher to simple and unadorned language. Calvin insisted that 'eloquence, therefore, is neither to be condemned nor despised which has no tendency to lead Christians to be taken up with an outward glitter of words or intoxicate them with empty delight, or tickle their ears with its tinkling sound.'[263] Calvin thus felt justified on occasion to give preference to one interpretation of a word over another based on the greater eloquence.

In his studies on Calvin's writing style, Higman points out how Calvin made use of imagery and metaphor, not as a simple literary adornment, but rather as an aid to clarity. Higman also observes that Calvin made extensive use of adverbs, relative pronouns and conjunctions which keep the sentence pattern clear. Although Calvin was schooled in humanism, he turned his back on Latin style of the humanist with its abundance of complex sentences, subordinate clauses, and participial constructions. In their place he substituted a regularized word order of subject, verb, object and the almost invariable use of expressed pronoun subjects, all in the interest of clarity.[264]

3.2.4. The Principle of Brevity

In the dedication to his commentary on Romans, Calvin indicated that *lucid brevity* was a most important principle in his method of exegeting the Scriptures:

> But both of us thought that the chief virtue of an interpreter is to be in clear brevity. And certainly since it is his task to unfold the mind of the writer he has undertaken to expound, the more he leads away from the author's meaning so the more he leaves his own purpose and is

---

262 CALVIN, *Comm. in Ps.* 16,10 (CO 31,157).
263 CALVIN, *Comm. in 1 Cor.* 1,17 (CO 49,322).
264 HIGMAN, *Three French treatises*, 27–31.

certain to wander from his goal [...] nevertheless I will not be able to be moved from my love of brevity.[265]

One of the main objects in his exegesis is to avoid lengthy doctrinal discussions, or even digressions into theological commonplaces, thus sparing his readers from both annoyance and boredom.[266] For that reason it is not surprising that we find such remarks as 'not to multiply instances [...],'[267] or 'I will not stop to refute the opinion of other men.'[268] The same methodological principle was repeated by Calvin in the introductory remarks to his Isaiah commentary.[269]

In a letter to Farel from September 1, 1549, Calvin spoke openly of the differences between the two of them in terms of stylistic emphasis on brevity. When Farel was about to publish a book, Calvin noted his regret about the style of the book, especially in connection with its intended audience: 'Because the readers of our time are so fastidious, and not possessed of great acuteness, I should wish the language to be so managed that one might allure them by the fluency of his expression.'[270] He did not, however, overly insist on this point, because he felt that his own style was perhaps 'over–concise'. This term (i.e. 'over–concise'), might seem rather questionable given that Calvin's commentaries, when translated into English, fill some twenty-two thick volumes of approximately 1,000 pages each. How could Calvin speak of brevity in connection with his own exegetical work? In an attempt to resolve this apparent contradiction, Battles remarked that 'the real test of brevity' is not measured in terms of length: 'With few exceptions his sentences and paragraphs are packed with thought and have all the condensation possible without sacrifice of the constituent matter.'[271] Thus for Calvin, when he spoke of 'brevity,' he meant the avoidance of superfluous verbosity. This penchant for brevity can be found in Calvin's works from very early on, in fact, from before the time he became a theologian. After all, in his commentary on Seneca (1532), he charged the Stoic philosopher with being too verbose. But of his own commentaries, Calvin clai-

---

265 CALVIN, Comm. in Rom., dedicatio (CO 10b,402f.): 'Sentiebat enim uterque nostrum praecipum interpretis virtutem in perspicua brevitate esse positam. Et sane, quum hoc sit prope unicum illius officium mentem scriptoris quem explicandum sumpsit patefacere, quantum ab ea lecturos abducit, tantundem a scopo suo aberrant, vel certe a suisfinibus quodammodo evagatur [...] unum aliquem exstare qui et facilitate studet, et simul daret operam ne polixis commentaries studiosos ultra modum detineret [...] ego tamen dimoveri non possum ab amore comendii.'

266 CALVIN, preface to the Institutes.

267 CALVIN, Comm. in Isa. 1,3 (CO 36,30).

268 CALVIN, Comm. in Ps. 11,7 (CO 31,126).

269 CALVIN, Comm. in Isa, praefatio (CO 36,19–24).

270 CO 13,374.

271 BATTLES, Introduction to the Institutes, lxx.

med: 'I have endeavored that no one may justly complain that there are here many things which are superfluous.'[272]

The dedication to Calvin's commentary on the first book of the Pentateuch gives some hints as to how he understood brevity. The commentary is quite long – the best-known English translation runs to over one thousand pages! – yet Calvin claimed that, fearing that he might die soon (however, the reference to 'death' in the English quotation below does not mean Calvin feared he would soon die), he had labored with special diligence to be concise as he wrote: 'Since in my progress I have often despaired of life, I have preferred to give a succinct exposition to leaving a mutilated one behind me.'[273] If a commentary of more than one thousand pages is supposed to be a 'succinct exposition,' all would agree with Breen's conclusion that Calvin's claim to brevity is not all that convincing.[274] However, Calvin scholarship is generally agreed on the justice of Calvin's comments on his exegetical method.[275] After all, for Calvin, brevity is not a matter of page-count, but rather diligence in covering the essential issues without becoming verbose or ending up in long digressions.

> Sincere Reader, possessed of sound judgement, will see that I have taken diligent care, neither through cunning nor negligence, to pass over anything perplexed, ambiguous, or obscure. Since, therefore, I have endeavored to discuss all doubtful points, I do not see why any one should complain of brevity, unless he wishes to derive his knowledge exclusively from commentaries. Now I will gladly allow men of this sort, for whom no amount of verbosity can satiate, to seek for themselves some other master.[276]

In the context of Calvin's exegesis on the concept of the גֵּר, we find some lengthier explanations in his commentary on Gn 18 and 19. In fact, his comments on the גֵּר go on for more than ten pages, and cover a variety of aspects. Calvin first of all argues how the unknown visitors who came to Abraham at Mamre, as well as Lot's visitors in Sodom, are to be considered strangers. He also elaborates in his commentary on this aspect of the 'stranger' when he goes

---

272 CALVIN, *Comm. in Rom.*, dedicatio (CO 10b,405).

273 CALVIN, *Comm. in Gen*, dedicatio (CO 20,121).

274 BREEN, 'John Calvin and the Rhetorical Tradition', 16.

275 PARKER, *Calvin's New Testament Commentaries*. In this work, Parker indicates that that Calvin was aware of the various exegetical methods practiced in his time, such as the double literal pattern of Nicholas of Lyra, the literal-prophetic model of Faber Stapulensis, the method of Erasmus where he combined allegorical and philological tools, the doctrinal model of exposition of Bucer, Bullinger, Oecolampadius, Luther and Melanchthon. We thus find references in his commentaries to the method of Luther (CO 39,36), Melanchthon (CO 38,131), Bucer (CO 38,404), Zwingli (CO 39,36), and Oecolampadius (CO 39,36). Cf. PARKER, 'Exposition and Method in Calvin,' 65–66 Cf. also the essays by KRAUS, GAMBLE, HAIRE, FUHRMANN, DE LONG, STEINMETZ, MCKANE, and PRUST in GAMBLE, *Calvin and Hermeneutics*; STEINMETZ, *Calvin in Context*; and the essays by SCHREINER, KOK, and MULLER in MULLER & THOMPSON, *Biblical Interpretation in the Era of the Reformation*.

276 CALVIN, *Comm. in Gen.*, dedicatio (CO 20,121).

on to argue, against a large part of the exegetical tradition of which Calvin himself mentions Nicholas of Lyra and Luther, that the sin that led to Sodom's destruction was not sexual, but rather the inhospitable attitude they showed towards visiting strangers. If, according to Calvin, the sin that led to Sodom's punishment was carnal in nature, it is rather strange that Lot's daughters go unpunished when they, too, later fell into carnal sins. This explanation of the inhospitality of the Sodomites, contrasted to the hospitality Lot showed towards the strangers who came to his house, is found in connection with several passages in Calvin's commentary, and covers multiple pages. So why did Calvin give such a lengthy discussion – or perhaps, digression – on the גר, when he himself had upheld brevity as his prime exegetical principle? It appears that in this context, Calvin felt it to be absolutely imperative to deal with the various views and opinions of other exegetes, and to show how they all ignored that very aspect of justice to strangers which for Calvin runs as a constant theme throughout this passage. Calvin explains that Lot and his daughters were spared because they were hospitable to the strangers. Moreover, the sin of Sodom was not only that they were inhospitable to the strangers who eventually stayed at Lot's place, but also that they despised the words of Lot, who himself was still a stranger there. Sexual sin could not have been the reason for the destruction of Sodom, because, argues Calvin, Lot's daughters would then be the first to be punished. In order to prove this point, which further illustrates the importance of the גר-concept in Calvin's thought, Calvin departed from his usual *brevitas* in his exegesis.

The above survey allows us to make several observations. First, if it is Calvin's aim to treat all difficulties and ambiguities in a particular text, then it is the text of Scripture that determines the length of the commentary. If all those issues were dealt with in a succinct manner, the principle of brevity has been respected, no matter how many pages the commentary.

A second remark concerns the relationship between Calvin's commentaries and his *Institutes*, where the two were intended to complement each other. The *Institutes* were somewhat like Philip Melanchthon's *Loci communes*, which dealt with major doctrinal topics systematically. The *Institutes* could thus be read alongside the commentaries to determine what Calvin thought of a particular doctrinal *locus*. But because Calvin would not allow himself to get lost in all kinds of excurses, he ridiculed those who wanted to derive everything from his commentaries. He also wrote:

> If after this road has [...] been paved, I shall publish any interpretations of Scripture, I shall always condense them, because I have no need to undertake long doctrinal discussions, and di-

gress into commonplaces. In this way the godly reader will be spared great annoyance and boredom, provided he approach Scripture armed with knowledge of present work. [277]

The principle of brevity thus meant not only avoiding verbosity within one
particular work, but also avoiding repetitions from one work to another. For
this reason Calvin time and again directs his readers to another volume of his
commentaries or else to his Institutes.[278] Both the Institutes, as well as the sum
total of Calvin's commentaries, were thus used by him to uphold and practice
his principle of *brevitas*.

In Calvin's Old Testament commentaries, we see that his treatment of the
גר-idea is limited to brief exegetical notes in forty-two places. Calvin's primary
concern was to help humble minds understand the Scriptures, and he found it
useless to outline the whole variety of opinions which would only confuse his
readers. He conscientiously chose to adopt a concise style: 'I determined to
treat things so briefly that without much lose of time, readers may peruse in
my work what is contained in other writings.'[279] Calvin's aim to be succinct is
also the reason behind one of the most interesting features of his commentaries. For at times, when there are contrasting views, he does nothing more than
note that those differences exist. In connection with a difficult passage from
one of the Pauline epistles, for example, Calvin writes: 'As there is some difficulty in Paul's words, interpreters differ as to the meaning. I shall not spend
time in setting aside the interpreting of others, nor indeed is there any need
for this.'[280]

There are occasions on which Calvin outlines the opposing views and treats
them at greater length, there are instance he renders the name on whose opinions they are. And there are instance where he does not identify the name. It
is not that he did not know who the particular commentator was, but he rather
thought that the context of his own commentary did not warrant the name of
these exegetes to be mentioned explicitly. Instead, we normally find such remarks as, 'I will not stop to refute the opinion of other men,'[281] or the like. This
feature, too, contributed to the *brevitas* of his exegetical work. And finally,
when Calvin did feel the need to refute the views of others, he always limited
himself to one or two sentences, thereby once more illustrating his principle of
brevitas.

---

277 CO 2,3–4.
278 Cf. CALVIN, *Comm. in Cor.* 9,5 (CO 49,440): 'on this point I (Calvin) have expressed myself more
     fully in the preceding epistle, and my *Institutes* will furnish a full discussion of it.'
279 CALVIN, *Comm. in Rom.*, dedicatio (CO 10b,405).
280 CO 52,388.
281 CALVIN, *Comm. in Ps.* 11,7 (CO 31,126).

3.2.5. The Principle of Natural Meaning

For Calvin, keeping to the natural meaning of a text not only avoids allegory, but also keeps one from any other speculative or imaginative interpretation. This principle of natural meaning promotes simplicity, and simplicity conversely keeps speculation at a minimum. However, one should not suppose that Calvin here aimed at a wooden literalness. He was aware that the Biblical writers used figures of speech just as any other people do in ordinary discourse. When Calvin spoke of the literal sense, he instead had in view the way people would naturally understand speech in daily discourse.

> Let us know that the true meaning of Scripture is the natural and obvious meaning; and let us embrace and abide by it resolutely. Let us not only neglect as doubtful, but boldly set aside as deadly corruption, those pretended expositions which lead us away from the natural meaning.[282]

Calvin made use of a number of expressions to point to this natural or obvious meaning. He sometimes calls it the 'the simple and genuine sense,'[283] or else 'the simple and natural interpretation,'[284] or even 'the plain and natural meaning.'[285]

Whatever terminology Calvin used, he employed this principle for the simple reason that he wanted to arrive at the natural meaning of the text. At times the principle of natural meaning is combined with that of utility: 'There is nothing more profitable than to adhere strictly to the natural treatment of things.'[286] On another occasion, Calvin opted for the natural meaning in connection with the principle of edification. Thus in the context of Jacob as stranger in Egypt blessing his sons, Calvin remarked:

> Since some interpreters perceived this prophecy to be noble and magnificent, they have thought that it would not be adorned with its proper dignity unless they should extract from it certain new mysteries. Thus it has happened that in striving earnestly to elicit profound allegories, they have departed from the genuine sense of the words and corrupted, by their own inventions, what is here delivered for the solid edification of the pious.[287]

Calvin thus sought after the natural meaning as the logical extension of his principle of simplicity, directed to fostering both utility and edification.

---

282 CALVIN, *Comm. in Ps.* 11,7 (CO 31,126).
283 CALVIN, *Comm. in Gal.* 4,22 (CO 50,237; COR 2/107).
284 CALVIN, *Comm. in Gen.* 9,5 (CO 23,146).
285 CALVIN, *Comm. in Isa.* 6,3 (CO 36,129).
286 CALVIN, *Comm. in Gen.* 6,14 (CO 23,122–23).
287 CALVIN, *Comm. in Gen.* 49,1 (CO 23,590).

3.2.6. The Principle of *Sitz im Leben*

Another important principle, and one which Calvin used specifically to arrive at the natural meaning, is his attention to context. Whenever he came across a problematic Hebrew or Greek term, Calvin's first rule was that 'the explanation must not be sought elsewhere than in the context.'[288] The definition and interpretation of individual words in a text must conform to the context of the passage. At times we thus see Calvin discarding other interpretations, not because they are impossible lexically or grammatically, but because 'context induces me to prefer the other view.'[289]

According to Kugel and Greer, in the first century one of the significant methods of interpreting Scripture was proof texting.[290] Justin Martyr, the leading second-century apologist, interpreted the Scriptures using this method of proof texting. In fact, his tendency to resort to proof texting was so strong that Shotwell argued that only rarely did Justin Martyr interpret the Old Testament to mean exactly what it said. Because for him, the Old Testament was one great mass of proof texts.[291]

It would be inaccurate to claim that all biblical exegetes before the sixteenth century were insensitive to the historical context. All the same, many Christian thinkers did not give much importance to the historicity of the text in their interpretation, since they thought that a historical interpretation did not support their Christian belief. Smally has observed that Biblical interpretation between 1100 and 1350 focused basically on the original meaning of the word and the text.[292] Throughout the Medieval exegetical tradition, however, allegory was greatly used, even though the excess in some writers led other biblical exegetes to ground themselves in the historical meaning of the text.[293] The renewal of biblical interpretation under Erasmus did not totally break with the medieval tradition.[294]

For Calvin, his interest in and attention to context did not begin with his Biblical interpretation, but much earlier on, with his commentary on Seneca's *De Clementia*. Battles has noted that Calvin corrected the text, analyzed its structure, vocabulary, and idioms, and sought to understand the text historically.[295] Both Battles and Torrance affirm that Calvin was influenced by the

---

288 CALVIN, *Comm. in Gen.* 16,12 (CO 23,229).
289 CALVIN, *Comm. in Eph.* 4,32 (COR 2/16,252).
290 KUGEL & GREER, *Early Biblical Interpretation*, 3,127.
291 SHOTWELL, *The Biblical Exegesis of Justin Martyr*, 29.
292 cf. SMALLEY, 'The Bible in the Middle Schools,' 3,219.
293 See EVANS, *The Language and Logic of the Bible*, 67–71.
294 Cf. SMALLEY, *The Study of the Bible in the Middle Ages*, 83–195.
295 BATTLES, *De Clementia*, 63.

style and rhetorical skills of Cicero.[296] This influence is evident, for example, in his rejection of syllogistic reasoning in his Old Testament exegetical work. Like Cicero, Calvin maintained the relationship between the text and the author's intent. Calvin relied on what Cicero called 'intrinsic arguments,' which sought to lay bare the truth inherent in the subject matter, and to allow its force to convince.[297] Bouwsma has similarly shown that Calvin stood in the rhetorical tradition of the Latin fathers, who in turn were orators after the style of Cicero and Quintilian.[298]

Jerome Friedman has noted that Calvin's sensitivity to context significantly affected his approach to the Old Testament, and that particularly in the context of the נר.[299] The qualities that led Hunnius in the sixteenth century to charge Calvin with being a Judaizer, led Philip Schaff three centuries later to designate Calvin as the founder of modern historical-grammatical exegesis.[300] Calvin rarely loses sight of the fact that, before one can explain how a passage applies to an individual in his own time, one must first determine its meaning for the original audience of the writer. This further shows that he looked not only to the historical situation, but also the immediate literary context. Calvin was very mindful of the historical situation of the text, whether it be Joseph as stranger in Egypt, Amos as a stranger-prophet in Israel, Jonah as stranger-prophet in Nineveh, or Cyrus as a stranger-king. He always emphasized both the intention of the prophet (consilium prophetae), as well as circumstances of the time (circumstantias temporis). In the preface to his lectures on Lamentations, Calvin ties the writer's intent to the historical context. He says that the exegete must inquire when the book was composed (quando hic liber compositus), and what the original intent of the author (autoris consilium) was in order to arrive at the true meaning of the text.[301]

Although Calvin considered the grammatical, syntactical and philological tools to be extremely important for his exegetical work particularly in connection with the נר, he never allowed himself to be bound strictly by them. Thus, nine times he interpreted the term תושב ('foreigner') as uncircumcised non-Israelites living in the midst of Israel. However, he used the same term for Abraham when the latter was pleading with the Hittites to buy land to bury his wife.[302] In Ps 39,13, he used the same noun in connection with David who iden-

---

296 BATTLES, *De Clementia*, 81; TORRANCE, *The Hermeneutic of Calvin*, 100.

297 TORRANCE, *The Hermeneutic of Calvin*, 100–11.

298 BOUWSMA, *John Calvin*, 117–25.

299 FRIEDMAN, *The Most Ancient Testimony*, 114.

300 SCHAFF, 'Calvin as a Commentator,' 466.

301 CALVIN, *Praelect. in Lam.*, praefatio (CO 39,505).

302 CO 23, 321–322.

tifies himself with his forefathers because of the similarity of their situation.[303] In connection with Ps 16,4, Calvin himself says that, in translating the word גֵּר, he not only follows grammar approach but also the principles of common usage of language.[304] Elsewhere, Calvin argues that context alone is sufficient justification to go against the consensus of scholars: 'The other reading, I confess, is the more common one, but as it is somewhat meager, I have not hesitated to prefer the one that contains the fuller meaning, and beside, is much better suited to the context.'[305] And again, in expounding on the opening phrase in the prophecies of Isaiah, Calvin writes: 'Almost all the commentators consider the clause to end with words "for the Lord has spoken"; [...] but the context demands that we connect the words in a different manner.'[306]

Further, when multiple translations are possible, Calvin considers it a matter of choice. In his exegesis of Nu 15,30, about the 'proud soul' which can refer to either the 'native' or the 'stranger,' Calvin remarks: 'Since either version is probable, and makes no difference in substance, I have allowed myself freely to choose that which expressed the meaning more clearly.'[307] However, he is still extremely concerned not to depart from the original meaning of the text: 'I have been unwilling to depart from its ordinary sense; nor do I curiously insist on the words, except so far as it is necessary to ascertain the actual substance.'[308]

On numerous occasions when a particular word or phrase made a passage difficult to interpret, Calvin appeals to the context as the highest arbiter. This is evident in cases where he writes such things as, 'those who interpret this passage as alluding [...] introduce a forced and far-fetched sense, which is contradictory by the context.'[309] Or else, 'I rather prefer the former exposition, because it corresponds better with the context.'[310] And again, 'the other meaning is more suitable to the context.'[311] Many other examples could be given that indicate the importance Calvin gave to context in his biblical exegesis.

Calvin appears to have distinguished between and employed three different layers of context in connection with his exegesis of the גֵּר. There is first of all the immediate sentence or paragraph. Consideration of this first level might

---

303 CALVIN, *Comm. in Ps.* 39,13 (31,44).
304 CALVIN, *Comm. in Ps.* 16,4 (CO 31,152): 'I would, therefore, be much disposed to adopt this sense were it supported by the common usage of the language; but as grammarians observe that there is not to be found another similar passage in Scripture.'
305 CALVIN, *Comm.* in 2 Cor. 1,20 (COR 2/15,30–31).
306 CALVIN, *Comm. in Isa.* 1,2 (CO 36,28).
307 CALVIN, *Comm. in Mosis reliq. libr.*, Nu 15,30 (CO 24,366).
308 CALVIN, *Comm. in Mosis reliq. libr.*, Lv 23,40 (CO 24,596).
309 CALVIN, *Comm. in Mosis reliq. libr.*, Ex 4,13 (CO 24,56).
310 CALVIN, *Comm. in Col.* 2,13 (CO 52,107).
311 CALVIN, *Comm.* in 1 Thess. 2,12 (CO 52,150).

lead Calvin to change the punctuation, or tense or mood of the sentence: 'The verb in Hebrew is indeed in the past tense; but, since it is plain from the context that their hope for what was to come was founded on God's former mercies, I have preferred making the meaning clearer by translating it in the future.'[312] The second layer of context is the surrounding paragraphs or chapters, and their thrust. In connection with the meaning of a disputed verse, Calvin remarked: 'As I have already said, the context will quickly remove all doubt; for the commencement of the following chapter clearly explains and confirms what is here stated; and he who made this division has improperly separated things which ought to have been joined together.'[313] The third layer of the context is the broad background of a writer's style, and pattern of his word usage. The broader context might include consideration of the overall historical setting for a passage. For instance, Calvin rejected a possible interpretation of Jes 2,22 with the words: 'Neither can this interpretation be admitted, which does not agree either with the time or the occasion.'[314] The three levels one can distinguish within Calvin's attention to the context highlight once more the importance of the principle of the *Sitz im Leben* for his exegetical work.

3.2.7. The Principle of Unity of Scripture

For Calvin, the concept of the נר in the Old Testament is at bottom susceptible to a twofold division. This is clear from his exegesis of Ez 14,7, where he distinguishes two categories. The first is composed of people who transacted business among the Israelites, but who remained pagans, continuing in their uncircumcised state. However, there is also a second group. This one concerns those people who were not born of the Israelite race, nor were 'indigenous to the soil,' but had still been circumcised and in terms of religion had become members of the Israelite congregation. For this second class, the Lord wished them to be considered in the same class and rank as the Israelites themselves, and that they thus also be subject to the same law as the native Israelites.[315] This division of the 'strangers' into multiple categories dominates Calvin's hermeneutics in connection with the 'stranger'-concept in his Old Testament commentaries.

In the historical context where the people of Judah were in bondage in Babylon, concerned about the broken walls of the city in their native land, the prophet Isaiah comforts them by prophesying that they will receive help with

---

312 CALVIN, *Comm. in Mosis reliq. libr.*, Ex 15,14 (CO 25,160).
313 CALVIN, *Comm. in Isa.* 2,22 (CO 36,77).
314 CALVIN, *Comm. in Isa.* 2,22 (CO 36,77).
315 CALVIN, *Praelect. in Ezech.* 14,7 (CO 40,305–06).

the rebuilding of Jerusalem's walls. In his exegesis of Jes 60,10, where the text reads וּבָנוּ בְנֵי־נֵכָר חֹמֹתָיִךְ ('the sons of foreigner will build the wall'), Calvin sees king Cyrus as the person, a 'stranger' (cf. גֵּר), as the one chosen to help later with the rebuilding of the temple. Help will thus come in the form of a person who is also a 'stranger.' Similarly in Sach 6,15, the prophet in a similar context prophesied that וּרְחוֹקִים ׀ יָבֹאוּ וּבָנוּ בְּהֵיכַל ('Even those from afar shall come and build the temple of the Lord'). At this point, however, Calvin distances himself from other exegetes who think that here, too, the text speaks about Cyrus. Calvin's argument is that, historically, the time of Zechariah was much later than Cyrus, and that the wall of Jerusalem had already been rebuilt. Calvin instead interprets this verse as a reference to Jesus Christ who would come to build the hearts of the people. Further, Calvin understands the building of the temple not in terms of a Solomon's temple, or the rebuilding authorized under Cyrus, but rather as a spiritual temple. And the contribution of materials from far off refers not to materials that can waste away, but rather to the doctrine and gift of the Holy Spirit.[316]

From his commentary on Isaiah to his commentary on Ezekiel, Calvin interprets all those who are circumcised as one category that belong to holy community with various rights and privileges. All those who do not circumcised are kept in another category that do not belong to the congregation, consequently do not have any rights and privilleges. By this way of interpreting Calvin sees unity in the Scripture.

3.2.8. The Principle of *Equitas*

Preceding scholarship has by and large passed over the principle of *equitas*,[317] but the present study on Calvin's exegesis on the 'stranger'-concept has led to the conclusion that it should rightly be considered one of his exegetical principles. This principle arises from the way the people of Israel were commanded to treat the strangers who were in their midst. In relation to the treatment of 'strangers,' terms like, 'vex not,' 'oppress not,' and 'prevent not justice,' have a significant place in the principle of *equitas*. In his exegesis on Ps 15,6, Calvin essentially described it as the Golden Rule.[318]

In the sixteenth and seventeenth centuries, the principle of *equitas* was not only part of legal theory, but also undergirded the *ius gentium*, the law of nati-

---

316 CALVIN, *Comm. in Zach.* 6,15 (CO 44,215–17).
317 One exception is KLEMPA, *John Calvin on Natural Law*, 72–95.
318 CALVIN, *Comm. in Ps.* 15,5 (CO 31,147–48).

ons.[319] Through his legal background, Calvin had a thorough understanding of the principle of *equitas*, which comes up explicitly in his exegesis and exposition of the concept of stranger.

In his commentary on Daniel, Calvin noted what made Daniel a stranger among the Medes and Persians,[320] and argued that if people 'are not punished for any just reason, we ought to spare their persons, not through their worthiness, but through our own habitual sense of equity and rectitude.'[321] Later in the same chapter, he accuses the Medes and Persians of being robbers and tyrants, 'for scarcely one in a hundred of them showed a grain of equity, either when sent into any province or when discharging any magistracy'[322] to the refugees and foreigners. In his Institutes, Calvin also described the relationship between the constitutions of the nations, and the law of God.[323] Calvin found there to be a close connection between equity and natural law, which was of course the prevailing legal philosophy of his day. Differences in constitutions

---

319 In his work on law, Aristotle employed *equitas* as a central principle, and both Thomists and Nominalists followed suit. Ockham normally used the Greek term *epieikeia*, which had been Aristotle's term, though Aquinas in following Augustine preferred *equitas*. The concept played a significant role in discussions on law. Both terms encompassed the same basic notion, and in Aquinas they are often replaced by the synonymous phrase *ratio iustitiae*. For example: 'Quam tamen in aliquibus servare est contra aequalitatem iustitiae, et contra commune bonum, quod lex intedit [...] bonum est autem, praetermissis verbis legis, sequi id quod poscit iustitiae ratio et communis utilitas.' (*ST* IT, ii, q. 120, a.1) Medieval theologians derived their conception of *equitas* from the Greeks' *epieikeia*. Equity is an aspect of law which appeals to a higher good in order to avoid an injustice being done by overzealous enforcement of a specific ordinance. Ockham used it very effectively in his political tracts against papal excesses (BAYLEY, 'Political Philosophy of William of Ockham,' 202–203).

320 CALVIN, *Praelect. in Dan.* 5,7 (CO 40,702): 'As, therefore, they wished to retain their good opinion, as being God's counselors, no wonder they despised this stranger.' Cf. *Praelect. in Dan.* 6,1–2 (CO 41,2): 'His own army abounded in numbers, and we know how every conqueror is surrounded in war by many dependents, all of whom wish to share in the spoil. Darius, therefore, would never have noticed a stranger and a captive, and admitted him to such great honor and power, unless he had understood him to be a known Prophet of God, and also a herald in denouncing destruction against the Babylonish monarchy'; *Praelect. in Dan.* 6,10 (CO 41,11): 'When, therefore, he prayed to God, he kept Jerusalem in sight, not that his eyes could penetrate to so distant a region, but he directed his gaze towards Jerusalem to shew himself a stranger among the Chaldeans, although he enjoyed great power among them, and was adorned with great authority, and excelled in superior dignity'; *Praelect. in Dan.* 6,13 (CO 41,14): 'The effect is the same as if they had said, "He is lately a captive among thy slaves; thou art supreme lord, and his masters to whom he was subject are under thy yoke, because thou art their conqueror; he is but a captive and a stranger, a mere slave, and yet he rebels against thee!"'; *Praelect. in Dan.* 6,28 (CO 41,35): 'But lest he should be ungrateful to God, he desires to express his sense of the uncommon benevolence with which, though an exile and a stranger, and subject to reproach among other captives, he was treated and even honored among the Medes and Persians.'

321 CALVIN, *Praelect. in Dan.* 2,24 (CO 40,582).

322 CALVIN, *Praelect. in Dan.* 2,40 (CO 40,599–600).

323 CALVIN, *Institutes* IV.20.16.

should be accepted, Calvin continued, 'provided they all equally press toward the same goal of equity.' According to Calvin, the law of God is nothing but a variation of natural law, governed by the principle of equity:

> It is a fact that the law of God which we call the moral law is nothing else than a testimony of natural law and of that conscience which God has engraved upon the minds of men. Consequently, the entire scheme of this equity of which we are now speaking has been prescribed in it. Hence, this equity alone must be goal and rule and limit of all laws.[324]

For Calvin, a good understanding of the principles of *equitas* is a required precondition to exegete Ex 22,21 ('thou shall neither vex a stranger, nor oppress him: for ye were strangers in the land of Egypt').[325] Calvin harmonized Ex 22,21 with Lv 19,33 ('and if a stranger sojourn with thee in your land, ye shall not vex him'), but before commenting on the verbs יָנָה ('to maltreat, vex, suppress') and לחץ ('to oppress, squeeze'), Calvin laid down the principle of *equitas*: 'before I pass on to the other iniquities, I have thought fit to introduce this precept, wherein the people are commanded to cultivate equity towards all without exception.' He further added that one who broke the principle of *equitas* in his treatment of the 'stranger' would never go unpunished.[326] The concept of *equitas* in relation to possessions also plays a role in Calvin's dismissal of the practice of usury against strangers and foreigners.[327]

3.2.9. The Principle of Harmony

Commentators from the early church right through to the modern period have noted a problem when they came across repetitions, overlap, inconsistency, and seeming contradictions in the Hebrew text. Scholarship has sought to address these issues by referring to the sources, composition, various stages of development, and changes by redactors, and so forth. These practices have been applied particularly in scholarship on the first five books of Old Testament, and over the centuries have resulted in significant changes. Also in connection with the idea of the גֵּר, their legal and religious position, their privileges, etc., modern scholars have pointed to problems and contradictions in the biblical text. For Calvin, however, these are not contradictions, but rather various aspects of truth that need to be harmonized. Calvin harmonizes the text on the basis of content, as well as its relation to the historical context. This is

---

324 CALVIN, *Institutes* IV.20.16.
325 Cf. CALVIN, *Comm. in Mosis reliq. libr.*, Ex 22,21 (CO 24,672–73).
326 CALVIN, *Comm. in Mosis reliq. libr.*, Lv 19,33 (CO 24,673): 'No iniquity, indeed, will be left unavenged by God, but there is a special reason why He declares that strangers, widows, and orphans are taken under His care; inasmuch as the more flagrant the evil is, the greater need there is of an effectual remedy.'
327 CALVIN, *Comm. in Mosis reliq. libr.*, Lv 19,33 (24,673–74).

true especially in Calvin's commentary on the Harmony of the Law, where his commentary proceeds on the basis of the subject. Calvin harmonizes the idea of the גֵּר according to subject: the idea of equity,[328] just judgment,[329] harvest law,[330] sacrificial ceremonies,[331] oppression,[332] eating holy food,[333] and observance of the Sabbath.[334] Calvin harmonized the text not only between the books but within the book and within the chapter.[335] Calvin's purpose in combining and harmonizing these texts is to be able to arrive at a most complete understanding of the concept of 'stranger.'

3.3. Summary

In his exegesis of the גֵּר in the Old Testament commentaries, Calvin uses simple, useful, historical and contextual, brief explanations. Calvin, whenever possible, tries to combine and harmonize the texts pertaining to the גֵּר together in order to provide one exegetical note. What undergirds all of his exegetical work on the stranger-motif is the search for the truth that leads to spiritual edification.

---

328 Ex 22,21 and Lv 19,33–34.
329 Ex 22,26–27 and Dt 24,6.10–13.17–18.
330 Lv 19,9–10; 23,22 and Dt 24,19–24.
331 Lv 22,17–25 and Dt 17,1.
332 Lv 25,35–38 and Dt 23,19–20.
333 Dt 14,21; Ex 22,31 and Lv 17,15–16.
334 Ex 16,23–30.
335 E.g. Nu 18,1–7 and 18,22–23; Lv 24,7 and 25,19–22.

4. The Exegetical Trajectory

4.1. Introductory Matters

This chapter focuses on the exegetical trajectory of Calvin's understanding of the stranger-motif, whether the word is mentioned directly or else implied indirectly in the MT, as reflected in his Old Testament commentaries. As was noted in the introductory chapter, with the exception of an article by Herman Selderhuis, very little research has been carried out on this topic at all. It therefore goes without saying that no survey of scholarship will be necessary. However, there are several elements that must yet be noted before we deal with Calvin's exegesis.

In this chapter, all of the exegetical comments on the גֵּר found in Calvin's Old Testament commentaries will be collected, so as to gain an understanding as to what Calvin says about the 'stranger.' To avoid unnecessary repetition, some occurrences will be passed over. In other cases, several texts are treated together, following Calvin's own method as in the Harmony of the Law.

Translations from Calvin are taken as reconstructed and compiled by Richard F. Wevers. As in chapter two, this chapter is also arranged chronologically according to the life of the Genevan Reformer.

As has also been noted in the introductory chapter, the methods of citation from the sixteenth century differ significantly from contemporary practices, and so Calvin's citations should not be viewed from the perspective of today's standards.[336] Calvin does cite the names of his sources in the Institutes, whereas the commentaries generally contain vague references; consequently, it is much more difficult to track down the sources in Calvin's commentaries, which

---

336 BLAND, *Issues* , 59.

form the basic source of the present study, than for example in the Institutes. However, as Anthony Lane has pointed out, when Calvin makes critical comments on a particular work, he does directly identify the source.

Another important factor to consider, as has been observed by Anthony Lane, Richard Muller, David Steinmetz, Heiko Oberman, Richard Gamble, T.H.L. Parker, Hans-Joachim Kraus, J.L.M. Haire, and Wilhelm H. Neuser, is whether Calvin had books available to him, as well as the time needed to read them. As Ford Lewis Battles remarked, it is also important to consider where Calvin may have read the books that were available to him.[337]

When Calvin refers to a source, it cannot be taken for granted that he had actually consulted that particular source directly. He knew how to get maximum usage out of a minimum of sources. He knew how to borrow quotations from others, and how to use them even without having primary sources in hand. It is further highly possible that Calvin used intermediary sources. One's approach must therefore be critical when attempting to find out which authors influenced Calvin, and where Calvin cited them from. After all, mere parallels do not mean that Calvin used a particular source. It might well be that parallels between Calvin and another source go back to another primary source. It further needs to be remembered that in the commentaries, most interpreters used different methods, but often did still end up with similar conclusions. Looking at the conceptual similarities, Karl Reuter observes that Calvin was influenced by Bernard of Clairvaux, whereas similarity in thought led T.F. Torrance to conclude that John Major was highly influential on him. Thus Lane notes that seeking parallels between Calvin and earlier writers is a precarious way of establishing influence and dependence.[338] If a study on Calvin's sources proceeds from the basis of identifying similarities and parallels, it would be nothing less than a Herculean task, as it would require searching through all major commentaries that precede Calvin, and were available to him. And even if such efforts produce parallels in thought, Lane remarks that it would be more from mere luck than from a sound methodology.

Comparative studies presuppose that Calvin was influenced by certain earlier sources or persons, and are in nature more ecumenically and polemically motivated than historical. Secondly, Calvin indicates his view on earlier writings by citing them wherever it was necessary. Finally, there are studies which try to determine the influences on Calvin, but as Lane points out, this is a most difficult task. In fact, the identification of Calvin's sources is a separate study in itself, and does not come directly within the scope of the present one.

---

337 BATTLES, *Sources*, 40; cf. STEINMETZ, 'Calvin and the Patristic Exegesis,' 101.
338 LANE, *Calvin Student of the Church Fathers*, 9.

In method, Calvin employs basic grammatical and syntactical boundaries for his translations and interpretations. When that is not possible, as in the case of Ps 16,4, Calvin tries to find a similar passage to direct him in his translation and exegesis. When he does not find a similar passage, and the basic grammar does not help him arrive at a clearer understanding of the meaning, Calvin resorts to the sense supported by common language usage. In other words, for Calvin, the *context corrects*.

In the exegetical sections on the stranger-motif, we find phrases from Calvin himself which give us an indication of certain exegetical principals: 'I chose to interpret this way,'[339] 'omitting those subtleties,'[340] 'the context corrects.'[341] All of these could serve as indicators for the reader to help gain an understanding of the exegetical trajectories in Calvin.

4.2. The Old Testament Texts and their Exegetical Trajectories

4.2.1 Isaiah Commentary

Isaiah 14,1

Here Calvin emphasizes that the גֵּר will be joined (וְנִלְוָה) to Israel; that is, the stranger is one of the נִלְוִים.[342] It is not only the גֵּר (14,1), but also the בֶּן־נֵכָר ('sons of the stranger' – Jes 56,3.6) and even the גּוֹיִם ('nations' – Sach 2,15) joined the Lord and His people. Calvin points out that not only nations (plural),[343] but also individual men (singular), join the Jews.[344] Interestingly, Jes 14,1 shares with other texts such as Dt 10,19, a positive attitude towards the גֵּר. In Dt 10,19, the native is commanded to love the גֵּר for historical reasons.[345] However, in Jes 14,1, the integration of the גֵּר is not based on historical, but rather eschatological, grounds. Calvin writes: '[...] is not limited to a short period, but

---

339 CALVIN, *Comm. in Isa*.14,1 (CO 36,273).
340 CALVIN, *Comm. in Gen.* 13,16 (CO 23,194). .
341 CALVIN, *Comm. in* Ps. 16,4; 148,11–14.
342 It seems the verb לוה (niphal) was used to designate the non-Israelites who joined Israel and Yahweh. Cf. Nu 18,2.4; Jes 56,3.6; Jer 50,5; Sach 2,15.
343 Sach 2,15: 'Many nations shall join themselves to the Lord on that day'; Jer 3,17: 'At that time all nations shall come together [in Jerusalem]'; Sach 8,22: 'Many people and strong nations shall come to seek the Lord.' Cf. Jer 3,17; Sach 8,20–22; Jes 49,22–23.
344 Cf. texts such as Sach 8,23: 'In those days ten men [...] shall take hold of a Jew and [...] say "let us go with you, for we have heard that God is with you."' See further in Jes 60,23.
345 'Remember you are גֵּרִים in Egypt, therefore [...]' Cf. Dt 23,8; 26,5. These clauses express motives that are historically rooted.

extends to the whole [...]"[346] Further, Jes 14,1 is oriented towards the future, and presents an eschatological view of Israel, which mirrors that great event of her past:

- Yahweh chose Israel (Ex 19,5) and brought her to Palestine (Ex 19,17), and he will choose Israel again and will bring her back home (Jes 14,1);
- As other people joined Israel before (Nm 11,4), the rG will then join Israel too (Jes 14,1);[347]
- As they are freed from their former slavery (Ex 1,14), they will be freed from their present captivity (Jes 14,1).[348]

It must be noted that the motif of the blessings to the nations becomes more faint in the post-exilic times. The motif of nations bowing down before Yahweh-Israel, on the other hand, becomes more and more prominent in the exilic and post-exilic prophecies.[349]

Another significant feature of Jes 14,1–2 is the distinction drawn between the plural and singular forms of the Hebrew for 'stranger': on the one hand, it is said that the Israelites will possess the nations, but the individual גר will on the other hand be joined with Israel. What is the reason for this difference in attitude? This can be explained quite easily from the fact that an individual can with facility be incorporated into the religion of Israel, is not politically organized at all, and consequently does not pose a threat to the nation of Israel. On the contrary, as עמים גוים they could fight against Israel for a concrete, individual religious identity. The difference in attitude towards these two categories of strangers is thus based on the way Israel as nation relates, and can relate, to them. The present study deals with the גר both as individual, as well as compo-

---

346 CALVIN, *Comm. in Isa.* 14,1 (CO 36,273): 'Non restringitur ergo hoc beneficium ad exiguum tempus, sed ad totam ecclesiam pertinet.' Realistically, Israel could not withstand a Babylonian army, and salvation did not come as expected. So were the gods of the nations simply idols, as the prophets claimed (cf. Jes 40,18–20; Jer 10,1–16)? How long would they have to wait to see Yahweh's punishment on their enemies (cf. Thr 1,21–22; 3,64–66)? It was under these circumstances that eschatological sentiments grew. Calvin interpreted these concrete events, and transformed them into a universal event which involved all nations.

347 It seems the integration of גר in Jes 14,1 follows the pattern of the first exodus. However, there is a remarkable difference between the 'mixed multitude' in Ex 12,38 and the גר of Jes 14,1. The reference to the גר in Jes 14,1 is no longer marginal, but it now describes the new Israel. It is a community in which there will be only one law for both the native-born and the גר (Ex 12,49; Lv 24,22; Nu 9,14; 15, 15.16.29).

348 CALVIN, *Comm. in Isa.* 14,2 (CO 36,274): 'The Lord softened the hearts of the nations, who regarded that people with deadly hatred, so that by their guidance he brought them back to their native country, and bestowed on them their former liberty. But so far were many of the nations from assisting the Jews, after their return from Babylon, that all the neighbors earnestly entered into a league to distress them.'

349 Cf. Jes 25,6–8; 49,22–23; 60,3.10–12.14.16; 61,5; Sach 2,10–17; 14,16.

sed as communities.[350] The tension between the singular and plural uses becomes clear when the terms גר and עמים are opposed to each other as they are in Jes 14,1. While the גר will join Israel (14,1a), the עמים will be possessed by Israel (14,2a). The same tension is found in Calvin's commentary on the Harmony of the Law.[351]

To sum up, Calvin holds to an eschatological notion with respect to the גר in Jes 14,1. Yahweh will ultimately vindicate Israel for the humiliation suffered under its former enemies. The very presence of the גר within the Yahweh community is a sign of Israel's vindication. In Calvin's exegesis, the distinction between גר as individual and as peoples is sharp. While the integration of the individual remains clearly in view (Jes 56,3ff.), as nations the גר are still seen as a threat and are rejected.

Isaiah 56,3–5

In the Harmony of the Law, Calvin identifies the בֶּן־נֵכָר as one who is uncircumcised, and does not belong to the community, which consequently deprives him of his privileges. In his commentary on Isaiah, on the other hand,[352] Calvin identifies the בֶּן־נֵכָר as being part of the congregation, with the rights and protection this would normally entail.[353] Calvin indicates that the imperatives (cf. שִׁמְרוּ מִשְׁפָּט וַעֲשׂוּ צְדָקָה) are addressed to the Jews with respect to their

---

350 The consistent use of the noun גר in the singular form is well illustrated in Dt 29,10, where גר is used in singular form even though it is surrounded by other nouns in the plural: וְגֵרְךָ טַפְּכֶם נְשֵׁיכֶם. In Ez 47,22 we find the only plural usage of the noun גר in a text similar to the texts in the laws of the Pentateuch and in Jes 14,1.

351 In his commentary on the Harmony of the Law, Calvin points to the differences in attitude on the part of Israel towards foreigners. Their attitude towards strangers as individuals is found in Ex 23,9.12; and as people (Ex 23,20–33). A more distinct difference is found between (Dt 24,14.17.19–21) the laws ensuring their humane treatment to stranger and (Dt 20,10–15) the laws dealing with the welfare measure.

352 In his translation of Jes 56,3–5, Calvin rendered בֶּן־נֵכָר as 'son of stranger,' while in his commentary on the same passage he translates בֶּן־נֵכָר as 'sons of foreigner' (Cf. CALVIN, Comm. in Isa. 56,3–5 [CO 37,293.295–98]). Luther takes it as 'Fremde,' the Geneva Bible and LXX translate with 'stranger'; the Jewish Tanakh reads 'alien,' the Vulgate 'filius advenae,' and some of the lexical derivatives 'foreigner.' The editor of the English translation of Calvin's commentary remarks the following in a footnote: 'The essential meaning of this verse is, that all external disabilities shall be abolished, whether personal or national. To express the latter, he makes use of the phrase בן נכר, (ben nekar,) which strictly means not 'the son of the stranger, 'as the common version has it, but 'the son of strangeness,' or 'of a strange country;' נכר (nekar) corresponding to the German Fremde, which has no equivalent in English.' In Jes. 60,8 בן נכר is translated as 'son of stranger,' yet with the meaning of not belonging to the congregation.

353 CALVIN, Comm. in Isa. 56,3.4; 60,10 (CO 37,295–97.361–62).

treatment of their neighbors.[354] In remarking that the גֵּר had equal rights with the Jews, Calvin added yet another category, namely סָרִיס (eunuch), that enjoys the same rights as the natives and the גֵּר.[355] These three groups (Jews, strangers and eunuchs), Calvin notes, have the same rights with respect to the Sabbath-laws.[356]

4.2.2. Genesis Commentary

Genesis 15,13

According to Calvin, in Gn 15,13 God's promise to Abraham is that his seed shall be גֵּר in a foreign land. Although the two nouns 'seed' and 'stranger' are in the singular, the reference to 400 years indicates that these nouns point to the children (note the plural!) of Israel in Egypt. A closer look at the commentary reveals that Calvin links two separate actions:

The initial sojourn: יהת גר יהיה זרעֲךָ seed shall be a stranger (singular)
The later slavery: ועבדום וענו אתם they shall afflict them (plural)

In Calvin's commentary on Deuteronomy, this very idea of sojourning and slavery is significant for the treatment of the stranger who resides in Israel's midst.[357] In his commentary on Gn 15,13, but not in the commentary on the Harmony of Law, Calvin relates the term גֵּר with the Egyptian oppression.[358]

We further draw attention to verse 7 of the same chapter:

---

354 CALVIN, *Comm. in Isa.* 56,1 (CO 37,294). For this text ('Keep ye judgment, and do righteousness'), with the concepts 'judgment' and 'righteousness,' Calvin understands all the duties men owe to each other, and which consist not only in abstaining from doing wrong, but also in rendering assistance to the neighbor. It is in what follows that Calvin explains that these words were addressed to the Jews.

355 According to the law, eunuchs could not to be received into the Hebrew nation (Dt 23,1); in this respect, their situation was the same as that of the foreigners as noted above. Cf. CALVIN, *Comm. in Isa.* 56,3 (CO 37,295–96). Calvin also observes: 'by calling them "foreigners" and "eunuchs," he describes under both classes all who appear to be unworthy of being reckoned.'

356 CALVIN, *Comm. in Isa.* 56,3 (CO 37,295–96): 'they may not say that they are rejected, or unworthy, or "foreigners," or excluded by any mark; for the Lord will remove every obstacle. This may refer both to Jews, who had been brought into a condition similar to that of foreign nations.'

357 CALVIN, *Comm. in Deut.* 6,21 (CO 24,225); 16,11.12 (CO 24,599); 24,17–18.19–22 (24,677–78.696).

358 Recent scholarship differs on this point. VAN SETERS, 'Confessional Reformation,' 456, argues that in the exilic period, there was a conscious confessional shift from Yahweh as the God of the Exodus to Yahweh as the God of the Patriarchs. WELLHAUSEN, on the other hand, suggested that this verse was the work of a later redactor.

And Yahweh said unto Abraham,
I am the LORD that brought thee out of Ur of the Chaldees [מֵאוּר כַּשְׂדִים]
to give thee this land to inherit it.

Calvin suggests that the above text is in the form of a covenant. A similar covenant format can be found in Calvin's commentary on Ex 20,2:[359]

I am Yahweh
Who brought you out of the land of Egypt [מֵאֶרֶץ מִצְרַיִם]

This text shows similarities with the one cited above, although there is of course the variation in place names; Ur of the Chaldees in the former, and Egypt in the latter. This observation has both chronological[360] as well as theological[361] significance for the idea of the גֵּר. Chronologically, by including this period of sojourn (גֵּר) in Gn 15,13, Calvin shifts the focus from the exodus to Abraham as the point of departure for Israel's history. Calvin sees the Egyptian sojourn as an interlude between the promise to Abraham, and its fulfillment in the con-

---

359 CALVIN, *Comm. in Mosis reliq. libr.* Ex 20,2 / Dt 5,6 (CO 24,209–11); Lv 25,8 (CO 24,588).

360 CALVIN, *Comm. in Gen.* 15,12 (CO 23,217–18): 'It is, however, asked, how the number of years here given agrees with the subsequent history? Some begin the computation from the time of his departure out of Charran. But it seems more probable that the intermediate time only is denoted; as if he would say, "It behoves thy posterity to wait patiently; because I have not decreed to grant what I now promise, until the four hundredth year: yea, up to that very time their servitude will continue." According to this mode of reckoning, Moses says [Ex 12,40], that the children of Israel dwelt in Egypt four hundred and thirty years: while yet, from the sixth chapter [of Genesis], we may easily gather, that not more than two hundred and thirty years, or thereabouts, elapsed from the time that Jacob went down thither, to their deliverance. Where then, shall we find the remaining two hundred years, but by referring to the oracle? Of this matter all doubt is removed by Paul, who [G 3,17] reckons the years from the gratuitous covenant of life, to the promulgation of the Law. In short, God does not indicate how long the servitude of the people should be from its commencement to its close, but how long he intended to suspend, or to defer his promise. As to his omitting the thirty years, it is neither a new nor infrequent thing, where years are not accurately computed, to mention only the larger sums. But we see here, that for the sake of brevity, the whole of that period is divided into four centuries. Therefore, there is no absurdity in omitting the short space of time: this is chiefly to be considered, that the Lord, for the purpose of exercising the patience of his people, suspends his promise more than four centuries.'

361 CALVIN, *Comm. in Gen.* 15,12 (CO 23,217): 'It is, however, to be observed, that before one son is given to Abram, he hears that his seed shall be, for a long time, in captivity and slavery. For thus does the Lord deal with his own people; he always makes a beginning from death, so that by quickening the dead, he the more abundantly manifests his power. It was necessary, in part, on Abram's account, that this should be declared; but the Lord chiefly had regard to his posterity, lest they should faint in their sufferings, of which, however, the Lord had promised a joyful and happy issue; especially since their long continuance would produce great weariness.'

quest, in the verses that come between verses 13 and 16. Calvin brings out
three elements that are important theologically:

- the sons of Abraham must be wanderers before they arrive at the Promised
  Land;
- they must be slaves;
- they must be treated inhumanly and tyrannically.

To sum up, the word גר implies wandering, it includes the experience of being
slaves, and suffering under cruelty. This experience of being גר is a prelude to
experiencing the benefits of God's promise. These miseries are intended to
strengthen faith, and more importantly, to manifest the power of God. By including both the promise of God to Abraham, and the exodus experience in Gn
15,13, Calvin sees chronological and theological significance for the idea of גר
in the stipulations of the covenant.

Genesis 12,1

Calvin clearly distinguishes Gn 12,1 from other texts which speak about the
reasons for Abraham moving from his native land.[362] In the context of Gn 12,1,
the reason for Abram's move is the command of God, in contrast to other situations where the reason for moving may be impulsion by disgust and disap-
pointment with one's own country or its miseries and crime, foolish hope, or
whatever other allurements there may be. The verb that denotes 'movement'
in this context is not גור but הלך ('to go, to proceed, to move, to walk') and the
ו-prefixed to the qal imperfect changes the tense of the verb to render the
meaning 'went out' or 'departed.'

More importantly, according to Calvin, the term גר is related to the other
verb (ה)לֶךְ־לְךָ ('you go out'), which is in the imperative form and which Calvin
translate as 'get out thee.' The imperative is not only connected to the move
from the land and the country where Abram was dwelling, but also to the
words מבית אביך ('from your Father's house'). After noting this point, Calvin
goes on to explain that being a stranger means not only being deprived of the

---

362 Calvin disagrees with the commentators who suggest that Abram already at that time did not
     have a settled base, and was on the sojourn with his father Terah. If this is true, says Calvin,
     God's command to Abram 'to leave your land, your country and your father's house' would be
     superfluous. In support of this argument, Calvin also refers to Gn 15,7, where the Lord assures
     Abram that it was He Himself who brought Abram to Ur of the Chaldees. He thus affirms that
     before the command of God came to Abram to move from his native land, Abram was 'settled
     in his nest, having his affairs underanged, and living quietly and tranquilly among his rela-
     tives, without any change in his mode of life.' (CALVIN, *Comm. in Gen.* 12,4 [CO 23,178–79])

privillege to live in one's country, but also having to depart from one's father's house. Calvin writes:

> For since exile is in itself sorrowful, and the sweetness of their native soil holds nearly all men bound to itself, God strenuously persists in his command to leave the country, for the purpose of thoroughly penetrating the mind of Abram. If he had said in a single word, Leave thy country, this indeed would not lightly have pained his mind; but Abram is still more deeply affected, when he hears that he must renounce his kindred and his father's house.

There are two terms which imply a second time of sojourning for Abram, this time shortly after his departure from Haran. In verse 8 the hiphil verb עתק ('to remove') is related to the qal נסע ('to journey') in verse 9. Calvin suggests that the cause of such an immediate move was that the inhabitants of Sichem, namely the Canaanites, did not make life easy for Abram. That Abram moved to the east of Bethel indicates that these verbs reflect a movement within the boundaries of the land promised to Abram's posterity.[363]

Calvin highlights a third and final aspect to the notion of moving in the context of Gn 12. The verb גור ('to sojourn') is here linked with Abram for the first time, and more importantly, the verb ירד ('to go down') qualifies the act of moving. Here, the destination was Egypt, and the motive for the movement was the famine.[364]

According to Calvin, Abram was without a settled residence (Ἀστατούμενος).' He was not only a stranger, but a wretched wanderer in the land of which he was the lord. The forefathers Abram, Isaac and Jacob should be strangers in their own land before their posterity inherit the land. They were strangers driven into exile with hunger and famine. All these, according to Calvin, are not only to test the faith of forefathers but also reveal to them that God is the protector of strangers.[365]

The very promise of God to Abram[366] presupposes that Abram should first be regarded as a stranger before inheriting the land of promise. This experience of being a stranger is one of being exhausted by continual and fruitless upheaval; he will be without stable and permanent possessions. Calvin remarks on the paradox of the present situation: Abram was lord of that land in which

---

363 Gn 12,8–9.

364 CALVIN, Comm. in Gen. 12,10 (CO 23,183): 'he "went down into Egypt to sojourn there." For he intimates, that Abram, nevertheless, retained in his mind possession of the land promised unto him; although, being ejected from it by hunger, he fled elsewhere, for the sake of obtaining food.'

365 CALVIN, Comm. in Gen. 12,17 (CO 23,186): 'When they were but a few men in number; yea, very few, and strangers in it. When they went from one nation to another, from one kingdom to another people; he suffered no man to do them wrong; yea, he reproved kings for their sakes; saying, "Touch not mine anointed, and do my prophets no harm."'

366 Gn 12,1: וְשַׂמְתִּי אֶת־זַרְעֲךָ כַּעֲפַר הָאָרֶץ אֲשֶׁר ('And I will make thy seed as the dust').

he was scarcely permitted to drink the water, since he was still a stranger and foreigner there.

This concept of Abram as stranger can be explained from what follows immediately below.

Genesis 14,13

MT   One who had escaped came and told Abram the Hebrew (העברי)

LXX   One who had escaped came and told Abram the migrant (περατη)

Calvin   And there came one that had escaped, and told Abram the Hebrew (Ebraeo)

The Septuagint renders the Hebrew noun העברי with the neologism περατη as 'wanderer' or 'migrant' in following Philo and Origen. In his nineteenth homily to the book of Numbers, Origen states that the word העברי means 'travelers (transeuntes)[367] in close proximity,' while Philo's etymological explanation leads him to render the Hebrew as 'migrant.'[368]

Another argument centers on the identity of the וַיָּבֹא הַפָּלִיט וַיַּגֵּד לְאַבְרָם ('one who escaped and came to Abram'). Calvin discards the argument of some who think that the messenger is a relative of Abram, and instead posits that he is a fugitive who had lost all his belongings in war, and narrowly escaped being taken captive. He not only sought to deliver a message to Abram, but he also sought refuge from the war and attempted to gain something from Abram's kindness.[369]

In the context of verse 13, it is a fugitive seeking refuge with Abram, while in the context of verse 14 it is Lot who is taken captive. In both cases, according to Calvin, the cause is war. Hence, war is one of the key factors for people ending up as strangers, captives and refugees.

In narrating the story of Abram overthrowing the kings to deliver Lot, Calvin points out that Abram had great wealth that the earth could not hold, that he had many people serving him, the power and force to overthrow kings, a great family that could be numbered with the kings, and that Abram was able to make a covenant with kings. And yet, in spite of that all, Abram could not be considered a king because he was a stranger and sojourner.[370] As Calvin points out, that is the misery of a stranger and foreigner.

---

367 PG 12.725: 'Hebraei *transeuntes* interpretantur.' (italics added)

368 Mig 20 (LCL 4.143).

369 CALVIN, *Comm. in Gen.* 14,13 (CO 23,199): 'With respect to the messenger who had related to Abram the slaughter at Sodom, I do not accept what some suppose, that he was a pious man. We may rather conjecture that, as a fugitive from home, who had been deprived of all his goods, he came to Abram to elicit something from his humanity.'

370 CALVIN, *Comm. in Gen.* 14,13 (CO 23,198).

Genesis 23,4

In the phrase גֵּר־וְתוֹשָׁב אָנֹכִי עִמָּכֶם ('I am a stranger and sojourner'), the use of the pair גֵּר־וְתוֹשָׁב indicates that both stranger and alien are allowed to live together among the other inhabitants. Calvin at times confirms this idea, noting that the fathers lived as strangers in the land of Canaan.[371] Similarly, Calvin brings in Ps 39,13, where the phrase כִּי גֵר אָנֹכִי עִמָּךְ תּוֹשָׁב ('for I am stranger before thee and sojourner') is found, to indicate that these two texts have similar elements. In Ps 39 the point of reference is God, whereas in Gn 23,4 Abraham is said to be a stranger before the sons of Heth. These two-noun formulae introduce a petition:

The following textual comparison is interesting:

Gn 23,4	גר ותושב אנכי עמכם
Ps 39,13	כי גר אנכי עמך תושב

The pair גֵּר־וְתוֹשָׁב functions as hendiadys in Gn 23, while it is in a parallel structure in Ps 39. This comparison highlights the different points of designation for the second noun תוֹשָׁב. Although the texts have a similar function – i.e. to support the petition made in the first person[372] – in Gn 23 we find no clause providing the motive. In both instances, Calvin attributes these nouns to an individual such as Abram and David, both of whom are actually part of the elected community. Both were pleading for their miserable situation and seeking piety. According to Calvin, Abraham had a precarious place among the Hittites, because he could not even bury his dead in a tomb without first requesting their permission; he further did have the humility needed to win their recognition.

In summary, strangers are those who lead a precarious life, and do not possess any land.

Genesis 17,8 and 28,4

Calvin translates the term מָגוֹר ('sojourning place') as *terram peregrinationum* ('the land of wanderings'), using the plural ending. Calvin argues that the plural in the Hebrew text here appears to be significant, since Jacob was a stranger

---

371 Cf. CALVIN, *Comm. in Gen.* 17,8 (CO 23,239); 28,4 (CO 23,388); 36,7 (CO 23,478); 37,1 (CO 23,480); Ex 6,4 (24,78–79).

372 CALVIN, *Comm. in Gen.* 23,4 (23,323–24): 'this introductory sentence tends to one or other of these points; either that he may more easily gain what he desires by suppliantly asking for it; or that he may remove all suspicion of cupidity on his part.'

many times in the country which in promise already belonged to his posterity.[373] All the same, the present situation of the fathers was one of wandering and an unsettled mode of life. It is interesting to see that Calvin uses the idea of *peregrinatio* to characterize the lives of the forefathers in Canaan, just as he uses the same idea to portray the life of the Psalmist on earth.[374] In short, although the forefathers did receive God's blessing of land, by applying the term מגור to the forefathers, Calvin indicates that at present their lives are those of wanderers, and that they lead an unsettled way of life. Thus the גר is one who leads an unsettled life, and that of a wanderer.

Genesis 17,12.27

Calvin's exegesis on Gn 17 treats the covenant established between God and Abraham. For both verse 12 and verse 27, Calvin lists the beneficiaries: כל־זכר לדרתיכם ('every male child of their generation'), יליד בית ('home born') and בן־נכר ('children of strangers'), and מקנת־כסף ('those purchased at a price'). In his commentary, Calvin includes a separate group: the slaves. All of these categories have a similar status before Abraham.

The term מכל is formed from the combination of two separate words: the preposition מן ('from') and the masculine singular absolute form of כל (all), which results in the meaning 'from all.' However, the masculine noun כל is singular in form, which could also be rendered as 'any.' Hence the phrase could be translated as 'from any stranger.' Calvin, as well as the Geneva Bible, understands the phrase as 'of any.' The LXX takes it as ἀπὸ παντὸς ('from every'), while the literal and better translation is 'from any [sons of a stranger].' Because the Hebrew preposition can be translated in a variety of ways ('from,' 'of' or 'by'), the sense of the text could be drastically changed depending on which particular form is chosen. The following chart illustrates the variation in meaning:

MT	or	bought with money	*from any*	son of stranger
LXX		and he that is bought with money	*of every*	son of a stranger
GB	as	he that is bought with money	*of any*	stranger
Calvin	or	bought with money	*of any*	stranger

---

373 CALVIN, *Comm. in Gen.* 28,4 (CO 23,388): 'Even the plural number seems to express something significant, namely, that Jacob would be a wanderer not once only, but in various ways and perpetually.'

374 In addition, Calvin connects Abraham's walk 'before Yahweh' (התהלך לפני) in Gn 17,1b to Israel and the Psalmist (cf. Ps 39,13; 119,54) who also portray themselves as גרים 'before Yahweh' (גרים אנחנו לפניך).

If one follows the MT as it is, the text would mean that the slaves are purchased from strangers with money. This in turn implies that the strangers who lived in Israel had slaves with them, either to serve them or else to sell to the natives. Does the text thus mean that there was a group subordinate (i.e. the slaves) to the strangers?[375] Or does it mean that the strangers are sold as slaves? In this context, translating the phrase מכל as 'of any' does not make the meaning any clearer.

Calvin in many places also states that slaves are either brought in as captives after a victory,[376] or else are purchased with money.[377] In short, Calvin identifies slaves as belonging to the broader category of the גר on account of their miserable situation.[378]

Genesis 20 and 21

In connection with Gn 20 and 21, Calvin recounts yet another occasion in Abraham's life on which he was forced to move. Three verbs are used to describe this move: נסע ('to journey'), ישׁב ('to dwell') and גור ('to sojourn'). Wherever Calvin uses this last verb (גור), he takes the verbs that either precede or follow as reflecting the meaning of this instance of sojourning. In his exegesis it is also clear that the verb גור refers to a specific event in the life of a concrete person, a concrete reason for moving,[379] a definite destination.[380]

Calvin's exegesis also reveals that the verb גור is often associated with people who go abroad. They usually depart from a town or city in Israel, and the persons who do the sojourning are Israelites. The remarkable difference, in spite of their common etymological root, in Calvin's exegesis between the verb

---

375 According to Calvin, the patriarchs had slaves and servants while they sojourned as strangers. One example is Hagar (a 'bond servant') in the house of Abraham (Cf. CALVIN, *Comm. in Gen.* 21,20 [CO 23,305–06]).

376 CALVIN, *Comm. in Gen.* 14, 21.

377 CALVIN, *Comm. in Gen.* 37, 27. It was the Ishmaelites who bought Joseph from his brothers as slave for money, and sold to Potiphar, the officer of Pharaoh. From this account it is clear that such sojourners (foreigners) may bring slaves with them to sell.

378 According to Calvin, slaves are not counted among the number of men. However, the power of God that brings forth *mercy* brought them together into one community of faith. Further, in his explanation of the narrative of Potiphar's wife and Joseph (Gn 39), Calvin refers to Joseph as a Hebrew, slave and גר.

379 CALVIN, *Comm. in Gen.* 20,1 (CO 23,286): 'Therefore, there is nothing discordant with facts, in the supposition, that Abraham, seeing the place was under the curse of the Lord, was, by his detestation of it, drawn elsewhere. It is also credible, that (as it happened to him in another place) he was driven away by the malice and injuries of those among whom he dwelt.'

380

Person	Destination	Reason	Protected by	Other Verbs
Abraham	Gerar	avoiding the curse	Abimelech	נסע and ישׁב

A separate chart illustrating a similar sequence in Calvin's commentaries can be found below.

גור and the noun גֵר is related to the subjects involved in each case. The verb
גור is generally associated with Israelites who make a sojourn in order to depart from their town,[381] while the noun גֵר is associated with non-Israelites who
come to live among the Israelites.

Here in the context of Gn 20 and 21, Abraham is the subject of the verb גור;
the destination is Gerar, the city of the Philistines; the reason for the move is to
avoid the curse of Sodom; and it was Abimelech who protected the stranger.
Calvin identifies Abraham as 'stranger' here not only because of his sojourn,
but also because in this context Abraham had 'been constrained, as a wanderer,
and without a fixed abode, to move his tent from place to place, during sixty
years.'[382] Calvin's second exegetical remark focuses on the remarkable fact that
a covenant was established between Abraham and Abimelech. After all, strangers were normally not regarded as possible covenant partners. Calvin points
that strangers were commonly even prohibited from digging a well, or even
from drinking from one. However, Abraham, although a stranger, could not be
ignored because his servants were so numerous that his company was virtually
equivalent to an entire nation.

Genesis 50,16

In Gn 50,16, Calvin uses the context of the narrative to translate the piel verb
צוה as *mandarunt*, and understands the unknown messenger as a 'stranger.'
Calvin further concludes that this stranger must be one of the servants who
had traveled with Jacob to Egypt.[383]

---

381 From Calvin's commentaries, the following list can be gleaned:

In Egypt	Abraham	Gn 12,10
In Gerar	Abraham	Gn 20,1; 21,23
In Philistia	Abraham	Gn 21,34
In Haran	Esau	Gn 32,5
In Sodom	Lot	Gn 19
In Meshech	The Psalmist	Ps 120,5
In Ham (Egypt)	Jacob	Ps 105,23

382 CALVIN, *Comm. in Gen.* 21,22 (CO 23,306).
383 The text of the narrative of Jacob's death reads וַיְצַוּוּ אֶל־יוֹסֵף ('and they sent a word to
Joseph'), but Calvin translates *Propterea mandarunt ad Joseph* ('Therefore they sent a messenger
to Joseph'). From the fact that a message was sent, Calvin infers that there must also have been
a messenger to bring it. Although the MT does not refer to such a messenger, much less his
identity, Calvin thinks that there must have been a messenger sent from Jacob's family, who
was further highly regarded by Joseph: 'they engage messengers of peace, in whom Joseph
might have greater confidence [...]. The most probable conjecture is, that some domestic witnesses were chosen from the number of their own servants; for though Moses makes no mention of such, when he relates that Jacob departed into Egypt; yet that some were brought with

Genesis 26,3, 12, 17

In his exegesis, Calvin once again points out that the verb גּוּר refers to a concrete Hebrew personality (Isaac), moving out of the Promised Land, with a clear destination (Gerar), for a clear purpose (to avoid famine), and that he was protected by another notable personality (Abimelech).

Calvin clearly illustrates his understanding of what the condition of a stranger is when he describes the situation of Isaac as a 'wandering, uncertain, and changeable kind of life, but almost consumed them with hunger' due to the severity of the famine. In Calvin's exegesis, the verb גּוּר ('to sojourn') in verse 3 goes together with the verb יָשַׁב ('to dwell') in verse 6. Calvin further notes that the reason for the sojourn was famine, the subject of the verb גּוּר was Isaac, the movement was from Beer Lahai Roi to Gerar, and finally that it was also Abimelech who played the role of protector in face of the Pharaoh of Egypt in the case of Abraham. Calvin's exegesis also clearly illustrates that in both cases, that is, earlier for Abraham in Egypt and now for Isaac in Gerar, the life of a stranger in a foreign land is dangerous and precarious.

For both passages,[384] Calvin singles out the verb יָרֵא ('to fear') as the key factor leading Abraham and Isaac to claim that their wives (Sarah and Rebekah) were their sisters. This once again illustrates that strangers always lead a threatened existence and a life of fear. When Calvin considers the Isaac when he finds himself in such a threatening situation, he identifies himself with him (the stranger) when he writes: 'therefore, we are surrounded on all sides with so many dangers.'[385]

Calvin goes on also to point to God's twofold role when a stranger is abused. God is the protector who prevents the stranger from being abused, and the avenger in those cases when the stranger does end up being oppressed.[386] Yet God's intervention resulted not only in Isaac being considered equal in status with the natives of Gerar, but also in him receiving special privileges and even protection from Abimelech.

Calvin distances himself from those who suggest that the verb זָרַע ('to sow') in verse 12, and the term קָנָה ('possession') in verse 14, indicate that Isaac

---

him, may easily be gathered from certain considerations.' (CALVIN, *Comm. in Gen.* 50,16 [CO 23,617]).

384 CALVIN, *Comm. in Gen.* 12,11 (CO 23,184) (Abram); *Comm. in Gen.* 26,7 (CO 23,359) (Isaac).

385 CALVIN, *Comm. in Gen.* 26,7 (CO 23,359).

386 CALVIN, *Comm. in Gen.* 26,11 (CO 23,361). Calvin points out that it was not customary to avenge the wrongs inflicted on strangers; however, in the context of Isaac-Abimelech, divine intervention ensured the proclamation of a special edict to maintain and protect strangers by giving them a special legal status equal to that of the natives.

owned land to cultivate.[387] As he sees it, strangers do not possess any land for themselves.[388] Calvin dismisses the suggestion that Isaac did have land to sow and reap, by pointing out that the impending movement suggested by the verbs in verse 17 (הלך ['to go'] חנה ['to pitch tent'] ישׁב ['to dwell']) makes this unlikely. He notes that the possession of land gives one a fixed or settled life, in contrast to the wandering, uncertain and unstable character of the life of a גר.[389] Yet how does Calvin account for the term קנה ('possession')? From the context (i.e. the verb in Gn 26,17 indicates that Isaac moved on), as well as the notion of a גר (i.e. the גר as one who does not possess land and leads the life of a wanderer), he proposes that the Hebrew term should instead be translated 'hired field.' Thus, concludes Calvin, Isaac rented a field for sowing and reaping, but never possessed even a square inch of land for himself.

Genesis 47

The verbal form גור is once again connected to definite circumstances: this is true for the verbal subject (children of Jacob), destination (Egypt), reason for the move (severe famine), and protector (Pharaoh). In Calvin's exegesis it is further also connected to other verbs of movement (ישׁב). Calvin points out that in this context of Jacob's family moving to Egypt, the law of hospitality was violated, and that the people of Israel were oppressed as slaves. It was Pharaoh who extended hospitality to Jacob and his posterity to live in Egypt; it was one of the later Pharaohs who oppressed the children of Israel as slaves.[390] Calvin further notes that Jacob, as גר, was considered to be a man of low standing, and did not have any authority, and for that reason asked his son Joseph

---

387 CALVIN, *Comm. in Gen.* 26,12 (CO 23,361): 'It may, however, be asked, how could Isaac sow when God had commanded him to be a stranger all his life? Some suppose that he had bought a field, and so translate the word קנה (kanah) a possession; but the context corrects their error: for we find soon afterwards, that the holy man was not delayed, by having land to sell, from removing his effects elsewhere: besides, since the purchasing of land was contrary to his peculiar vocation and to the command of God, Moses undoubtedly would not have passed over such a notable offense.'

388 Calvin maintains the same in his exegesis of the negotiations between Abraham and the sons of Heth regarding the burial plot for Sarah (Gn 23,4).

389 CALVIN, *Comm. in Gen.* 26,12 (23,361–62): 'To this may be added, that since express mention is immediately made of a tent, we may hence infer, that wherever he might come, he would have to dwell in the precarious condition of a stranger. We must, therefore, maintain that he sowed in a hired field. For although he had not a foot of land in his own possession [...].'

390 CALVIN, *Comm. in Gen.* 47,5 (23,567–68): 'Therefore the law of hospitality was wickedly violated when the Israelites were oppressed as slaves, and when the return into their own country, for which they had silently covenanted, was denied them; though they had professed that they had come thither as guests; for fidelity and humanity ought to have been exercised towards them, by the king, when once they were received under his protection.'

to bury him in Canaan with his fathers. Thus for Calvin, a 'stranger' is someone of low standing, without authority. In the narrations of Jacob moving to Egypt in Genesis 47, Calvin indicates that it was Jacob's sixth movement after leaving his father's House with the blessings and promise of his father Isaac.[391]

Genesis 18 and 19

In this passage, Calvin identifies the שְׁלֹשָׁה אֲנָשִׁים סֹלְבָּאל (three men)[392] and שְׁנֵי הַמַּלְאָכִים (two messengers)[393] as 'strangers' on account of their miserable condition: 'wearied with their journey, and [he] has no doubt that they are overcome by heat; he considers that the time of day was becoming dangerous to travelers; and therefore he wishes both to comfort, and to relieve persons thus oppressed.'[394] Calvin further observes that the angels presented themselves to him as unknown guests, and in this instance as well as Lot's invitation to the messengers at Sodom, he extols the virtue of hospitality they showed to these unknown strangers. Unwillingness to extended hospitality to strangers is the most disgraceful thing a human being could do. The people of Sodom had an 'outrageous attitude to abuse, dishonour and injure' the strangers, explains Calvin. Consequently, for Calvin, it was this very tendency to abuse strangers that became one of the key factors that led to the destruction of Sodom. Lot and his daughters, on the other hand, were spared from destruction on account of the hospitality they showed. Calvin disagrees with the Greeks who suggested that the sin of Sodom was carnal in nature:

> I think the word has here a different meaning; as if the men had said, We wish to know whom thou bring, as guests, into our city. The Scripture truly is accustomed modestly to describe an act of shame by the word know; and therefore we may infer that the men of Sodom would have spoken, in coarser language, of such an act: but, for the sake of concealing their wicked design, they here imperiously expostulate with the holy man, for having dared to receive unknown persons into his house.[395]

If the reason for the destruction of Sodom and Gomorrah was sexual immorality, Lot and his daughters would have been the first to be punished.[396] Calvin further notes in this context of the destruction of Sodom that Lot was despised by the natives because he was a stranger. In short, unknown strangers are to be given hospitality, and this was considered a great virtue.

---

391 CALVIN, *Comm. in Gen.* 48,5 (CO 23,581).
392 CALVIN, *Comm. in Gen.* 18,2 (CO 23,250).
393 CALVIN, *Comm. in Gen.* 19,1 (CO 23,267).
394 CALVIN, *Comm. in Gen.* 18,2 (CO 23,250)
395 CALVIN, *Comm. in Gen.* 19,5 (CO 23,268).
396 Lot was willing to give up his daughters to the people of Sodom to do as they wished. Later, Lot's daughters would also have immoral relations with their father.

4.2.3. Psalms Commentary

In his Psalms commentary, Calvin mentions the idea of גֵּר seventeen times.[397] Out of these seventeen times, Calvin brings up the topic directly from the MT (i.e. because the word גֵּר occurs there) nine times, while for the remaining eight occurrences, the topic is brought into the discussion through contextual considerations or common language usage (i.e. גֵּר does not occur in the MT). Calvin translates the noun בֶּן־נֵכָר as 'children of stranger' three times, and each time he portrays them as enemies of the natives.[398] In the context of his exegesis of Ps 18,44, Calvin further identifies בֶּן־נֵכָר as the nations once conquered by David, who lived under him, did not belong to the community of Israel, and kept their independence.[399] In connection with Ps 144,7, he notes that the בֶּן־נֵכָר are the people who do belong to Israelite community by blood, and yet are internal foes who continually frustrate the author of the Psalms.[400] In the first case, בֶּן־נֵכָר refers to foreign nations which violently attack the children of Israel; in the second, the term refers to the internal adversaries who stir up slander.[401]

In his commentary on the Psalms, Calvin takes the term גֵּר directly from the MT on four occasions in order to point to the concept of 'stranger.'[402] In all cases, except Ps 94,6, Calvin observes that the term refers to David and his situation. In the case of Ps 94,6, Calvin does not directly identify the one to whom the term גֵּר refers. All the same, he does place the subject גֵּר among other subjects – עַמְּךָ ('thy people'), נַחֲלָתְךָ ('thy inheritance'), אַלְמָנָה ('widow'), וִיתוֹמִים ('fatherless') – to indicate how they all suffer at the hands of their oppressors, whom Calvin notes are the neighboring nations who were not well disposed towards Israel. Further, he points out that the twofold duty is: 1) cultivating equity and justice; and 2) keeping them under special care, because

---

397 Calvin, *Comm. in Ps.* ad locum: Ps 16,4; 18,7.44.45; 39,13; 45,1; 69,9; 72,4; 94,6; 105,20; 109,17; 119,19; 120,5; 144,7.11; 148,14.

398 According to Calvin, in spite of the inclusion of the word בֵּן in the expression 'children of a stranger,' it still simply means 'strangers.' Cf. Calvin, *Comm. in Ps.* 72,4 (CO 31,666): 'it is an idiom quite common in Hebrew.'

399 Calvin, *Comm. in Ps.* 18,44 (CO 31,189): 'Those whom he terms the children of stranger or of strangers, are the nations who did not belong to the people of Israel, but who, previous to their being conquered by him, formed a distinct and an independent community by themselves.'

400 Calvin, *Comm. in Ps.* 144,7 (CO 32,409): 'He calls them strangers, not in respect of generic origin, but character and disposition. It were a mistake to refer the term to the uncircumcised, for David rather animadverts upon degenerate Jews who gloried in the flesh; and shortly afterwards he hints that he had to do with internal foes rather than a foreign enemy, who would openly assault him with violence and arms.'

401 Calvin, *Comm. in Ps.* 144,7 (CO 32,409): 'I have no doubt David's reference here is to false, treacherous, and perfidious persons.'

402 Calvin, *Comm. in Ps.* ad locum: Ps 39,13; 94,6; 119,19; 120,5.

according to Calvin, they are exposed to injury. Consequently, any injuries inflicted against these groups are considered acts of impiety, and contempt against divine authority. And one of the reasons why the Psalmist mentions the גר is to incite God to action as Defender of the גר.

Returning now to Calvin's discussion of the three other occurrences of the term גר, in which he identified the referent as David, we can note that Calvin argues that this term applies to David due to the miserable situation in which he finds himself. For Calvin, the phrase כִּי גֵר אָנֹכִי עִמָּךְ תּוֹשָׁב כְּכָל־אֲבוֹתָי ('I am a stranger and sojourner like all my fathers') in Ps 39,13 stresses two aspects: being estranged and being dependent. These two dimensions are illustrated by the metaphorical use of the noun גר. Whenever Calvin uses the noun גר for human beings, the dimension of dependency is emphasized. David sees himself as a protégé of Yahweh in a relationship based on mercy. The term גר is here used to form part of a desperate appeal for help.[403] The particle כִּי introduces a statement of self-abasement in the first person (אָנֹכִי). In this prayer for help, the author of the Psalm distinguishes two historical moments: 1) that of his forefathers; and 2) that of his own generation before Yahweh, because the ancestors of the Psalmist reside in the land of Canaan as גרים. The entire statement in Ps 39,13 stresses the state of estrangement: however, there is this difference, in that for the Psalmist's ancestors the estrangement was territorial, while for his own generation it was religious. In other words, in this prayer the term גר acquires a new, religious aspect. Calvin indicates that the reference to being a גר before Yahweh highlights how short the human span of life really is.[404]

Psalm 119,19

In Ps 119,19, the Psalmist refers to himself with the words גֵר אָנֹכִי בָאָרֶץ.[405] Calvin poses the question as to why David may have depicted himself as a stranger on earth. For him, the answer is found in the translation of the term בָאָרֶץ ('on the earth'), since it makes a difference theologically whether one

---

[403] According to Calvin, the three nouns (תְּפִלָּתִי ['my prayer'], שַׁוְעָתִי ['my cry'], דִמְעָתִי ['my tears']) with the first-person singular suffix are not only poetic rhetoric, but is the way in which David bemoans his miserable condition. David confesses his dependence on God, and portrays himself as a stranger.

[404] CALVIN, *Comm. in Ps.* 39,13 (CO 31,404): 'he adds expressly, *before God,* not only because men are absent from God so long as they dwell in this world, but in the same sense in which he formerly said, *My days are before thee as nothing;* that is to say, God, without standing in need of any one to inform him, knows well enough that men have only a short journey to perform in this world, the end of which is soon reached.'

[405] Calvin translates this phrase as: 'I am a stranger on the earth.'

translate it as 'on the earth'[406] or 'in the land.'[407] In Calvin's commentaries, the noun גֵּר is used in combination with the expression בָּאָרֶץ fourteen times.[408] Here he remarks significantly that life in this world is short, and that it will quickly pass away.[409]

Psalm 120,5.

Two elements need to be observed in Calvin's interpretation of the verb גּוּר and the noun גֵּר in connection with Ps 120,5. Both the verb and the noun are always associated with other verbs that indicate a kind of movement; in this case it is שָׁכַן ('to dwell or to settle') of the second part of the verse. In the context of Ps 120, the particle of interjection, together with the preposition לְ with the first person singular suffix, אוֹיָה־לִי ('alas for me'), is an indicator for the condition of the גֵּר.[410] From Calvin's commentary it is clear that this term מֶשֶׁךְ was disputed. Calvin himself is of the opinion that the poetic parallelism of this Psalm[411] implies that the term מֶשֶׁךְ, which is found at the end of the first line of the couplet, is to be taken with the term at the end of the second line (i.e.

---

406 So Luther, the Geneva Bible, and few modern scholars, among whom GUNKEL, Psalms, 518; KRAUS, Psalmen, 987; WEISER, Psalmen, 486.

407 So NRSV; KELLERMANN, TWAT I, col 991.

408 a) with proper places names: 'the land of Egypt' (CALVIN, Comm. in Mosis reliq. libr., Ex. 22,20; 23,9; Lv 19,34 [CO 24,672–74]), 'the land of Israel' (Comm. in Mosis reliq. libr., Dt 10,19 [CO 24,674–75]).
   b) with a possessive suffix: 'in his land' (CALVIN, Comm. in Mosis reliq. libr., Dt 23,8 [CO 24,555–57]), 'in your land' (Comm. in Mosis reliq. libr., Dt 24,14 [CO 24,671]; Lv 19,33 [24,673–74]).
   c) qualified by an adjective: 'in a foreign land' (CALVIN, Comm. in Mosis reliq. libr., Ex 2,22 [CO 24,29]; 18,3 [CO 24,182–83]), 'in the land that is not theirs' (CALVIN, Comm. in Gen. 15,13 [CO 23,206]).

409 CALVIN, Comm. in Ps. 119,19 (CO 32,222): 'The great concern of the unholy and worldly is to spend their life here easily and quietly; but those who know that they have their journey to pursue, and have their inheritance reserved for them in heaven, are not engrossed nor entangled with these perishable things, but aspire after that place to which they are invited. The meaning may be thus summed up: "Lord, since I must pass quickly through the earth, what will become of me if I am deprived of the doctrine of thy law?" We learn from these words from what point we must commence our journey, if we would go on our way cheerfully unto God.'

410 CALVIN, Comm. in Ps. 120,5 (CO 32,298): 'David exclaims, Alas for me! because, dwelling among false brethren and a bastard race of Abraham, he was wrongfully molested and tormented by them, although he had behaved himself towards them in good conscience.'

411 Parallelism, in many varieties, is one of the main features of Hebrew poetry. In this context, the parallel is such that the last word of the first line in the couplet has a meaning very close to that of the last word of the second line.

קְדָר), which refers to a place. If that is the case, then מֶשֶׁךְ, which is poetically linked with קְדָר, must also be a place name.[412]

After establishing that the term מֶשֶׁךְ is a place name, Calvin goes on to identify the מֶשֶׁךְ community as Arabians, and קְדָר as the Ishmaelites among whom David dwelled as גּור.[413] This leads to the next issue. How were these two nations connected to David? Did David literally sojourn among these peoples? Calvin remarks that these two nations are referred to metaphorically in order to emphasize that there is a certain cruelty that exists among the Jews. He identifies the cruelty that made David feel as a stranger in the midst of his own people as 'venomous tongues' and 'false accusations.' These made him feel as a person in exile. According to Calvin, 'although David was living in his own country, he yet was a stranger in it, nothing being more grievous to him than to be in the company of wicked men.'

Psalm 69,9.

Calvin also treats Ps 69,9, where David refers to himself as 'stranger' and 'alien' (זוּר and נכר). This is the only place where Calvin translates the term נכר, re-

---

412 Calvin rejects the interpretation of the term מֶשֶׁךְ as an appellative noun: 'Some would have the word Mesech to be an appellative noun; and because מֹשׁ mashak, signifies to draw, to protract, they think that the Prophet bewails his protracted banishment, of the termination of which he saw no prospects.' (CALVIN, *Comm. in Ps.* 120,5 [CO 32,297]) As is usually the case, Calvin does not give any indication as to who the 'some' might be. The editor of the English translation makes the following notes: 'This is the sense in which the word is rendered in most of the ancient versions. Thus the Septuagint has ἡ παροικία μου ἐμακρύνθη, "my sojourning is protracted;" and it is followed by the Syriac, Vulgate, and Arabic versions. Aquila has προσηλύτευσα ἐν μακρυσμῷ, "I was a stranger for a long time;" and Symmachus, παροικῶν παρίλκυσα "I have protracted sojourning." Bishop Patrick and Dr. Hammond, following these authorities, render מֶשֶׁךְ, mesech, adverbially. But though this is a meaning which the word will bear, yet as Calvin observes, there is little room for doubting that it is here a proper name. The parallelism which enables us in many instances to determine the accurate interpretation of a word in Hebrew poetry when other helps entirely fail, decidedly favors this interpretation. The term corresponding to מֶשֶׁךְ mesech, in the next hemistich, is קְדָר kedar and as it is universally admitted that this is the name of a place, it cannot be justly questioned that such is also the case with respect to מֶשֶׁךְ mesech. To render it otherwise is destructive of the poetical structure of the passage. "If," says Phillips, "the adverbial sense be intended, then the expression should not have been גרתי מֶשֶׁךְ, but something analogous to רבת שכנה in the next verse. Many localities have been mentioned for the geography of Mesech, as Tuscany, Cappadocia, Armenia, etc., which proves that the particular district called by this name is uncertain." It is however obvious that some barbarous and brutal tribes of Arabs are intended.'

413 CALVIN, *Comm. in Ps.* 120,5 (CO 32,297): 'The Mesechites and Kedarenes, as is well known, were Eastern tribes; the former of which derived their origin from Japhet, as Moses informs us in Genesis 10:2; and the latter from a son of Ishmael. (Genesis 25:13) [...] as immediately after he adds *Kedar*, by which term the Ishmaelites are unquestionably intended, I have no doubt that *Mesech* is to be understood of the Arabians who were their neighbors.'

ferring to David, as 'alien.' The editor of Calvin's commentaries suggests that in this context, the concept of estrangement has a domestic nature.[414] It is worthwhile observing that Calvin here translates the term זוּר as 'stranger' and further identifies David as its referent, because elsewhere he identifies the זוּר as an uncircumcised stranger who lives among the Israelites. This once again underlines that Calvin in his exegesis does not simply follow grammatical and syntactical boundaries rigidly. In this case he used the context, as well as common language usage, to translate and interpret the idea of estrangement as found in the Old Testament.

Contextual Considerations

Aside from the above considerations on the meaning of גֵר in the Psalms, Calvin brings some contextual reflections to bear on this concept. Calvin himself notes that, wherever needed, he will proceed from the common usage of the language in order to arrive at a proper understanding of the גֵר. The different kinds of people who declare the praises of God are listed in a social hierarchy, in descending order.[415] What is interesting is that the list starts with the מֶלֶכ (king), and ends with the עַם־קְרֹבוֹ ('the people near unto him'). In his exegetical comments, Calvin explains that these 'people near unto him' are 'strangers.' He first identifies 'the children of Israel' as 'the people near unto him,' and a little further identifies them as 'an unknown despised stranger.' Later he even adds that they are 'a single people,' and 'a people poor and despised.' According to Calvin, the striking reality is that this category – i.e. the 'strangers' – are at the very bottom of society. Calvin similarly interprets the term אֶבְיוֹן ('afflicted') in Ps 72,4 as 'strangers.' The same is true for Calvin's rendering of the term אַחֵר, which literally means 'other' or 'another,' in Ps 16,4.[416] Most commentaries and translations refer this term to other gods, because the context speaks of people who hurry to offer sacrifices to other gods. Given the context and uniqueness of the passage, Calvin translates אַחֵר as 'stranger' to indicate

---

414 Ps. 69,9. 'David reflects his situation as stranger and alien towards his own blood brothers who are children of his father but of other mothers. The relationship between the brothers who are born of the same mother is always stronger. On the other hand, a kind of malice remains between the brothers who are born of the same father and a different mother always. David was looking for a kind of love and affection from his brothers when that affection of lacked he felt he was זוּר and נֵכָר among his bothers.'

415 Ps 148,11–14: 'Kings of the earth, and all peoples; princes, and all judges of the earth. Young men, and also virgins; old men, with children. Let them praise the name of Jehovah: for exalted is his name only, his praise is above the earth and the heavens. And he hath exalted the horn of his people: praise is to all his merciful ones, to the children of Israel, a people which is near to him. Hallelujah.'

416 יִרְבּוּ עַצְּבוֹתָם אַחֵר מָהָרוּ ('Their sorrows shall be multiplied who offer to an other').

that there is no relationship between the true God and the false gods. Calvin notes that it is common language usage that leads him to arrive at this interpretation.

To sum up, in his commentary on the Psalms, Calvin understands the term גר as 'stranger.' However, as was illustrated in the above, he also used contextual factors and common language usage to identify this 'stranger'-concept in passages where the term גר is not explicitly found in the MT.

4.2.4. The Harmony of the Law

Deuteronomy 14.

References to the concept of גר are found in Calvin's commentary on verses 21 and 29 of Deuteronomy 14. Both occur at the end of paragraphs each containing two different laws. Calvin deals with the regulations concerning the eating of carcasses in the first part of the chapter (vv. 1–21), and with the law of the tithe in the second part (vv. 22–29). In both paragraphs, Calvin places emphasis on two themes: that of food, and that of being charitable to the גר. While the second paragraph is treated on its own, Calvin harmonizes the first with Ex 22,31 and Lv 17,15–16.[417]

In the first paragraph, two nouns – גר ('stranger') and נכר ('alien') – are distinguished, according to Calvin in order to denote different groups that lived in Israel's midst. He notes that the noun גר, which is the one most often used in the Harmony of the Law, refers to 'those strangers who, although born of heathen parents, had embraced the Law. Circumcision, therefore, connected them with God, just as if they had derived their origin from Abraham.' The other category, grouped together under the term נכר ('alien'), are 'other strangers whom uncircumcision separated from the children of Abraham as profane and excommunicated.' What is striking is that in his commentaries on the Psalms and on Isaiah, on the other hand, Calvin does include the נכר and בן־נכר among the congregation of the Lord. This suggestion is, therefore, that although Calvin sees two separate groups of 'strangers' in Israel, i.e. the circumcised and the uncircumcised, he does not rigidly apply this distinction wherever that particular phrase occurs in the biblical text.

---

417 CALVIN, *Comm. in Mosis reliq. libr.* Dt 14,21; Ex 22,31; Lv 17,15–16 (CO 24,351–52). It is interesting to see how Calvin deals with these texts. For Dt 14,21, Calvin distinguishes the native from the stranger as if the stranger was not part of the holy community; in connection with Lv 17,15–16, Calvin keeps both native and stranger in one category, and applies the same dietary regulation to them.

This leads to the question as to why Calvin distinguishes various classes of strangers and foreigners. Could this be linked something along the lines of Weber's in-group and out-group moral dualism?[418] A close reading of Calvin reveals that in this context, the Law plays a central role between Israel's faith and a faith that is not of Yahweh. There is the נכר ('alien') who has adequate economic powers to engage in business relations with the Israelites, and there is the גר ('stranger') who is in a very vulnerable position. These two groups were dealt with differently in both cultic and economic matters by the native Israelites. The strangers were not subject to the food laws, but they were still included among those who were to be shown generosity by the native Israelites.

With respect to the dietary regulations, Calvin argues there would have been no harm in giving meat prohibited for Israelites to the 'strangers,' or else to sell it to the 'aliens.' For 'Gentiles were permitted to eat indifferently of all sorts of food, since no distinctions were placed between them; but the prohibition of certain meats was a mark of separation between them and the elect people of God.'

Those chosen to be holy were prohibited from eating from a carcass. All the same, it was permitted to give such meat to strangers or else to sell it to aliens. According to this law, the stranger and the alien do not belong to the congregation of Israel; this food law clearly separates Israelites from non-Israelites. However, this same food law also draws a distinction not only between 'stranger' and Israelite, but also between 'stranger' and 'alien.' For the Israelites are commanded to show charity (cf. נתן 'to give') to the 'stranger,' but to the 'alien' (מכר) they are allowed to sell meat. The distinction between the stranger and the alien is here thus made on an economic basis. The stranger needs charity, but the alien has the means to buy. This is the only place where Calvin brings these three groups (Israel, stranger and alien) together.

Calvin remarks that this food law involves a seeming contradiction. On the one hand, according to Calvin Mosaic law prohibits Israelites from eating from a carcass in Deuteronomy 14,21, and thereby creates a distinction between Israelites and non-Israelites. The food laws in Lv 17,15–16, on the other hand, place the native and the stranger under one law, to which both must be obedient.

In short, the food regulations make a basic distinction between Israelite and non-Israelite. And according to Calvin, the law makes a further distinction within the non-Israelite group by distinguishing the 'stranger' (גר) from the 'alien' (נכר) with respect to the exercise of charity. Calvin thus differentiates

---

two groups of foreigners, the 'strangers' and the 'aliens,' according to Israel's religion.

The second paragraph (vv. 22–29) concerns tithing laws. Calvin places the גר among the other beneficiaries of the tithes received, namely, the Levites, widows and orphans. Although the MT mentions only these four categories, in his commentary on the Harmony of the Law Calvin adds the category of the 'poor.' One of the basic criteria for benefiting from the tithe is that one 'possessed no inheritance in land.' In other words, all of these groups are poor, and thus need to be protected from hunger through the law of the tithe. In this way, Calvin combines these four groups (stranger, Levite, widow, and orphan), and places them all under the protection of the one tithing law.

Deuteronomy 16,11 and 11,14.

For Calvin, the 'stranger,' as well as other collective subjects, are all under the same obligation of celebrating the Feast of Tabernacles.[419]

Exodus 6,16.

This passage contains a genealogy of Levi, whose purpose is to ensure the purity of the priestly line, lest it be infiltrated by a 'stranger.' Calvin emphatically states that for the sake of the purity of worship, the defense against apostasy, and the careful observance of the priestly activities, it is imperative to have a genuine genealogical account that starts from Abraham, and runs through to Levi. In other words, according to Calvin, the stranger can never take up the priestly office of the Old Testament.[420]

Exodus 22,21 and Leviticus 19,33–34.

Interestingly, Calvin in his exegesis combines these two texts which instruct the Israelite not to mistreat the גר. The particle לא followed by the verb ינה in the hiphil imperfect form renders the meaning 'do not oppress' or 'do not be

---

419 Dt 16,11 and 11,14: 'thou, and thy son, and thy daughter, and thy manservant, and thy maidservant, and the Levite that *is* within thy gates, and the stranger, and the fatherless, and the widow, that *are* among you.'

420 CALVIN, *Comm. in Mosis reliq. libr.* Ex 6,16 (CO 24,83): 'to make it appear more dearly that the people was not brought out by any stranger, but that he, who was to be the witness among his brethren of the power, and grace, and truth of God, was divinely chosen from the genuine stock of Abraham.'

violent.'[421] This verb is often used in the context of those in power oppressing the poor and weak.[422] Here Calvin points out that strangers are weak because 'they have no one who would submit to ill-will in their defense, they are more exposed to the violence and various oppressions of the ungodly.'

The second verbal phrase, composed of the verb לחץ preceded by the particle of negation לא, renders the meaning 'do not press' or 'do not oppress' in a physical sense. This verb is consistently used by Calvin in the context of the oppression of Israel by foreigners.[423] In the present context of the commandment forbidding Israel to oppress the strangers in their land, Calvin refers back to Israel's experience as גרים in the land of Egypt as a motive for this command. Calvin writes:

> on this ground, that the people, who had themselves been sojourners in Egypt, being mindful of their ancient condition, ought to deal more kindly to strangers; for although they were at last oppressed by cruel tyranny, still they were bound to consider their entrance there, viz., that poverty and hunger had driven their forefathers thither, and that they had been received hospitably, when they were in need of aid from others.

The experiences of the Israelites when they themselves were גרים in Egypt thus functions as a motive for them to treat the גר with equity.

Exodus 12,38 (וגם־ערב רב 'mixed multitude').

When the Israelites went up out of Egypt, an unknown 'mixed multitude,' who according to Calvin were united with Israel, also left with them. So who are the people of this 'mixed multitude' whom Calvin in his commentary identifies as 'strangers'? Further, Calvin dismisses the argument of some (Calvin did not indicate to whom he refers as 'some' neither the searching of the sources does come under the periphery of this study directly) that this mixed multitude refers to the servants of Jacob. Calvin disapproves the argument because Jacob himself was under severe famine and he does not have enough food to supply to his servants. According to Calvin, the servants of Jacob must have left him long before Jacob leaving to Egypt on account of famine. He further lists three possible identifications for these 'strangers': 1. They may be Egyptians who had integrated with Israel; 2. They could be a mixture of people from the neighboring countries who looked for shelter in face of their poverty; 3. They may be a

---

421 The LXX, Syriac and Targumim use the second person plural form, without an object; in the MT, the second person masculine singular form is used.

422 It is interesting to note that in Jes 49:26, Calvin uses the same term in reference to a foreigner oppressing an Israelite (CALVIN, Comm. in Isa. 49,26 [CO 37,213–14]).

423 Cf. CALVIN, Comm. in Mosis reliq. libr. Ex 3,9 (CO 24,38); Praelect. in Amos 6,14 (CO 43,117–18); Comm. in Ps.106,42 (CO 32,132–33); Praelect. in Jer. 30,20 (CO 38,633–35).

group of Egyptians who left together with the Israelites due to the great number of calamities that reduced Egypt to a state of poverty.

Exodus 12,43–49.

Calvin notes that initially the celebration of the Passover was not intended for any 'alien' (כָּל־בֶּן־נֵכָר). Similarly the foreigners (תּוֹשָׁב) and hired servants (שָׂכִיר) were prohibited from partaking of the Passover meal. However, the גֵּר was allowed to eat with the native-born, and according to Calvin there was to be one law governing these two groups. In other words, Calvin identifies different categories of non-Israelites among those who reside among the Israelites. For him, the תּוֹשָׁב refers to a foreigner or a temporary resident whose exact identity is unknown. However, when Abraham approaches the Hittites to purchase the cave of Machpelah, Calvin identifies him as a גֵּר and תּוֹשָׁב. Similarly, Calvin identifies the speaker of Ps 39,13 – that is, David – as גֵּר and תּוֹשָׁב, as were his fathers before him as well. The term תּוֹשָׁב occurs eleven times in Calvin's commentaries,[424] and with two of these occurrences the term תּוֹשָׁב is juxtaposed with גֵּר.[425] Three times Calvin refers to the the תּוֹשָׁב-group in connection with the legislation regulating holy food.[426] In the context of the holy meal in Ex12,43–47, Calvin mentions four groups: the foreigner, temporary resident, hired worker and slave. Of these four, only the slaves are permitted to partake of the holy food, and that only after they have been circumcised. Once again, it is clear that Calvin pays careful attention to terminological sequences in his interpretation of the גֵּר-concept.

Exodus 29,33.

Calvin translates the noun זָר as 'stranger,' but for him this group of people is prohibited from partaking of the holy food. As observed above זָר is one of the terms with which Calvin categories non Israelites among Israelites. However, he keeps this category of non Israelites outside the holy community. They are uncircumcised people live among Israelites due to commercial purposes.

---

424 CALVIN, *Comm.* ad locum: Gn 23,4; Ex 12,45; Lv 22,10; 25,6.23.35.40.45.47; Nu 35,15; Ps 39,13.
425 Gn 23,4; Ps 39,13.
426 Ex 12,43–47; Lv 22,10–13; 25,6.

Leviticus 17,8.10–14.15.

Calvin distinguishes five parts in the ceremonial laws contained in this text.[427]
The first is addressed to the Israelites alone, while the remaining four are addressed to both Israelites and the strangers. In his commentary, Calvin draws a clear distinction between different kinds of 'strangers':

> I do not understand "the strangers" to be all such visitors as may have journeyed amongst them on matters of business, but those who had devoted themselves to the worship of God; for many foreigners, abandoning their superstitions, were circumcised, and it behooved that such as these should be expressly laid under the bonds of the Law, lest, if it had not referred to them, they should have withdrawn themselves from obeying it.

Once again, Calvin does not directly identify who these strangers who are allowed to take part in the religious regulations may be. However, the noun זר makes clear that these are uncircumcised people who are yet part of the holy community. The stranger in this context has a similar status to the native; both have to purify themselves if they transgress the law against eating the meat of carcasses, which contrasts with what Calvin wrote in connection with Deuteronomy 14,21.

4.2.5. Commentary on Amos

Amos 1,1 – בְּנֹקְדִים מִתְּקוֹעַ ('among the herdmen of Tekoa')

From the masculine plural noun נֹקְדִים ('shepherds') with the prefix בְּ ('among'), Calvin infers the *ignobilitas* of the prophet Amos as just one among many hired shepherds.[428] He sees his position confirmed against that of other interpreters[429] in the preposition מִן ('from'), prefixed to the proper name תְּקוֹעַ ('Tekoa'), which for him indicates that Amos came from an unfamiliar place; the preposition מִן appears to suggest a move from one place to another. Inte-

---

427 Slaughtering of domestic animals (verses 3–7); prohibitions against sacrifices offered outside of the tabernacle grounds (verses 8–9); regulations regarding the holy food (verses 10–12); regulations regarding the slaughtering of game (verses 13–14); regulations regarding the meat of an animal found already dead (verses 15–16).

428 Two points should be noted here. First, Calvin agrees that the term נֹקֵד was used in the Ancient Near East to indicate that someone was rich and wealthy; as example, he points to the King of Moab who was said to be rich with innumerable cattle. However, Calvin also points out that the same term can be used simply to denote the hired shepherd. In the context of Am 1,1, נֹקֵד has the latter meaning. Secondly, in arguing for the *ignobilitas* of Amos, Calvin discards other interpretations with the words, 'they are therefore mistaken, as I think [...] I do not then doubt.' This is yet another example of an instance where Calvin does not identify his opponents. Cf. CALVIN, *Praelect. in Amos* 1,1 (CO 43,2–4).

429 Calvin again does not identify those with whom he disagrees, but merely observes: 'interpreters have not observed this preposition' (CALVIN, *Praelect. in Amos* 1,1 [CO 43,2]).

restingly, for Calvin this preposition implies the idea of 'migration.'[430] Therefore, Calvin observes that 'he is not called a shepherd of Tekoa, but from Tekoa,'[431] and that Amos was at that time living in a town that was not his own,
where he did not belong. He concludes:

> He (Amos) therefore dwelt there as a stranger in a land not his own. Had he been rich, and pos-
> sessing much wealth, he would have surely dwelt at home: why should he change his place?
> Since then it appears evident, that he was a sojourner in the land of Israel.[432]

4.2.6. Commentary on Daniel

In his treatment of the book of Daniel, Calvin draws parallels between the captive, stranger and slave on account of their condition.[433] Daniel's captivity from
his native land to an unknown kingdom is for Calvin the reason for Daniel's
identity as 'stranger.'[434] This status was also the main reason why Daniel was
accused of pride, contempt and insolence, remarks Calvin.[435]

4.2.7. Commentary on Jeremiah

Calvin introduces the idea of גר three times in his commentary on Jeremiah,
twice in reference to non-Israelites, and once in reference to God.[436] In both
instances involving non-Israelites, the noun is found as a collective subject
alongside the words יתום ('orphan') and אלמנה ('wodow').[437] In both places,
Calvin demands that there be legal protection for these groups because they
are destitute of protection, subjected to many wrongs, and exposed as prey.[438]

---

430 Calvin observes that the prophet 'migrated into the Kingdom of Israel and remained there as
  stranger.' (CALVIN, *Praelect. in Amos* 1,1 [CO 43,2]) Cf. Am 2,4–5.
431 The preposition מִן expresses the idea of separation or removal. It can thus be translated as:
  'out of, from, on account of, off, on the side of, since, above, than, and so that not.' (BDB B5520);
  For Calvin, the text here refers to a separation on the part of Amos for financial reasons.
432 CALVIN, *Praelect. in Amos* 1,1 (CO 43,2).
433 CALVIN, *Praelect. in Dan.* 6,13 (CO 41,14–15) (captive-stranger-slave), *Praelect. in Dan.* 6,28 (CO
  41,34–36) (exile-stranger-captive).
434 CALVIN, *Praelect. in Dan.* ad locum: 5,7; 6,1–2.13.28; 12,5–7.
435 CALVIN, *Praelect. in Dan.* 6,13 (CO 41,14–15).
436 CALVIN, *Praelect. in Ier.* ad locum: Jer 7,6; 22,3 (in reference to non-Israelites); Jer 14,8 (in reference to God). When God does not respond immediately to the crisis of the Israelites, he is referred to as 'stranger' and 'wayfarer.'
437 Jer 7,6; 22,3.
438 The nouns מׁשׁפט and צדקה (Jer 22,3) are used with a verb in imperative form, which Calvin
  notes is addressed to the kings, judges and natives. Three verbs ינה ('to defraud'), חמס ('to be
  violent') and דם־נקי שׁפך ('to shed innocent blood') are used in the imperfect with the particle of negation אל to indicate the way the גרים are to be defended.

Calvin further also points out that these groups all come under the one category of נקי ('innocent').[439]

4.2.8. Commentary on Jonah

Jonah 1,2 – קוּם לֵךְ אֶל־נִינְוֵה (Surge, proficiscere Nineven)

According to Calvin, the two imperative verbs קוּם and לֵךְ indicate that Jonah was a stranger, who was not known to Assyria, and was of low rank. However, in contrast to his explanation of Amos' *ignobilitas* (see 4.2.5 above), he here does not give any reasons to justify his suggestion that Jonah was of a low condition. Calvin also notes: 'Jonah was a stranger and of a humble condition: that he therefore so touched the heart of the king.'[440] As Calvin explains, a 'stranger' is one who finds himself in a foreign country without any holdings there.[441]

4.2.9. Commentary on Ezekiel

Ezekiel 14,7 – וּמֵהַגֵּר אֲשֶׁר־יָגוּר בְּיִשְׂרָאֵל (Et e peregrino qui peregrinatur apud Israelem)

Although the word גֵר occurs five times in the book of Ezekiel,[442] Calvin's commentary deals with only one of these texts (Ez 14,7).[443] Ez 14,1–11 is a textual unit framed by a narrative introduction and a concluding formula.[444] Calvin repeats his interpretation of verse 6 in his treatment of verse 7, and from the phrase וּמֵהַגֵּר אֲשֶׁר־יָגוּר בְּיִשְׂרָאֵל ('of the stranger that sojourneth in Israel') in verse 7 he concludes that the imperatives of verse 6 are directed to the house of Israel. He further links this phrase with other, similar passages in the Harmony of Law, where it occurs with minor variations.[445] Calvin goes on to define the גֵר, and points out that in terms of the law and the promise, the status of the גֵר is the same as that of the native-born:

---

439 CALVIN, *Praelect. in Ier.* 22,3 (CO 38,373): 'orphans have no knowledge or wisdom, they are exposed, as it were, to plunder; and also widows, because they are in themselves helpless; and strangers, because they have no friends to undertake their cause.'

440 In the case of Amos, Daniel, Jonah and Joseph, Calvin suggests that their *ignobilitas* was the 'platform where the Hidden Power of God could be exercised to touch the heart of kings.' (cf. CALVIN, *Praelect. in Ion.* 3,1–2 [CO 43,246–47])

441 CALVIN, *Praelect. in Ion.* 3,6–8 (CO 43,252–57).

442 Ez 14,7; 22,7.29; 47,22.23.

443 This was the last Bible book on which Calvin wrote a commentary before his death.

444 ZIMMERLI, *Ezekiel I*, 302.

445 I.e. Nu 15,15–16; Lv 17,3.8.10.13; 20,2; 22.18. This similarity between the text points to the closeness of the author(s) of the books.

When he adds strangers, he doubtless speaks of the circumcised who professed to be worshipers of the true God, and so submitted to the law as to refrain from all impieties. For there were two kinds of strangers, those who transacted business there, but were profane men, continuing uncircumcised. But there were others who were not sprung from the sacred race, and were not indigenous to the soil, but yet they had been circumcised, and as far as religion was concerned, had become members of the Church; and God wishes them to be esteemed in the same class and rank as the sons of Abraham. The law shall be the same for the stranger and the home-born, wherever the promise is concerned.[446]

Ezekiel pronounces the same punishment over the גֵּר as well as the אֶזְרָח ('native') when they set up idols in their hearts, yet Calvin argues that the punishment for the אֶזְרָח is more severe than for the גֵּר, since the אֶזְרָח are 'by nature heirs of eternal life.'[447] This meaning of this law thus appears to be somewhat ambiguous. The phrase וּמֵהַגֵּר אֲשֶׁר־יָגוּר בְּיִשְׂרָאֵל ('stranger who sojourns in Israel') could be a standard formula, since it is hard to determine when the prophet was in Babylon as captive.[448] Calvin provides no such explanation, but it could well be that this phrase refers to 'Israel' as people rather than as land as is also the case in other passages.[449] It may also imply that the strangers were allocated land among the Jews during their exile in Babylon.[450] Thus in this context, the word גֵּר refers to a non-Israelite who has embraced the religion of Israel, and therefore enjoys both legal and religious benefits.[451]

4.3. Summary

4.3.1. The גֵּר and (Etymologically-Distinct) Related Concepts

As was noted earlier, in Calvin's commentaries, four different terms are used in relation to groups of people Calvin identifies as 'strangers': גֵּר ('stranger'), תּוֹשָׁב ('foreigner'), נֵכָר ('alien'), and זָר ('outsider').[452] The term זָר literally comes from the verb meaning 'to be estranged,' and thus signifies 'he who has been separated.' Calvin always contrasts this term to גֵּר. Interestingly, in the Old Testament commentaries, גֵּר is always found in masculine form, whereas

---

446 CALVIN, *Praelect. in Ezech.* 14,7 (CO 40,305).
447 CALVIN, *Praelect. in Ezech.* 14,7 (CO 40,305).
448 ZIMMERLI, *Ezekiel I*, 303.
449 Cf. 2 Ch 15,9.
450 EICHRODT, *Ezekiel*, 592. Cf. ZIMMERLI, *Ezekiel II*, 526. Both scholars also think that this text could contain additions from a later editor.
451 Calvin here lists two prerequisites for a גֵּר to be included among the Israelites: 1) profession of worshiping the true God; and 2) submission to the laws (CALVIN, *Praelect. in Ezech.* 14,7 [CO 40,305]).
452 BLOCK, 'Sojourner,' 561–64.

both נכר and זר occur in the feminine as well.[453] Furthermore, the terms נכר and זר are in various contexts used adjectivally to qualify a number of different subjects,[454] but גר always occurs as substantive.

The term גר is a technical term used not to identify an individual, but for the most part rather to indicate a legal status; the terms נכר and זר, on the other hand, do not have a special legal significance. According to Calvin, only with the גר did the Israelites have a relationship of mutuality. In contrast, the זר is an enemy; with the נכרי, no communion *in sacris* is possible; and with the נכרי a commercial relationship can be maintained, but for the rest they were kept at arm's length.[455]

The analysis of Calvin's commentary on Ex 12,43–49 revealed that Calvin used the term תּוֹשָׁב to indicate both meaning based on the contxt. Calvin identifies both Abraham and David as תּוֹשָׁב which renders the notion of belongingness. Three times this group is addressed in connection with the regulations regarding the holy food; in six instances, this group is kept separate.

All the same, Calvin's predominant use of the term גר (and its verbal form גור, 'to sojourn') is to identify and classify different categories within the larger group of the non-Israelites. A quick glance at his commentary reveals that the verb גור is predominantly used in the narrative parts of his exegesis.[456] What is significant is that Calvin used the verb גור in the context of Israelites going overseas. Further, wherever Calvin employed this verb, he did so in connection with specific events in the life of concrete Old Testament personalities.[457] It is

---

453 The feminine form of זרר occurs in Ex 30,9; Lv 10,1; Nu 3,4; 26,61; the feminine form of נכרהי is found in Ex 2,22; 18,3; Is 28,21; Jer 2,21.

454 The term נכרי is used to qualify the nouns 'land' (Ex 2,22), 'people' (Ex 21,8), 'man' (Dt 17,15), 'wine' (Jer 2,21), and 'clothing' (Sach 1,8), and is even used of God's actions (Jes 28,21). Similarly, the participle זר is used adjectivally with 'incense' (Ex 30,9), 'fire' (Lv 10,1), 'man' (Dt 25,5; Lv 22,12), a 'god' (Ps 44,8.21), Yahweh's work (Jes 28,21), and 'children' (Hos 5,7).

455 CALVIN, *Praelect. in Ezech.* 14,7: 'Those who transacted business there, but were profane men, continuing uncircumcised.'

456 See the narratives in CALVIN, *Comm.* ad locum: Gn 12,10; 19,9; 20,1; 21,23.34; 26,3; 32,5; 35,27; 47,4; Ex 3,22; 6,4; Jer 35,7; 42,15.17.22; 43,2.5; 44,8.12.14.28.

457 Cf. CALVIN, *Comm.* ad locum:
Gn 19,19 – Lot sojourning to Sodom
Gn 12,10 – Abraham and Sarah in Egypt
Gn 20,1 – Abraham and Sarah in Gerar
Gn 21,23 – Abraham in Beer-Sheba
Gn 26,3 – Isaac and Rebecca in Gerar
Gn 32,5 – Jacob at Laban's
Gn 47,4 – Joseph in Egypt
Jer 42,15.17.22 – Jeremiah is discussion with the Israelites who wanted to migrate in Egypt.

also interesting to observe that wherever the verb גור is employed, its subject is involved in dialogue.[458]

On the other hand, the noun גר is predominantly found in Calvin's work on the Harmony of the Law, in particular in connection with legal prescriptions. Here no specific Old Testament figure (e.g. Abraham, David, etc.) is identified, and the גר is rather an anonymous figure in a theoretical situation. With the exception of three instances,[459] no personal events are connected to the noun גר. It is further interesting to observe that the noun גר does not involve any action. The commentaries also reveal that גר does not refer just to an individual, but rather to the legal status of one in the community where he lives. By virtue of one's status as גר, one enjoyed specific rights and privileges: rest on the Day of Atonement,[460] the right not to be oppressed,[461] to gather fallen grapes,[462] to benefit from the communal meal during the offering of the first fruits,[463] to take shelter in a city of refuge,[464] to be protected by the law,[465] to enjoy the Sabbath rest,[466] to receive free meat[467] and to benefit from the tithes collected every third year.[468] One more element brought out in Calvin's exegesis concerns the use of the noun (גר) over against the verb (גור): here the גר is not involve in any specific action, and is seldom introduced in the context of a dialogue.[469]

---

458 Gn 19,19 – Abraham dialogues with the angel
     Gn 21,23 – Abraham dialogues with Abimelech
     Gn 26,3 – Isaac dialogues with Abimelech
     Gn 32,5 – Jacob dialogues with Esau
     Gn 47,4 – Jacob dialogues with Pharaoh
     Cf. also Jes 33,14; Jer 42,15.17.22; 43,20. Calvin also employs the verb גור frequently where Yahweh's speaks: Jes 52,4; Jer 44,8.12.14.28; 49,18,33; 50,40, and in the context of story-telling: Gn 12,10; 20,1; 21,34; 35,27; Jer 43,5.
459 Gn 20,10; Ex 2,22 ; 18,3.
460 Lv 16,29.
461 Ex 22,20.
462 Dt 24,21.
463 Dt 26,11.
464 Nu 35,15.
465 Dt 1,16.
466 Dt 5,14.
467 Dt 14,21.
468 Dt 14,29.
469 The noun גר was used by Calvin in the context of a dialogue by a human being (Gn 23,4), by Yahweh (Gn 15,13), and in the context of prayer (Ps 39,13; 119,19).

4.3.2. Nature and Character

Verbal (גור) and Nominal (גר) Forms

In his Old Testament commentaries, Calvin generally associated the verb גור with other verbs of movement that highlight the departure or initial movement of a person or nation from hometown or place of origin to a new location. In Gn 20,1, for example, the verb 'journeyed,' which denotes a certain kind of movement, is placed alongside the verb גור.[470]

In fourteen other instances, for Calvin the verb גור in infinitive construct form with the prefix ל is intended to continue the idea of the previous finite verb, which is always one of movement.[471] It is further interesting to note that for Calvin, the verb גור conveys the idea of the final intention or purpose of the movement:

Gn 19,9 [...] this fellow *came* to *sojourn* and he would [...] judge
Gn 47,4 [...] they said: we have *come* to *sojourn* in the land
Gn 12,10 [...] Abraham *went* down to Egypt to *sojourn* there
Jes 23,7 your city [...] whose feet *carried* her to *settle* afar?

On the contrary, the idea 'גר among you,' according to Calvin, relates the noun גר not to any expressions that indicate the initial move, but rather to the actual residing of the person in his new home.

Moving and Settling

The following chart clearly shows how Calvin understood and interpreted the verb גור and its noun גר.

The verb גור as it occurs with other verbs of movement:

Jer 42,17	dwell [...] sojourn	(לגור [...] לבוא)
Gn 19,9	came [...] sojourn	(גור [...] בא)[472]
Gn 12,10	went down [...] sojourn	(לגור [...] וירד)[473]
Gn 20,1	journeyed[...] sojourned	(לגור [...] ויסע)[474]
Jes 23,7	dwell [...] sojourn	(לגור [...] יבלוה)

---

470 CALVIN, *Comm. in Gen.* 20,1 (CO 23,285): 'Postea profectus est inde Abraham ad terram Meridianam, et habitavit inter Cades et Sur, peregrinatusque est in Gerar.'
471 ירד- Gn 12,10; Jes 52,4; בוא – Gn 9,9; 47,4; Jer 42,15.17.22; 43,2; 44,8.12.14.28; יבל – Jes 23,7; שוב – Jer 43,5; and נעו ... נצו – Thr 4,15.
472 CALVIN, *Comm. in Gen.* 19,9 (CO 23,265) : 'praeterea [...] perigrinandum.'
473 CALVIN, *Comm. in Gen.* 12,10 (CO 23,172): 'descendit [...] peregrinaretur.'
474 CALVIN, *Comm. in Gen.* 20,1 (CO 23,285): 'habitavit [...] peregrinatusque.'

The noun גֵּר as it occurs in contexts not involving migration:

Ex 12,49	גֵּר in your midst	(הגר בתוככם)
Lv 19,33	גֵּר in your land	(הגר בארצכם)
Lv 22,18	גֵּר in Israel	(הגר בישראל)[475]
Dt 14,29	גֵּר within thy gate	(הגר אשר בשריך)[476]
Dt 29,10	גֵּר in thy camp	(גרך אשר בקרב מחניך)[477]

However, when the nominal and verbal forms occur together, one can observe that the idea of migration or movement fades away, and expressions that do not suggest motion, such as 'the גֵּר among you'[478] or 'the גֵּר with you,'[479] appear in Calvin's commentary.

When Calvin places the verb גּוּר in the context of other verbs of movement, he argues that these other verbs state the reason for the sojourn. When such a movement from Palestine to other places takes place, the reasons are famine,[480] war[481] or the threat to personal safety.[482] However, when such a movement takes places within Palestine, the reason concerns the material need of the Levites.[483]

In contrast, when it comes to the nominal form (גֵּר), Calvin does not make direct connections to the surrounding words to suggest that these indicate the reason for becoming a גֵּר. This omission of the reason or cause means that the noun גֵּר instead stresses the present situation of being a 'stranger,' rather than the reasons of the past that led the state of estrangement. Further, it is significant that in his Harmony of the Law, Calvin most frequently uses the noun גֵּר to suggest that the גֵּר was already living in the community for some time.[484]

---

475 CALVIN, Comm. in Mosis reliq. libr. Lv 22,18 (CO 24,539): 'et e peregrinis Israel.'

476 CALVIN, Comm. in Mosis reliq. libr. Dt 14,29 (CO 24,479): 'et peregrinus, et pupillus, atque vidua, qui sunt intra portas.'

477 CALVIN, Comm. in Mosis reliq. libr. Dt 29,11 (CO 25,46–47): 'et peregrini tui qui habitant in medio castrorum tuorum.'

478 CALVIN, Comm. in Mosis reliq. libr. Lv 17,8 (CO 24,468).

479 CALVIN, Comm. in Mosis reliq. libr. Nu 15,14 (CO 24,538).

480 Gn 12,10; 26,3; 47,4.

481 Jer 39,1–10; 42,15.17.22; 43,2.8.12.14.28; Thr 4,15.

482 Cain (Gn 4,16), Jacob fleeing to his uncle Laban out of fear for his brother Esau (Gn 32,5; 27,43), Moses (Ex 2,15), and the fugitive slaves (Dt 23,17).

483 Dt 18,1.

484 Calvin refers to the noun גֵּר in connection with the feast of Weeks (Dt 16,11) and of Tabernacles (Dt 16,14); tithes (Dt 14,29; 26,12–13); and the harvest (Dt 24,19–21). In several places Calvin uses this word in the context of the future of the community (Jes 14,1; Ez 47,22).

Expatriate vs. Colonist

The Use of גור *For 'Expatriates'.* Above it has already been observed that in his exegetical works, Calvin places the verb גור alongside verbs of movement which for him identify the reason for the departure. In addition to this, it is significant to note that Calvin points out that the move has a specific direction: from *within* the territory identified by the Israelite territory, to various locations *abroad*. The person who is the subject of the verb thus departs from Israel for another, foreign country. The following shows the various directions in which the subject of the verb גור sojourns according to Calvin's Old Testament exegetical works:

The Israelites sojourned to:

Philistia (Gn 21,33);
Egypt (Gn 12,10);
Mesech (Ps 120,5);
the nations (Thr 4,15).

Individuals, on the other hand, sojourned to specific cities:

Lot went to Sodom (Gn 19,9);
Isaac went to Gerar (Gn 20,1);
Jacob went to Haran (Gn 32,5).

On a few occasions, Calvin places the verb גור alongside verbs that identify movement within Israelite territory.[485]

The Use of גר *For 'Colonists'.* On the other hand, the noun גור was used in many places to refer to foreigners living in Israel. Here the direction of the movement of migration is the opposite of that in the situation as outlined above: it is now a person who begins in a foreign country and travels to Israel.[486] The גר,[487] the בן־נכר[488] and even the גוים[489] are expected to join (לוה) the Lord and His people as part of the pilgrimage of the nation towards Israel. This general movement towards Israel is described in Zechariah 8,22 as follows: 'In those days

---

485 Cf. Jes 11,6; 23,7; 33,14; Ps 5,5; 15,1; 61,5; Jer 49,18.33; 50,40.
486 In his exegesis of Jes 14,1, Calvin remarks that the גר will be joined (ונלוה) to Israel (CALVIN, *Comm. in Isa.* 14,1 [CO 36,272–73]).
487 Jes 14,1 ('stranger').
488 Jes 56,3.6 ('son of stranger').
489 Sach 2,15 ('nation as stranger').

ten men from nations of every language shall take hold of a Jew, grasping his garment and saying, let every one go with you, for we have heard that God is with you.'

To sum up, Calvin used the term זר to identify Israel's enemies. The term נכר is generally used to identify temporary residents with whom the Israelites may have business relations, but are for the rest generally kept at a distance. The term תושב is used in a mixed sense, both inclusively and exclusively. The term גר is always used not to identify an individual, but rather a legal status, and that of one who is under the protection of the natives. The related verbal form (גור) is mostly used for Israelites who go abroad.

The 'Stranger': Contextual Derivatives

Calvin understands those who are forced to leave their homeland and move to another territory on account of their *personae miserae* as 'strangers.' For that reason, there are instances when he introduces the 'stranger'-concept in his commentaries even when the MT does not explicitly include the words גור or גר:

Person:	Reason:	Movement from:	Movement to:
Amos	*ignobilitas*	Tekoa	Northern Kingdom
Daniel	war/captive	Jerusalem	Babylone
Jonah	*ignobilitas*	Northern Kingdom	Ninevah/Assyria

Similarly, unknown visitors and unfamiliar people are identified by Calvin as 'strangers.' These include Abraham's three guests at Mamre, the two men who visited Lot in Sodom, and the man who negotiated between Joseph and his siblings.

The Place of the גר

Calvin's exegesis shows that the term גר refers not to an individual, but rather to a legal status which places this class of people in a certain relationship with the natives. Yet how was this group formed? Calvin touches on this issue two separate times. First, in his exegesis of the term ונם־ערב רב ('mixed multitude') found in Ex 12,38, where it is to characterize the people who left Egypt together with the Israelites during the exodus. Here Calvin gives three possibilities as to where this group may have originated from: 1) they may have been the offspring of the Egyptians and Israelites through inter-marriage;[490] 2) they may have come from the surrounding nations and joined Israel because of the misery they themselves were suffering; 3) finally, they may be a group of Egyptians who decided to join Israel after the numerous calamities they themselves faced as a nation.

The other place where Calvin treats the possible origin of the גור group is in his commentary on Ps 140. Here Calvin suggests that this group may well be composed of those who were conquered by David, live under him, and yet maintained their separate identity. These 'strangers' would thus be from the indigenous population of Palestine who had been conquered by the Israelites.[491] This group would have come out of the occupation of the land of Canaan, which recent scholarship has characterized in terms of a conquest or infiltration model.[492]

Calvin elsewhere suggests that the descendants of Ishmael and Esau may well have joined the community of Israel. Further, that a גור group may have emerged through the establishment of (disparity) treaties as recorded in Gn 34 and Joshua 9,3–27. In the latter case, the Gibeonites were not equal with Israelites, but even as hewers of wood and drawers of water they still enjoyed a special status (Jos 9,23–26).[493]

גור and עלה ('to sojourn' and 'to return')

Calvin notes that when the Patriarchs have the intention of returning to the Promised Land, the reason for leaving is external. Although Jacob's original reason for escaping to Haran was an internal family dispute, he urged Laban to send him back to his home town for external reasons. Abraham also refused to send his son Isaac to Bethuel along with his servant when the latter went to look for a bride for him. According to Calvin, Isaac could have experienced a change in heart had he accompanied the servant to Bethuel, thus endangering his reception of the Lord's promise. Though Jacob went to Egypt on account of a severe famine, he made his son Joseph swear to him that he would be buried in the promised land.

---

490 Note that MILGROM, *Religious Conversion*, 175, argues that the only way to become part of the community was through inter-marriage.

491 DE VAUX, *Ancient Israel*, 74 ; KILLERMAN 'gur,' 545.

492 GOTTWALD, *Tribes*, 191–228. Gottwald gives various models of the Israelites occupation of the land of Canaan which would naturally allow for the strangers to be part of the Israelite community.

493 BLENKINSOPP, 'Are There Traces,' 207–09, 213–19.

גּוּר
Abraham went to sojourn in Egypt (Gn 12,10)
Jacob went to sojourn in Egypt (Gn 47,4)

עלה
and he returned (Gn 13,1)
and he returned (Gn 50,7–9)

Reasons For Be(com)ing a גֵּר

Calvin lists various causes for both the Israelites being forced to leave their home country and end up as 'strangers,' and for the non-Israelites coming into Israel to dwell there as 'strangers.' They may be driven by famine,[494] war, and other vicissitudes; abhorrence of their own country;[495] crime and false allurements;[496] lack of human aid;[497] and finally, by a divine calling.[498]

The Nature of the גֵּר

On the basis of the above analysis of the exegetical trajectories in Calvin's Old Testament commentaries, one can draw the following conclusions as to the nature of the גֵּר. Calvin states that the גֵּר is a one who leads a life that is filled with continual journeying and upheaval.[499] They pitch their tent here and there without having a settled residence.[500] They leave their own country to live in a strange, foreign country.[501] Although they may be powerful in force, in the land of their sojourning they are not considered equal with kings,[502] or even judges.[503] They are wanderers without a fixed abode.[504] They do not enjoy the earthly benefits that come with being bound to a particular geographical location.[505] They experience no such thing as a peaceful resting place, and do not have the comforts of the hearth to come home to.[506] They are hated by all, exposed to contempt and reproach, wander about without a home, are driven

---

494 CALVIN, *Comm. in Gen.* 12,10 (CO 23,183).
495 CALVIN, *Comm. in Gen.* 12,1 (CO 23,174).
496 CALVIN, *Comm. in Gen.* 12,1 (CO 23,174).
497 CALVIN, *Comm. in Mosis reliq. libr.* Dt 10,19 (CO 24,674–75).
498 CALVIN, *Comm. in Gen.*12,1 (CO 23,174).
499 CALVIN, *Comm. in Gen.* 13,16 (CO 23,194).
500 CALVIN, *Comm. in Gen.* 12,8 (CO 23,182).
501 CALVIN, *Comm. in Gen.* 11,3 (CO 23,164).
502 CALVIN, *Comm. in Gen.* 14,3 (CO 23,196–97).
503 CALVIN, *Comm. in Gen.* 19,9 (CO 23,270).
504 CALVIN, *Comm. in Gen.* 21,22 (CO 23,306)
505 CALVIN, *Comm. in Mosis reliq. libr.* Ex 2,22 (CO 24,32).
506 CALVIN, *Comm. in Mosis reliq. libr.* Ex 2,22 (CO 24,32).

this way and that, and suffer from nakedness and poverty.[507] They are people of low standing, finding neither favour nor having any authority.[508]

The Condition of the גֵּר

In his exegetical work on Gn 26, Calvin characterizes the difficult condition against which the stranger must struggle every moment as follows: a troublesome, intolerable, wandering, uncertain, and instable mode of existence, overcome by hunger and precarious situations.[509] In other contexts he goes on to explain their sad state: they are exposed to violence and other injurious treatment;[510] their life is unstable, and subject to innumerable changes;[511] their abode is precarious, and they cannot possess even a tomb without requesting special permission;[512] they are a most alienated people;[513] and they are continually exposed to violence and various kinds of oppression, against which they cannot defend themselves.[514]

507 CALVIN, *Comm. in Gen.* 13,16 (CO 23,194).
508 CALVIN, *Comm. in Gen.* 47,8 (CO 23,569).
509 CALVIN, *Comm. in Gen.* 26,3 (CO 23,358).
510 CALVIN, *Comm. in Mosis reliq. libr.* Lv 25,40 (CO 24,703).
511 CALVIN, *Comm. in Gen.* 15,10 (CO 23,216–17).
512 CALVIN, *Comm. in Gen.* 23,4 (CO 23,323–24).
513 CALVIN, *Comm. in Mosis reliq. libr.* Lv 19,18 (CO 24,613–14).
514 CALVIN, *Comm. in Mosis reliq. libr.* Lv 19,33 (CO 24,673–74).

5. Position and Protection of the גֵּר

5.1. Introductory Matters

For there were two kinds of strangers, those who transacted business there, but were profane men, continuing uncircumcised. But there were others who were not sprung from the sacred race, and were not indigenous to the soil, but yet they had been circumcised, and as far as religion was concerned, had become members of the Church; and God wishes them to be esteemed in the same class and rank as the sons of Abraham. The law shall be the same for the stranger and the home-born, wherever the promise is concerned, and the same sentiment is repeated in many places. Thus the word foreigners is now to be explained.[515]

In chapter four we observed that the non-Israelites who live in Israel are, for etymological and contextual reasons, grouped into the following four categories: גֵּר ('stranger'), תּוֹשָׁב ('temporary resident'), נֵכָר ('foreigner'), and זָר ('alien'). They all have their own place and duties in Israelite society. Calvin groups these four into two larger categories according to faith and practice. The term זָר, according to Calvin, refers to 'one who does not belong to the community' in which he finds himself. The term comes from the root 'to turn aside' or 'to depart,' and could bear the simple meaning 'outsider.' It also denotes a person who usurps a position to which he has no right, a person who does not belong to the nation. In extension of the latter signification, the terms can thus also mean 'enemy.'[516] Calvin places this noun in opposition to גֵּר.

The term נֵכָר refers to a person who belongs to another race. Calvin often understands this term to have a religious connotation, thus 'idolater.' For reli-

---

515 CALVIN, *Praelect. in Ezech.* 14,7 (CO 40,305).
516 Cf. Is. 1,7; Jer 5,19; 51,51; Ex 7,21; 28,10; Ob 1,11.

gious reasons, Israelites are also forbidden to marry a נכר. On four occasions, Calvin uses inclusive language in reference to a נכר. A תושב is a one who lives among the Israelites as a temporary resident, a traveler, or businessman. Two times Calvin applies either the term, or else the situation, of the תושב to the situation of Abraham and David. Two times the term is juxtaposed with גר.

The term גר refers to a person whose permanent residence is in another nation. Calvin deals with this term on many occasions in reference to non-Israelites who live among the Israelites, who have accepted their faith and thus form part of the congregation.

In the present chapter, the noun גר will first be placed alongside other nouns of *ignobilitas* like widow and orphan. The chapter will thereafter consider the place of the גר among other non-Israelites who live in Israel. In the third place, this chapter will deal with the relationship between גר and the homeborn/native. Finally, the chapter will identify the nation (Israel) as גרים.

5.2. The Triad: גר-orphan-widow

According to Calvin, strangers have 'no one who would submit to ill-will in their defense, they are more exposed to the violence and various oppressions of the ungodly, than as if they were under the shelter of domestic securities.'

The *widow*, likewise, is a woman who 'on account of the weakness of her sex, is exposed to many evils, unless she dwells under the shadow of a husband';

As to the *orphan*, 'many plot against orphans, as if they were their prey, because they have none to advise them.'

Since all three groups are destitute of human aid, God intervenes to assist them; and if they are unjustly oppressed, He declares that He will be their avenger.[517]

Calvin thus positions the גר as collective subject alongside other groups of people (widow, orphan) who have a similar nature, character, need and *ignobilitas*.

5.2.1. Statistical Account

The nouns stranger, orphan and widow form a collective subject and appear as such twenty-two times Calvin's Old Testament commentary.[518] These twenty-

---

517 CALVIN, *Comm. in Mosis reliq. libr.*, Ex 22,21–23 (CO 24,672–74).
518 Ex 19,10; 22,17.21; Lv 19,10; 23,22; Dt 10,18; 11,14; 14,29; 24,17.19.20.21; 26,11.12.13; 27,19; 29,11; Ps 94,6; 146,6–9; Jer 7,6; 22,3; Sach 7,10; Mal 3,5.

two occurrences could be grouped into two categories: 1) laws related to generosity;[519] and 2) laws related to the execution of justice.

5.2.2. Law of Generosity

In his commentary on the Harmony of the Law, Calvin treats Dt 24,19–22;[520] Lv
23,22[521] and Lv 19,9–10[522] as one unit. Why did he do this? It is because in Dt
24,19–22, Calvin places the גר alongside 'orphan' and 'widow' as a collective
subject, whereas in the two texts from Leviticus, the words 'orphan' and 'widow' are not found, and it is instead the word 'poor' which stands as collective
subject alongside גר:

	Stranger	Orphan	Widow	Poor
Dt 24,19	גר	יתום	אלמנה	
Dt 24,20	גר	יתום	אלמנה	
Dt 24,20	גר	יתום	אלמנה	
Lv 19,10	גר			עני
Lv 23,22	גר			עני

Calvin includes the entire group together on the basis of one common principle, namely, that they do not posses land to cultivate for themselves: 'indeed by
name the orphans, and widows, and strangers, yet undoubtedly He designates
all the poor and needy, who have no fields of their own to sow or reap.' In his
commentary on Ps 146,9 where the same triad is found, Calvin similarly remarks that it includes 'all those [...] who are destitute of human help.' They are
landless *personae miserae*. As was noted in chapter four, for Calvin being landless is one factor for the *ignobilitas* of a stranger, which in turn brings them

---

519 I.e. Lv 19,10; 23,22; Dt 14,29; 16,11.14; 24,19.20.21; 26,12.13.

520 Dt 24,19–22; '19. When thou cuttest down thine harvest in thy field, and hast forgot a sheaf in
the field, then shalt not go again to fetch it: it shall be for the stranger, for the fatherless, and
for the widow; that the Lord thy God may bless thee in all the work of thine hands. 20. When
then beatest thine olive-tree, thou shalt not go over the boughs again: it shall be for the stranger, for the fatherless, and for the widow. 21. When thou gatherest the grapes of thy vineyard,
thou shalt not glean it afterward: it shall be for the stranger, for the fatherless, and for the widow. 22. And thou shalt remember that thou wast a bond-man in the land of Egypt: therefore I
command thee to do this thing.'

521 Lv 22,22: 'And when ye reap the harvest of your land, thou shalt not make clean riddance of
the corners of thy field when thou reapest, neither shalt thou gather any gleaning of thy harvest; thou shalt leave them unto the poor, and to the stranger. I am the Lord your God.'

522 Lv 19,9–10: 'And when ye reap the harvest of your land, thou shalt not wholly reap the corners
of thy field, neither shalt thou gather the gleanings of thy harvest. 10. And thou shalt not glean
thy vineyard, neither shalt thou gather every grape of thy vineyard; thou shalt leave them for
the poor and stranger: I am the Lord your God.'

down to poverty. Thus it is the *ignobilitas* that is shared by the stranger, orphan, widow and poor that leads Calvin to bring them all together under one umbrella. However, a close reading of his commentaries also reveals that, although Calvin includes the triad stranger-orphan-widow and the poor in one broader category, he does keep them separate as for as the laws are concerned.[523]

Calvin writes that, because of the *ignobilitas*, the Israelites must be liberal and generous in regard to the law of the tithe (Dt 14,29). He discards the interpretation of other exegetes, whom he does not identify, that the tithe was to be apportioned only to the priests and Levites.[524] Calvin instead argues that the tithe must also be shared with the members of the triad, whose landlessness and the resulting poverty leave them in a state of hunger. Dt 14,29 does not explicitly mention the category of the poor, but in his exegesis Calvin does include them along with the stranger-widow-orphan triad on account of their *ignobilitas*.

Another interesting element is that, while dealing with the laws for the Feast of Weeks, Calvin finds equality there to be equality between the sons, daughters, male, female slaves, and Levites.[525] In this context, there is nothing special about the גֵר. However, Calvin's exegesis does show clear distinctions between when the גֵר is placed in the triad, as opposed to when the גֵר is found in combination with other nouns as above. When Calvin places the גֵר in the

---

523 The following chart will indicate the difference in law concerning these two groups:

		Stranger	Widow	Orphan
Dt 14,29	Tithe	x	x	x
Dt 16,11	Weeks	x	x	x
Dt 16,14	Booths	x	x	x
Dt 24,19	Harvest	x	x	x
Dt 24,20	Harvest	x	x	x
Dt 24,21	Harvest	x	x	x
Dt 26,11	Tithe	x		
Dt 26,12f	Tithe	x	x	x

	Poor and Needy
Dt 15,1–6	Fallow Year: no exaction of debts
Dt 15,7–11	Loans without interest
Dt 15,12–18	Fallow Year: liberation of slave
Dt 24,10–13	Pledge of a poor person
Dt 24,14–15	Daily pay for a poor day-laborer

524 CALVIN, *Comm. in Mosis reliq. libr.*, Dt. 14,29 (CO 24,482): 'It is rather a correction or interpretation of the Law, lest the priests and Levites alone should consume all the tithes, without applying a part to the relief of the poor, of strangers, and widows.'

525 CALVIN, *Comm. in Mosis reliq. libr.*, Dt 16,11 (CO 24,600–02).

triad, all three parties (the גר, orphan and widow) have equal status in virtue of their common poverty. However, when גר occurs outside of the triad, it is most often found in connection with the Israelites, thus a group that enjoyed a higher status in society. Finally, when in Calvin's exegetical works the גר is found as an individual subject outside of the triad, it does not necessarily refer to the poverty of a person, but is more closely linked with religious matters.[526]

Calvin states that the reason for generosity lay in the Israelites' own experience as strangers in the past:

> As regards strangers, God proves that he cares for them, because He is gracious in preserving them and clothing them; and then a special reason is again adduced, that the Israelites, when they were formerly sojourners in Egypt, had need of the compassion of others.[527]

The commentaries show a variation in the motive-clause. When גר stands as collective subject with 'widow' and 'orphan,' the motive-clause for the Israelites' generosity is זכרת כי־עבד ('remember that you were a slave'). The pattern of such clauses is the introduction of the verb זכרת ('memento'), and is used to support the command even where the term עבד ('slave') does not appear in the main clause in Calvin's translation.[528] On the other hand, when גר stands separate as subject, the motive-clause is כי־גרים הייתם בארץ מצרים ('for you are a stranger in the land of Egypt').[529] In such cases, the clause is thus introduced by the particle כי, where the particle-clause is then relative to the clauses containing the commands concerning the treatment of the גר.

The motive-clauses attached to these laws reflect an aspect of Calvin's theological thought. Laws requiring generosity are not easily enforced. If the law is to be obeyed, it is because the Israelites have been convinced that this is their duty, as opposing to being afraid of punishment. For that reason, these motive-clauses play a significant role in these laws. The motive-clause that occurs twice here is also found in Calvin's treatment of Dt 15,15, where he deals with the law demanding generosity to the released slave.

According to Calvin, the motivating clause contains two reasons for generosity to the needy. First, the Israelites are to remember their own slavery and the deliverance granted to them by God (Dt 24,18.22); second, God will bless the work of the Israelites if they are generous (Dt 24,19). In both cases, the Israeli-

---

526 גר is connected to איש and אה in Dt 1,16; with לוי, and, אתה in Dt 26,11; 28,43; with נשיכם and טפכם in Dt 29,10; and with והטף, והנשים, האנשים, and העם in Dt 31,12. Calvin did not speak about economic reasons in these texts.

527 CALVIN, *Comm. in Mosis reliq. libr.*, Dt 10,17–19 (CO 24,674–75): 'Quoad peregrinos, [eos sibi curae esse probat Deus, quod in illis alendis et vestiendis sit beneficus: deinde] specialis rursum adducitur ratio, quia Israelitae olim quum inquilini essent in Aegypto, indiguerint aliena misericordia.'

528 CALVIN, *Comm. in Mosis reliq. libr.*, Dt 24,17–18.19–21 (CO 24,677.696).

529 CALVIN, *Comm. ad locum*: Ex 22,20; 23,9.12; Lv 19,34; Dt 10,19.

tes are to follow the earlier action of God. Because God was kind to the Israelites when they were enslaved and liberated them, now the Israelites are to be
kind to the needy. Israel's relationship to the vulnerable is analogous to God's
relationship with Israel when they were in Egypt. Now that, on account of
God's acts, the Israelites have power, they are to use that power for the benefit
of the needy.

A similar principle is applied to the theology of land and harvest. God was
generous to the Israelites in giving them a bountiful harvest; now the Israelites
are to imitate God's generosity. Obedience to this commend of generosity is the
condition of God's blessing. In this both contexts, Calvin notes that the Israelites should not consider themselves to have rights to the entire yield of the
harvest.[530] According to Calvin, the farmer is not to go back over the field a
second time, because what remains belongs to the גר, widow and orphan. In
this way it becomes clear that the land and its produce are God's, and that it is
thus He who confers the harvesting rights.

For Calvin, the stranger, widow and orphan are vulnerable, landless, and
dependent on the land owning Israelites for their welfare. On the other hand,
though Calvin keeps Levites along with these vulnerable people in few occasions, he makes it clear that the Levites do not depend on the land owners but
with the benefit of tithe[531] and first fruits.[532] By including the Levites in the
harvest regulations, the regulations concerning the tithes and religious ceremonies, Calvin clearly points out that Levites enjoy a different status than the
triad stranger-widow-orphan. Levites are included only in religious matters,
and are thus paid religious workers.

There is a kind of rhetoric in Calvin's translation when he deals with Yahweh's action towards the triad in Ps 146,7–9 and Dt 10,18:

Ps 146,7–9	Dt 10,18
7a rendering right to unjustly oppress	18a He doth execute the judgment
7b giving bread to the hungry	18a giving him food and raiment
8b Jehovah loving the righteous	18ba (Jehovah) loveth the [...]

---

530 CALVIN, *Comm. in Mosis reliq. libr.*, Dt 24,19–21 (CO 24,696): 'God, therefore, permits every one to
     reap his corn, to gather his vintage, and to enjoy his abundance; provided the rich, content
     with their own vintage and harvest, do not grudge the poor the gleaning of the grapes and
     corn. Not that He absolutely assigns to the poor whatever remains, so that they may seize it as
     their own; but that some small portion may flow gratuitously to them from the munificence of
     the rich.'

531 CALVIN, *Comm. in Mosis reliq. libr.*, Dt 14,29; 26,12.13 (CO 24,482–83). Calvin harmonizes Dt 26,1–11
     with Nu 15,17–21, Ex 22,28; 23,19 and 34,26, focusing his comments on the laws of the first
     fruits (CO 24,307–09).

532 CALVIN, *Comm. in Mosis reliq. libr.*, Dt 16,11.12.14 (CO 24,599–600).

9a Jehovah guarding the גרים
9b he relieves the
  the *widow* and *fatherless*

18ba (Jehovah) loveth the גר
8a execute the judgment
  the *widow* and *fatherless*

Outside of Calvin's commentary on the Harmony of the Law, we find the pair 'widow' and 'orphan' in Jes 1,23 and Ps 68,6. In Jes 1,17 this pair appears together with the 'oppressed' (חמוץ), and in Jes 10,2 with the 'poor' (ענוו) and 'needy' (רלום). Calvin's reference to the help and generosity that must be extended to this cluster, indirectly indicates that there were two classes: the well-to-do upper class, and the impoverished lower class.[533]

The pair 'widow and orphan' takes a unique position in the above-mentioned texts in contrast to other places[534] where Calvin refers to this pair. Here they always function as the subjects of the verbs, most often verbs expressing accusations against the Israelites' oppression of the widow or orphan, or else prohibitions against oppression of the same.[535] In contrast, in Dt 10,18 and Ps 146,9 are the only two texts where Calvin refers to Yahweh as the subject of the verbs. These verbs refer to actions in relation to the widow and orphan, not actions done on behalf of, or against them. Further, according to Calvin it is in God's very nature to love the triad, deserted as strangers, widows and orphans are by human beings.[536] Calvin also juxtaposes God's acts in relation to the stranger, orphan and widow with those of humans.[537]

5.2.3. Legal Regulations

Throughout his exegetical works on גר , Calvin repeatedly notes that the גר is the one who is exposed to injuries and has no one to defend his cause. This understanding of what it is to be a גר becomes the starting-point for the formation of legal regulations for the גר. These legal regulations are combined with certain 'dos' and 'don'ts.'

---

533 FRICK, *The City in Ancient Israel*, 205, remarks that the rise of the monarchy introduced a hierarchical social structure. It created a royal family, a national cult class, a patrician class, and a peasant class.

534 Jes 1,23; Ps 10,2; 94,6; Ez 22,7; Mal 3,5.

535 Ex 22,21; Jer 7,6; 22,3; Sach 7,10.

536 CALVIN, *Comm. in Mosis reliq. libr.*, Dt 10,17–19 (CO 24,674): 'He confirms the foregoing decree by a reference to the nature of God Himself; for the vile and abject condition of those with whom we have to do, causes us to injure them the more wantonly, because they seem to be altogether deserted.'

537 CALVIN, *Comm. in Mosis reliq. libr.*, Dt 10,17–19 (CO 24,674): 'God distinguishes Himself from men, who are carried away by outward appearance, to hold the rich in honor, and the poor in contempt; to favor the beautiful or the eloquent, and to despise the unseemly.'

5.2.4. Prevent Not the Judgment

Calvin treats Dt 24,17 and Ex 22,26–27 as one exegetical unit. The interesting thing is that although the triad does occur in Dt 24,17 and not in Ex 22,26–27, Calvin relates the triad in the former to the 'poor' in the latter, thereby indicating that all of these categories suffer together because of their common injustice and poverty.[538] The motive-clause for charity to be shown to the strangers-widows-orphans and the poor is once again Israel's pas experience as slaves in Egypt:

> They should reflect that they were bondmen in the land of Egypt; for their condition there did not suffer them proudly to insult the miserable; and it is natural that he should be the more affected with the ills of others who has experienced the same. Since, then, this reason is a general one, it is evident also that the precept is general, that we should be humane towards all that are in want.[539]

Similarly Calvin applies the various verbs found in the imperative mood to bear on the Israelites who mistreat the גר, widow , fatherless and orphan

	Stranger	Fatherless	Orphan
Ex 22,21	לֹא־תוֹנֶה (vex not)	לֹא עַנִּי (afflict not)	לֹא עַנִּי
	לֹא־תוֹנֶה (oppress not)		
Lv 19,33	לֹא־תוֹנֶה (vex not)		
Jer 22,3	אַל־יָנָה (do no wrong)	אַל־יָנָה	אַל־יָנָה
	אַל־חָמָס (do no violence)	אַל־חָמָס	אַל־חָמָס
Jer 7,6	לֹא־תוֹנָה	:לֹא־תוֹנָה	לֹא־תוֹנָה
Sach 7,10	לֹא־תוֹנָה	לֹא־תוֹנָה	לֹא־תוֹנָה

Calvin begins his explanation by mentioning the fear of God. The fear of God is neither proved by ceremonies, nor by abstaining from doing wrong; it is rather acting justly towards one's brothers and sisters (in the broad sense of the word), and being ready to help the miserable.[540] According to Calvin, the ungodly will not injure, nor do harm these *personae miserae* because they are terrified by fear of God, since He is their avenger and defender. In this prophetic

---

538 CALVIN, *Comm. in Mosis reliq. libr.*, Ex 22,26–27 / Dt 24,6.17–13.17–18 (CO 24,678): 'What he had previously prescribed respecting the poor, lie afterwards applies to widows alone, yet so as to recommend all poor persons to us under their name; and this we gather both from the beginning of the verse (17), in which lie instructs them to deal fairly and justly with strangers and orphans.'

539 CALVIN, *Comm. in Mosis reliq. libr.*, Ex 22,26–27 / Dt 24,6.17–13.17–18 (CO 24,678).

540 CALVIN, *Comm. in Zech.* 7,10 (CO 44,227): 'As I have reminded you, that the fear of God is not really proved, except when a person cleaves to what is just and right, and is not restrained by fear or shame, but discharges his duty as it were in the presence of God and of his angels, so that he shows favor to the poor and miserable, who are without any to help them.'

context, Calvin binds these people together by their varying conditions as poor and miserable beings. In his commentary on the Psalms, Calvin calls this act of oppression 'impiety' and 'contempt of Divine authority.'[541] Calvin also thinks that such acts are not only unjust with respect to the highest level, but also in the basis of common social relationships.

In his exegesis of Mal 3,5 and Ps 94,6, Calvin lists the crimes executed against the stranger-widow-orphan triad. The significance of these texts lies in the way Calvin explains the prophet's intent. According to him, the prophet identifies the sins of the Israelites as being those of 'sorcerers, adulterers, and false swearers.' But in order to illustrate the gravity of their sins,[542] Calvin says the prophet refers specifically to their treatment of the גֵר, widow and orphan. For any crime against this group of people who already experience such misery instigates God into action against the oppressors. Any crime committed against the גֵר is considered to be war against God, because He is their defender, protector and avenger.[543]

To sum up, the noun גֵר occurs in combination with the words 'widow' and 'orphan' in less than twenty percent of the total number of occurrences in Calvin's Old Testament commentaries. The conditions that apply to the stranger in the triad גֵר-widow-orphan, do not always apply to the stranger when mentioned outside of the triad. The triad גֵר-widow-orphan always refers to a social category of helpless and marginalized people. On occasions, the word גֵר is used to indicate temporary residence, though not necessarily including a condition of poverty. For Calvin, the law always serves to protect the three groups of the triad.

5.3. גֵר and תּוֹשָׁב (Temporary Resident)

Calvin juxtaposes גֵר with תּוֹשָׁב four times in his commentaries, the latter occurring a total of twelve times in the commentary. In Gn 23,4, Calvin refers to Abraham as גֵר and תּוֹשָׁב. Similarly, in connection with Ps 39,13, Calvin identi-

---

541 CALVIN, *Comm. in Ps.* 94,6 (CO 32,20): 'To treat such objects with cruelty argues a singular degree of impiety, and contempt of divine authority, and is not only an outrage of common justice, but the infraction of a privilege of special protection which God has condescended to cast around them.'

542 CALVIN, *Comm. in Mal.* 3,5 (CO 44,467): 'By mentioning the *orphan, the widow,* and *the stranger,* he amplifies the atrocity of their crimes; for the orphans, widows, and strangers, we know, are under the guardianship and protection of God, inasmuch as they are exposed to the wrongs of men.'

543 CALVIN, *Comm. in Mal.* 3,5 (CO 44,467): 'Hence every one who plunders orphans, or harasses widows, or oppresses strangers, seems to carry on open war, as it were, with God himself, who has promised that these should be safe under the shadow of his hand.'

fies David as גר and תושב. However, this does not imply that these nouns have
the same meaning, because in his commentaries the laws that pertain to them
differ. In connection with the food regulations, the תושב and hired worker
(שכיר) are mentioned together. However, in all three places, the גר is completely absent from the context.[544] In his explanation of Ex 12,43–47 on the
Passover, Calvin lists who may, and may not, participate in the celebration. Of
the foreigner (בן־נכר), slave (עבד), temporary resident (תושב), and hired
worker (שכיר), only the slave is allowed to take part in the Passover meal. The
same is true for the eating of the priestly food. In this context, the slaves who
are bought with money and the slaves born in the household are linked with
the legislation.

What God here permits as regards strangers was everywhere customary
among the Gentiles, viz., that their power over their slaves should exist not
only until their death, but should continue in perpetual succession to their
children; for this is the force of the expression, "ye shall possess them for your
children," that the right of ownership should pass to their heir's also; nor is
there a distinction made only as to perpetuity, but also as to the mode of their
treatment.[545]

Furthermore, in the Sabbath year, the harvest belongs to the Israelite, man
servant, maid servant, hired worker, and temporary resident.[546] Once again,
one can observe that Calvin places temporary worker and hired worker in the
same category. In the context of the Israelite showing mercy (Lv 25,40), both
תושב and שכיר are listed. Once again, Calvin asserts that both share the same
social status in ancient Israel. In all these occasions, Calvin includes the גר in
his list.

References to גר and תושב are found in the law related to the year of Jubilee Lv 25,35–53. Calvin does not discuss the institution of the Sabbath year, but
he instead focuses on the well-being of the Israelite. That is, that the Israelite
does not become destitute, and that the rich do not abuse the poor:

> Yet God so mitigates His law as to lay no unjust burden upon sojourners, since He concedes
> more to them, with respect to Hebrew slaves, than to the natives of the land; for if they had
> sold themselves to their brethren, they went forth free in the seventh year, whilst their sla-
> very under sojourners was extended to the fiftieth year.[547]

In the context of the year of Jubilee and the redemption of the slaves, Calvin
uses the terms גר, תושב, and שכר interchangeably, where all stand in the same
social position. However, in the verses 47–51, the word גר refers specifically to

---

544 I.e. Ex 12,43–47; Lv 22,10–13; 25,6.
545 CALVIN, *Comm. in Mosis reliq. libr.*, Lv 25,44 (CO 24,704).
546 Cf. CALVIN, *Comm. in Mosis reliq. libr.*, Lv 25,6 (CO 24,585–87).
547 CALVIN, *Comm. in Mosis reliq. libr.*, Lv 25,47 (CO 24,705).

non-Israelites; this is illustrated quite clearly in that 'one of your brothers' is set directly against the גר and תּוֹשָׁב, which draws a clear line between insiders and outsiders. Although outsiders may become slaves, the Israelites are not permitted to become enslaved to other Israelites. In this context, the Israelites are set over against all these groups: גר, תּוֹשָׁב, and שָׂכָר. Calvin writes: 'He commands that he should be set free in the jubilee year, in which a general enfranchisement took place as regarded the children of Abraham.'[548] Here, Israelites have a special status because they were delivered by God out of Egypt. Although contrasted with the special privileges of the Israelites, according to Calvin the גר, תּוֹשָׁב, and שָׂכָר still share amongst themselves a more-or-less equal status.

5.4. The Stranger and the Native (גר and אזרח)

5.4.1. Statistical Note

The noun גר appears in Calvin's Old Testament commentaries together with other nouns אזרח[549] ('native'), תּוֹשָׁב[550] ('temporary resident'), and עני[551] ('poor') a total of eighteen times. The noun גר also occurs with other expressions like בית־ישׂראל ('house of Israel'), or בני ישׂראל ('children of Israel'). Sometimes the noun occurs together with a verbal form to denote a certain position, such as וכי־יגור גר ('if a stranger dwells with you'), or הגר הגר ('the stranger sojourns'). Four of these eighteen occurrences are attached to the Egypt motive-clause ('remember you were strangers in the land of Egypt');[552] four are found in comparisons with the impoverished;[553] nine are related to the religious regulations;[554] and one comes in the context of criminal law.[555] In most cases, Calvin understands the גר as being subject to the same laws as the Israelites.

---

548 CALVIN, *Comm. in Mosis reliq. libr.*, Lv 25,42 (CO 24,704).

549 CALVIN, *Comm.* ad locum: Lv 17,15; 18,26; 19,34; 24,16–22.

550 CALVIN, *Comm.* ad locum: Lv 25,35.47.

551 CALVIN, *Comm.* ad locum: Lv 19,10; 23,22.

552 CALVIN, *Comm.* ad locum: Lv 19,10; 19,33.34; 23,22.

553 CALVIN, *Comm.* ad locum: Lv 25,35.47 (3x).

554 CALVIN, *Comm.* ad locum: Lv 17,8,10,12,13,15; 18,26; 20,2; 22,18; 24,16.

555 CALVIN, *Comm.* ad locum: Lv 24,22

5.4.2. Social Status

According to Calvin, the law calls for equality between stranger and native. The Israelites are variously called 'sons of Israel' (six times), 'from the house of Israel' (three times), 'native' (six times), and 'sons of the native' (once). The term native is common, and appears only three times outside of Calvin's commentary on the Harmony of the Law.[556] For Calvin, the term native has significance, in terms of the sanctity attached to the land. The native derives importance from the purity of the land: the land is kept pure by right behaviour, and those who reside in the land are responsible to keep it pure. In this way of thinking, there is no room for a plurality of religions or legal system. For Calvin, land is much more than a geographical location where the chosen people happen to live. It is a land separated from other lands for God.

The laws in Lv 19,33–34 ('the stranger that dwelleth with you shall be unto you as one horn among you') fluctuate between the second person singular and the second person plural forms. Calvin describes a kind of relationship where the Israelite is a native, and the גֵר a guest in the land of Israel. According to the law, the Israelites may not oppress the גֵר, says Calvin. The verb תוֹנוּ found here is the same one Calvin refers to in connection with Ex 22,20. Calvin combines these two texts into one exegetical unit. The oppression referred to in this context of socio-economic. The demand to treat the גֵר as native-born is here not something in the religious domain, but rather refers to such socio-economic matters as receiving justice at the gate, paying fair wages, not making immoral demands of the גֵר or his family, etc. According to Calvin, the Israelites are to treat the גֵר as if they are their own. Calvin thus speaks about equality among all men.

Calvin does not include the גֵר with the native as those addressed in the particular laws concerned. A thorough survey of Calvin's commentary on the Harmony of the Law reveals that the גֵר is never included in the introductory formulae of the different section of the laws.[557] Generally speaking, Calvin translates the introductory phrase of the laws as:

וַיְדַבֵּר יְהוָה אֶל־מֹשֶׁה לֵּאמֹר ('And the LORD spake unto Moses, saying [...]')

The second part of the law has the notion of transmission:

דַּבֵּר אֶל־כָּל־עֲדַת בְּנֵי־יִשְׂרָאֵל וְאָמַרְתָּ אֲלֵהֶם ('Speak unto all the congregation of the children of Israel, and say unto them [...]')

---

556 CALVIN, *Comm.* ad locum: Ez 47,22; Jos 8,33; Ps 37,35.
557 CALVIN, *Comm.* ad locum: Lv 17,1; 18,1; 19,1; 20,1; 21,16; 22,1.18.26; 23,1.10.23.26.34; 24,1.13; 25,1.

In this second part of the law, the גֵר is never addressed directly. Most often it is the בְנֵי־יִשְׂרָאֵל ('sons of Israel')[558] or אֶל־אַהֲרֹן וְאֶל־בָּנָיו ('Aaron and the priests')[559] who are addressed, and in two instances בָּנָיו וְאֶל צַל־בְּנֵי יִשְׂרָאֵל אֶל־אַהֲרֹן וְאֶל ('Aaron and the children of Israel together').[560] In the body of the law, on the other hand, the 'stranger' is at times referred to, but then alongside other nouns like גֵר־עָנִי ('stranger and poor') or גֵר־אֶזְרָח ('stranger and home-born') or גֵר־תּוֹשָׁב ('stranger and foreigner'). One could suppose that from Calvin's point of view, the גֵר is not explicitly mentioned either in the introductory formula or in the transmission command because, being considered part of the people, the strangers are already under the בְנֵי־יִשְׂרָאֵל. This is not the case, however, for Calvin uses various expressions like 'the גֵר among you'[561] and the 'גֵר who lives among you'[562] to distinguish clearly and explicitly between the people of Israel themselves, and those who just live among them. The same can be concluded on the basis of the use of phrases like 'between the house of Israel' and the גֵר, and 'between the sons of Israel' and the גֵר. All these make it clear that the גֵר does not belong to any of these groups as such, although they could become considered as part of them.

5.4.3. Second Person אֶזְרָח vs. Third Person גֵר

The prime focus of the גֵר-laws in Calvin's commentary is on the principle of solidarity. Calvin interprets the law as guiding the attitude of the Israelite towards the גֵר. The Israelites are addressed in the second person, while the גֵר is referred to in the third person:

Ex 22,20   Thou shall not wrong or oppress a גֵר
Dt 24,21   when you gather the grapes of your vineyard
           Do not glean what is left; it shall be for the גֵר
Lv 19,33   when a גֵר reside with you [...] you shall not oppress him.
Lv 19,34   you shall love the גֵר as yourself

The function of these laws is to protect the גֵר, and to ensure he receives what is due to him in Hebrew society.

---

558 CALVIN, *Comm.* ad locum: Lv 1,2; 4,2; 7,23.29; 11,2; 15,2; 18,2; 20,2; 23,2.10.24.34; 24,2; 25,2; 27,2.
559 CALVIN, *Comm.* ad locum: Lv 21,1.17; 22,24.
560 CALVIN, *Comm.* ad locum: Lv 17,2; 22,18.
561 CALVIN, *Comm.* ad locum: Lv 17,10.13; 17,8.12; 18,26. הגר בתוכם
562 CALVIN, *Comm.* ad locum: Lv 20,2; 22,18. הגר בישראל

However, there are also laws that are common to the גר and the native.[563] One such concerns the regulations concerning carcasses, where Calvin remarks that the strangers were indeed subject to it: 'The strangers [...] but those who had devoted themselves to the worship of God; for many foreigners, abandoning their superstitions, were circumcised, and it behooved that such as these should be expressly laid under the bonds of the Law.'[564] On four occasions, Calvin places the words אזרח and גר together, and what is interesting is that all are in the context of prohibitive commands. The basic concern is to protect the holiness within the community. Laws are given to the natives to protect the גר, while other laws are addressed to native and גר equally in order to preserve holiness.

The laws concerning the protection of גר are:
* addressed only to the natives, where the גר are the beneficiaries
* aimed at the amelioration of the material condition of the גר
* not accompanied by any sanctions
* followed by the formula אני יהוה ('I am Yahweh')

The laws concerning the preservation of holiness in the community:
* include both native and גר
* aim to preserve holiness in the community
* have sanctions
* includes a cut-off formula

From Calvin's exegesis it is clear that when the laws deal with the preservation of holiness, the גר is just as much subject to the law as the native is. For example:

a. laws relating to the slaughtering of animals
Lv 17,10   the house of Israel and גר
Lv 17,3   the children of Israel and the גר

b. laws relating to sacrifices and offerings:
Lv 17,8 the house of Israel and the stranger
Lv 22,18   the house of Israel and the גר

---

563   Lv 17,15; 18,26; 24,16.22.

564   CALVIN, *Comm. in Mosis reliq. libr.*, Lv 17,12 (CO 24,620) Cf. Lv 17,12: 'Therefore I said unto the children of Israel, No soul of you shall eat blood, neither shall any stranger that sojourneth among you eat blood.'

c. other laws:

related to food	Lv 17,15	native and רֵג
related to sexual relations	Lv 18,26	native and the רֵג
related to Molech worship	Lv 20,2	the children of Israel and the רֵג
related to blasphemy	Lv 24,16	native and the רֵג
related to murder	Lv 24,22	native and the רֵג

When the laws do not deal with the issue of holiness within the community, they are addressed to the native, and the רֵג is mentioned only as beneficiary of the laws. For example:

d. laws concerned with the protection of the needy[565]
e. laws concerned with the impoverished Israelite brother[566]

The רֵג-laws that concern holiness include sanctions, and according to Calvin they have formulas of expulsion or annihilation in case one contravenes the laws. Their main aim is to preserve holiness, and the reference to the רֵג is always secondary.

In summary, the רֵג is one who lives in Israel, and consequently has a particular place in Hebrew society. The רֵג was referred to in the context of prohibitive laws with humanitarian import. However, when the main thrust of the particular law is the issue of holiness within the Israelite community, the רֵג is not considered to have the same status of the native in civil and religious matters.[567]

5.4.4. Religious Laws

In the context of the Passover celebration, Calvin juxtaposes the רֵג with the native. Although the Hebrew text juxtaposes the two in three places, Calvin's commentary treats only two of these places. The most significant place for him is the passage in Ex 12,43–49, because for him there is an opening here for the רֵג to change from the status of an outsider to one who is inside the community through the ceremonies that effect a change. It is notable, that Calvin still completely excludes the בֶּן־נֵכָר ('foreigner'), תּוֹשָׁב ('alien') and שָׂכַר ('hired

---

565 Lv 19,10,33,34; 23,22
566 Lv 25,35.47.
567 DRIVER, Deuteronomy, 165.

servant') from the celebration.[568] For Calvin, it is the whole notion of clean and unclean that either separates or includes the non-natives among the native.[569] He remarks that the Passover was given primarily to the natives: 'Moses, therefore, first of all, excludes all strangers who were unclean through their uncircumcision.' However, two groups of non-natives may, however, join in as well as long as they are circumcised according to the law: 'that servants bought with money (עבד) should be circumcised, (which was a necessary requirement;) and that free and independent persons (גר), if they chose to embrace the same.' The basic criterion for participation in the Passover is, therefore, circumcision, which thus clearly functions very much as did baptism did in the early church. This is the visible sign of membership in the holy community:

Circumcision was then like a hedge, which should distinguish heathen nations from the holy race of Abraham; if, then, any should wish to celebrate the passover together with the elect people, it was necessary that he should be circumcised, so as to attach himself to the true God; though God did not merely refer to the outward sign, but to the object, viz., that all who were circumcised should promise to study sincere piety.[570]

Calvin identifies these non-Israelites as follows: 'Nor does Moses refer only to that mixed multitude which had followed the Israelites out of Egypt; but prescribes a law respecting all strangers, who for many succeeding ages should come on business into the land.' Circumcision is the sign, for all time, of the covenant. Any male who is not circumcised is not a member of the community.

Once the requirements for participation in the Passover have been fulfilled, the stranger stands in a position of equal privilege as well as obligation over against the native. Calvin writes:

And this is expressed also in the words, "One law shall be to him that is home born, and unto the stranger", viz., that the ordinance of the sacrament should be solemnly observed by all, and that thus they should equally participate in the grace offered to them in common, and that

---

568 CALVIN, Comm. in Mosis reliq. libr., Ex 12,43 (CO 24,291): 'Since the passover was the sacred bond whereby God would hold the elect people in obligation to Himself, He forbids all strangers from partaking of it; because a promiscuous permission to eat of it would have been an unworthy profanation. And in fact, since this is a supplement to the First Commandment, it only addresses itself to those unto whom is directed the preface of the Law, "Hear, O Israel; The Lord our God is one Lord." We know that among the Gentiles none but the initiated were admitted to their sacred rites.'

569 CALVIN, Comm. in Mosis reliq. libr., Nu 9,6 (CO 24,297): 'A question is here introduced incidentally, viz., what must be done, if any sudden defilement should prevent any persons from celebrating the passover with the rest; since God would expunge from amongst His people whosoever should not observe this memorial of their redemption? Although the history is here touched upon, yet because the doctrine as to the just and pure observance of the passover is its main subject.'

570 CALVIN, Comm. in Mosis reliq. libr., Ex 12,43 (CO 24,291).

in this respect the condition of all should be equal, though it differed as to their inheritance of the land.

According to Calvin, these Passover stipulations were to be celebrated in the home, and not while traveling or on pilgrimage.[571] This custom is crucial to their self-identity, no matter where they live.[572] Thus, to sum up, for Calvin circumcision functions in the context of the Passover as a sign of membership in the community. For this reason, Calvin concludes that when the stranger is circumcised, he is considered member of the community, and equally shares in the rights and privileges that entails. It is only in the context of the Passover that this requirement binds the גר and the אזרח.

5.4.5. A Spatial Placement of גר

From Calvin's notion of holiness, one can understand the dimension of holiness in Hebrew society and thus also determine the place of the גר in society. The concept of graded holiness which flows out from the center is evident in the religious matters (the holy of holies, the tabernacle, Israel). It is also possible to see different levels of holiness. In the realm of ritual, there are the dimensions of holy, clean and unclean. There are accordingly sacrificial animals, and clean and unclean animals. However, the spatial dimension of holiness remains the clearest expression of the spectrum. In this scheme, the Israelites are at the center, and the non-Israelites are on the periphery:

God → Priesthood → Israelites → Non-Israelites

This spatial notion of holiness forms an important aspect in the understanding of the place of the גר in Israel. It helps us to understand the various social groups that could be found in Hebrew society. These groups may be ordered according to their distance from the holy realm of the cult:

Priests → Levites → Other tribes → Unclean Israelites → Non-Israel → the גר → the nation.[573]

The individual's status in terms of purity and impurity decide his role in society. The position of the גר always falls between the natives and the nations. From Calvin's treatment we can also observe that the nations closer to Israel

---

571   CALVIN, *Comm. in Mosis reliq. libr.*, Nu 9,6ff (CO 24,297). Cf. DE VAUX, *Ancient Israel*, 484–92; MCCON-VILLE, *Law and Theology in Deuteronomy*, 100–10.

572   SMITH, *The Religion of the Landless*, 76.

573   CALVIN, *Comm. ad locum*: Lv 19,10,33,34; 23,22.

are the ones which are more dangerous. The proximity of foreign elements could endanger the security of Israel through the seduction of idolatry. Thus in order to maintain the purity of society, laws were set in place to deal with the relationships between Israelites and Canaanites, and Israelites and the strangers.[574]

For Calvin, holiness is not limited to the priests, animals or sanctuary, but affects all: persons, animals, natives and גר. Because the גר receive his well-being from the same source (i.e. the land), he is also included in some laws.[575] Consequently, both native and גר are commanded to follow laws that were to be enforced in, and with respect to, the land.[576] It is clear from Calvin that the גר is bound only by the prohibitive commandments, and not by the performative commands. The גר is expected to keep the commandments that involve the purity of the community. He is not expected to observe the regulations and ceremonies that form part of Israel's religion. To illustrate this contrast, we can note how for example the regulations concerning sacrificial procedures are addressed also to strangers (Lv 17,8.10.12.13), while those dealing with profane slaughter appear to apply only to the Israelites (Lv 17,2–7) the regulation concerning blasphemy includes the strangers too (Lev. 24:16).

This also explains why the regulations concerning the גר in Hebrew society are of central importance for the prohibitions and instructions, as well as the severe penalties in case of disobedience. The גר who does not obey the laws shall be cut off from the congregation (Lv 17,8–9.10.13–14; 18,26–29), shall be put to death (Ex 12,19; Lv 20,2; 24,16.22; Nu 9,13–14), and shall bear their own guilt (Lv 17,15). It must be noted that these punitive or preventative prescriptions are essential to keep a positive place for the גר in society.

A similar sentiment is expressed in regard to the land. Calvin juxtaposes the גר with the native in relation to land-ownership: 'For although they might be reckoned among the people, yet did no portion of the land in consequence fall to their lot, nor was their condition improved as to temporal rights; but it was only that they might become members of the Church.' Since God dwells in the land of Canaan, having chosen His abode among the children of Israel, his sanctity is also profaned. In every respect, care should be taken lest the land, which is sacred to God, should be contaminated by bloodshed.

---

574 CALVIN, *Comm.* ad locum: Lv 18,3–5.24–30.
575 CALVIN, *Comm. in Mosis reliq. libr.*, Lv 17,8.10.12.13 (CO 24,469.619–20).
576 CALVIN, *Comm. in Mosis reliq. libr.*, Lv 18,26 (CO 24,646). Every adult in Israel and גר must heed the prohibitive commandments in order to keep the purity of the land.

5.4.6. Food Laws

As to the command, in the first passage, to give it to a stranger, or to sell it to an alien, that he might eat it, it does not appear reasonable, since that would be to supply the materials for sin, as though one should offer a sword to a madman, or transfer illicit goods to others. But the solution of this difficulty is easy: for the Gentiles were permitted to eat indifferently of all sorts of food, since no distinctions were placed between them; but the prohibition of certain meats was a mark of separation between them and the elect people of God. A more difficult question arises from a kind of contradiction, because Moses in another passage binds both the stranger and the home-born by the same law, and declares them to be alike unclean if they shall have tasted of carrion. But we must bear in mind that he sometimes calls those strangers who, although born of heathen parents, had embraced the Law. Circumcision, therefore, connected them with God, just as if they had derived their origin from Abraham; whilst there were other strangers, whom uncircumcision separated from the children of Abraham as profane and excommunicated. The sum is, that whosoever allege God's name, and boast themselves to be His people, are called to cultivate holiness, and to keep themselves pure from every stain.[577]

In his commentary on Dt 14, Calvin deals with two sets of laws regarding food and tithing. In both places Calvin calls the Israelites to be charitable to the גֵר. The law which deals with the first part of Dt 14 commands the Israelites not to eat anything that is already dead. However, they can give the meat to the גֵר who live in their midst, or they may sell it to the 'foreigner.' The reason for the prohibition to Israel is that the animal is not properly slaughtered, and its blood not drained (Dt 12,16). The meat is unfit to the Israelites because they are bound by the food laws. However, the meat may be eaten by those who do not belong to the congregation, and for that reason neither גֵר nor 'foreigner' are subject to this law. This food law thus clearly separates גֵר and Israelites. We also notice that in Calvin's exegesis, such meat on animals found already dead may be not given to widows and orphans, but is still permitted for the גֵר. Thus from Calvin it is clear that the גֵר referred to here is a non-Israelite.

In this food law, the גֵר is not only separated from the native, but also from 'foreigner.' For while the Israelites are commanded to show simple charity to the גֵר (i.e. they may give the meat to the strangers), they can sell it to the 'foreigners.' The differences between these two groups of non-Israelites are not only economic, but also have to do with their relationship to the Hebrew religion. The גֵר is the one 'who, although born of heathen parents, had embraced the Law. Circumcision, therefore, connected them with God, just as if they had

---

577 CALVIN, *Comm. in Mosis reliq. libr.*, Dt 14,21 (CO 24,352).

derived their origin from Abraham.' The 'stranger' also needs economic support. From Calvin's comments, it can also be observed that the Israelites are to be generous to other impoverished Israelites, but that this is not the case with respect to the 'foreigner.' When it comes to debts, the Israelites are commanded to cancel all the debts of another Israelite every seven years, but such a requirement does not exist for debts incurred by 'foreigners.' Further, in lending money, the Israelites are commanded to take no interest from other Israelites, but they may charge interest from a 'foreigner.'

5.4.7. Other Religious Ceremonies

In Dt 16, Calvin connects the food law with thanksgiving before God to remind the Israelites that God has brought them to the land of plenty. This act of God has to be reciprocated by being generous to the weaker groups.[578] The blessings of God involve sharing the gift of God with the Levites, poor and the גר, says Calvin. In his commentary, rejoicing and sharing are thus juxtaposed. The first fruits are presented at the temple, and this is followed by rejoicing with the members of household as well as with Levites and the גר (Dt 26,11). What is striking about Calvin's commentary here is that the גר is included as guest at the festal meal. However, we do not find the גר included as guest in his commentary on Nu 18,8–32 and Lv 27,30–33. This results from the different focus of the texts. For Nu 18 deals with the status of the Levites over against other tribes.[579] The differences in emphasis found in Numbers and Deuteronomy may arise from the different historical situations and theological *foci*. Also the list of people who benefit from the tithe and the first fruit are varied. In Dt 14,29 and 26,12–13 the intention of the tithe is to help the Levites and the marginalized; Dt 26,11 speaks of them as 'you and the Levites and the גר in your midst' (רבך־ אתה והלוי והגר אשר בק). It is interesting to observe from Calvin that the list he gives in relation to the feast of Weeks and of Tabernacles (cf. Dt 16,9–15) and the covenant-making ceremony (cf. Dt 29,11) are similar. These lists are intended to be inclusive of the different classes of society. In all of them, Calvin describes the גר as one who lives in the midst of the people, using the preposition קוב.

5.4.8. Summary

In relation to the natives, the גר is given religious and social privileges and protection. The גר is also given the option of becoming Israelite. If circumcised,

---

578 CALVIN, *Comm. in Mosis reliq. libr.*, Dt 14,29; 26,15 (CO 24,482–84).
579 MCCONVILLE, *Law and Theology*, 77; MAYES, *Deuteronomy*, 245.

he is permitted to participate in the Passover. Because circumcision is so significant, it separates Israelites and non-Israelites. But conversely, a circumcised גר is in effect an Israelite. For that reason, the Passover laws apply to the גר in a similar way as to the Israelite.

5.5. Israel as גרים

A question may also arise as to the Egyptians, why God lays His people under an obligation to them, because they sojourned in their land. For, it was barbarous and inhospitable cruelty in them to oppress the wretched fugitives who had trusted to their good faith. But God here refers to their first reception; as in Isaiah 52:4, where, comparing the Egyptians with the Assyrians, He says that the latter oppressed them like robbers, whilst the former had ruled over them not without a cause, because the people had gone down thither of their own accord. Although, therefore, the Israelites had been unworthily oppressed by their fierce tyranny, still God would have their old kindness acknowledged; since their dearth and famine had been relieved, and the refugees were kindly received, when the inhabitants of Canaan were perishing of hunger.[580]

God proves that He cares for the strangers because He graciously preserves and clothes them. But another reason for compassion to the strangers is added, for when the Israelites were formerly sojourners in Egypt, they need compassion from others.[581]

In Calvin's commentary on Dt 23,8 and 10,19, the noun גר, although referring to Israel as a community, is here used with a preposition and therefore includes a territorial dimension. From this it is clear that Calvin gives a new understanding to the Israelite slavery in Egypt in that he adds something positive to the experience in the 'house of slavery.'[582] In Calvin's exegetical work on Dt 23,8, we find five negative commands, followed by motive-clauses.

'You shall not abhor an Egyptian': the reason behind this command is that it was the Israelites themselves who went to Egypt, and not the Egyptians who conquered Israel as the Assyrians conquered Samaria. Given that Egypt is the only nation mentioned in Dt 23,3–8 that is not an immediate neighbor to Israel, and that the law concerns individual Egyptians and not Egypt as nation, the 'Egyptian' referred to here must be an individual immigrant. When we compare these notes with Calvin's comments on Ex 22,20, we note that the privileges

---

580 Dt 23,8: 'Thou shalt not abhor an Edomite; for he is thy brother: thou shalt not abhor an Egyptian; because thou wasts stranger in his land.'

581 Dt 10,19: 'Love ye therefore the stranger, for ye were strangers in the land of Egypt.' Cf. Ps 39,13.

582 Cf. Dt 5,6; 6,12; 7,8; 8,14; 13,5.10.

given to the Egyptian are nothing more than the basic rights of protection. The presence of this law suggests that a significant number of Egyptians must have lived in Israel, for otherwise no rule would have been needed to regulate their mutual relationship. From the nature of the command (i.e. negative), it can be deduced that the Israelites, or at least a significant number of them, reacted negatively against the presence of these immigrants in their territory.[583]

From Calvin's translation, it can be observed that the negative commands in Dt 23,8 do not require a motive-clause:

8a   you shall not abhor an Edomite
8b   you shall not abhor an Egyptian

Calvin further remarks that the historical reasons for these two prohibitions are entirely different. A positive attitude towards Egypt could hardly be possible before the Assyrian invasion of Samaria in 722. For the following texts, Calvin provides similar translations and comments:

	First Half	Second Half
Dt 10,19	you shall love the גר	because you were גרים in Egypt
Lv 19,34	you shall love the גר	because you were גרים in Egypt
Ex 22,20	you shall not ill-treat the גר	because you were גרים in Egypt
Ex 23,9	you shall not oppress the גר	because you were גרים in Egypt

However, Calvin does not follow exactly the pattern of Dt 23,8 because here the parallelism shown in the above verses is absent. The command to 'not abhor' does not refer to every גר, but only to the גר from Egypt. This explains why, although the motive is similar, the addressees of these laws are different. In Dt 23,8 the measure pertains only to the Egyptians, but in Dt 10,19, Ex 22,20 and Lv 19,33 the commands have reference to people of any nationality.

The Egypt-גר motive-clause thus is different from the Egypt-עבד (Egypt-slave) motive-clause. The Egypt-גר formula includes a positive notion, while the Egypt-עבד clause addresses the negative attitude towards the Egyptians.

The motive clause of the Egypt-עבד formula enjoins the Israelites to keep the commandments. The principle behind this command is that of gratitude, remembering God's salvific acts on behalf of Israel. This reminder is thus at the root of the commands concerning treatment of the stranger/needy.

---

583 The command in Dt 23,8 is formulated negatively as a prohibition, while the command in Dt 10,19 is formulated positively, which fact indicates that the community was divided on the issue of the integration of foreigners.

The motive clause of the Egypt-גֵּר formula, on the other hand, supports the content of the command. That is, the rationale of the motive-clause is based on the principle of reciprocity. What the Egyptians did for the Israelites during their initial sojourn in Jacob's time must now done by the Israelites themselves to the גֵּר in their midst.

Calvin also brings out a positive aspect in connection with Israel's sojourn in Egypt when he compares it with the Assyrian oppression. This positive aspect is very striking, and even seems to contradict other comments he makes when he speaks of Israel's experience in Egypt as slaves, using such expressions as 'the house of slavery'[584] and 'the iron furnace.'[585] Thus it seems as if there is a confusion in his understanding of the motive-clauses (i.e. with the Egypt-גֵּר formula and the Egypt-עבד formula). After all, how do these two formulas relate: 'remember that you were a stranger in Egypt,' and 'remember that you were a slave in Egypt?' Nevertheless, Calvin does maintain a clear-cut distinction between the two. According to him, in Dt 23,8, the formula Egypt-גֵּר refers to their 'first reception' in Egypt. The term 'first reception' thus refers to the initial sojourns by Abraham and Jacob in Egypt, when they received and benefited from the generosity of the Egyptians: it was the time of wellbeing and expansion. This initial moment was then juxtaposed with the later oppression formula.

On two other occasions (i.e. besides Dt 23,8 and 10,19), Calvin places the noun גֵּר in relation to Egypt. In Ex 2,22, Calvin refers to Moses as גֵּר in Egypt and in Gn 15,13 he refers to Abraham as גֵּר. It is clear from Calvin's translation on two different texts:

Gn 15,7:
And he said unto him, I *am* the LORD
that brought thee out of Ur of the Chaldees,
to give thee this land to inherit it.

A similar construction is found in Calvin's translation and exegesis of Ex 20,2:

Ex 20,2:
I am the Lord thy God
which have brought thee out of the land of Egypt
out of the house of the bondage.[586]

---

584 CALVIN, *Comm.* ad locum: Dt 5,6; 6,12.21; 7,8; 8,14.
585 CALVIN, *Comm.* ad locum: Dt 4,20; Jer 11,4.
586 Cf. Dt 5,6; Lv 25,8.

Gn 15,7   אנכי יהוה אלהיך אשר הוצאתיך <u>מארץ מצרים</u>

Ex 20,2   אני יהוה אשר הוצאתיך <u>מאור כשדים</u>

Calvin remarks that in Gn 15,7, a covenant was made with Abraham, Isaac and Jacob who were brought up out of the land of the Chaldees, but does not see the same being referred to in Ex 20,2. According to Calvin, the latter text rather refers to the fathers who had been in Egypt during the last two hundred years and then died in Egypt. He does maintain, however, that Ex 20,2 is a renewal or reinterpretation of the covenant found in Gn 15,7, and that 'thee' here refers to those who survived the Egyptian tyranny.

The structure of Calvin's translation is the same, except that in Ex 20,2 Ur of the Chaldeans replaces Egypt. With this, Calvin makes it clear that there is a shift from Abraham to the exodus as the point of departure for the story of Israel. Calvin thus holds the Egyptian sojourn as an interlude between the promise to the patriarchs and its fulfillment in Ex 20,2.[587]

Calvin similarly makes a clear distinction between the sojourn of the Israelites into Egypt, and their stay as slaves under Egyptians, in his exegesis of the historical credo found in Dt 26,5–6.

The historical credo begins with Jacob, the wandering Aramean. Why is he called an Aramean? Due to his mother, or due to his life in Aram (cf. Gn 31,41–42)?

Moment 1: Dt 26,5 ויגר שם ויהי־שם לגוי גדול   Initial Sojourn[588]

Moment 2: Dt 26,6 וירעו אתנו המצרים ויענונו   Later Oppression[589]

Thus according to Calvin, the Israelites' experience as גרים in Egypt was the foundation for them in turn to show compassion to the גר who is in their

---

587 In CALVIN, *Comm. in Mosis reliq. libr.*, Ex 20,2 (CO 24,210–11), Calvin gives clear indications as to the number of years the Israelites dwelled as 'strangers' in Egypt: 'It is, however, asked, how the number of years here given agrees with the subsequent history? Some begin the computation from the time of his departure out of Charran. But it seems more probable that the intermediate time only is denoted; as if he would say, "It behoves thy posterity to wait patiently; because I have not decreed to grant what I now promise, until the four hundredth year: yea, up to that very time their servitude will continue." According to this mode of reckoning, Moses says, [Ex 12,40], that the children of Israel dwelt in Egypt four hundred and thirty years: while yet, from the sixth chapter [Gn 6,1] we may easily gather, that not more than two hundred and thirty years, or thereabouts, elapsed from the time that Jacob went down thither, to their deliverance. Where then, shall we find the remaining two hundred years, but by referring to the oracle?'

588 Dt 26,5: 'A Syrian ready to perish was my father; and he went down into Egypt, and sojourned there with a few, and became there a nation, great, mighty, and populous.'

589 Dt 26,6: 'And the Egyptians evil entreated us, and afflicted us, and laid upon us hard bondage.'

midst. The motive-clause for the Egypt-גר formula thus reminds of the good they experienced due to the kindness of the Egyptians.

He recommends strangers to them on this ground, that the people, who had themselves been sojourners in Egypt, being mindful of their ancient condition, ought to deal more kindly to strangers; for although they were at last oppressed by cruel tyranny, still they were bound to consider their entrance there, viz., that poverty and hunger had driven their forefathers thither, and that they had been received hospitably, when they were in need of aid from others.

For Calvin, the other motive-clause for compassionate treatment of the גר in Israel, here attached to the Egypt-עבד formula, is based in spite of the memory of the bitter slavery on the reminder of the great salvific acts of God when Israel was still in slavery in Egypt.

Similarly, Calvin argues that the Israelites' own experience as גרים in the land of Egypt functions as a motive to obey the law, and to instruct their children in it throughout the generations: 'There was good reason why all the precepts of the Law should be observed, since by them it was that God desired His people, after their deliverance, to shew forth their sense of His loving-kindness.'[590]

The Egypt-עבד formula has the role of an introduction in the Israelite creed, particularly in relation to the Passover Haggadah.[591] In Calvin's commentaries, the Egypt-עבד formula becomes a sort of national, foundational primary confession for all Israelites.[592] This notion appears to be confirmed by some of Calvin's translations:

The גר	within thy gate	Dt 14,29
The גר	in thy land	Dt 24,14
The גר	in thy midst	Dt 16,11

In all of these contexts, Calvin makes the Israelite community the center, while the גר is someone who comes from the periphery. This difference is illustrated clearly between phrases 'the גר within thy gate' and 'you were גרים in the land of the Egyptians.' The first phrase speaks about the גר, while the second speaks

---

590 CALVIN, *Comm. in Mosis reliq. libr.*, Dt 6,20–21 (CO 24,225).

591 Cf. Dt 26,3ff.: 'And thou shalt go unto the priest that shall be in those days, and say unto him, I profess this day unto the Lord thy God, that I am come unto the country which the Lord sware unto our fathers for to give us. And the priest shall take the basket out of thine hand, and set it down before the altar of the Lord thy God. And thou shalt speak and say before the Lord thy God, A Syrian ready to perish was my father; and he went down into Egypt, and sojourned there with a few, and became there a nation, great, mighty, and populous: And the Egyptians evil entreated us, and afflicted us, and laid upon us hard bondage.'

592 CALVIN, *Comm.* ad locum: Dt 6,12.21; 7,8; 8,14; 13,6.11; 24,18; 26,8.

instead about being a גר. In the motive clause, it is not Israel that is at the center, but rather the land of Egypt. Behind the concept of the גר in these comments, there is clearly the perspective of the experience of bondage. These formulas are there to base and support the גר commands, that is, commands in which the noun גר is found both in main-, and in the (subordinate) motive-clause.

To summarize, there are two different motive formulas on the basis of which Calvin makes distinctions in the understanding of Israel's past in Egypt. The motive formulas – the Egypt-גר formula, and Egypt-עבד formula – do not represent two (re-)interpretations of the same event, but instead refer to two different stages of Israel's past in Egypt. The Egypt-גר formula refers to the initial sojourn during which Israel experienced well-being among the Egyptians in Joseph's time. The Egypt-עבד formula, on the other hand, is related exclusively to the theme of oppression under Pharaoh.

5.6. גר and the Cities of Refuge

In his exegesis of Nu 35,9–34, Calvin deals with the ramifications of blood-shed.[593] The land of Canaan must be purified from the shedding of innocent blood, because the land is holy, while the shedding of blood could render the land impure. It was for this exact reason, to keep the land pure, that the cities of refuge were established. 'God appointed the cities of refuge, not only to make distinction between sills of malice and error, but also lest innocent blood should be rashly shed.'[594] There were six cities of refuge, where Israelite, stranger and temporary resident could all enjoy the protection of the same privileges. The city of refuge, according to Calvin, is not a means of escape for murderers, but serves a slightly different function:

> Thus far we have seen how severely He would have murder punished: but, inasmuch as it would have been by no means just that he, who had not willfully but accidentally killed his neighbor, should be hurried away to the same punishment, to which willful murderers were subjected, an exception is added here, in order that he might escape who had killed another ignorantly, and unintentionally.[595]

---

593 Cf. also CALVIN, *Comm. in Ios.* 20,1–6 (CO 25,546): 'The nature of the asylum afforded by the cities of refuge has been already explained. It gave no impunity to voluntary murder, but if any one, by mistake, had slain a man, with whom he was not at enmity, he found a safe refuge by fleeing to one of these cities destined for that purpose. Thus God assisted the unfortunate, and prevented their suffering the punishment of an atrocious deed, when they had not been guilty of it.'
594 CALVIN, *Comm. in Mosis reliq. libr.*, Nu 35,10 (CO 24,637).
595 CALVIN, *Comm. in Mosis reliq. libr.*, Nu 35,10 (CO 24,638–38).

All three groups (Israelite, stranger, temporary resident) are referred to together. The slave is not mentioned, presumably because, as part of a particular
household, they do not have free choice. But all the other three groups enjoy
the same protection provided by the cities of refuge. They have the same status
so as to guard the purity of the land. As Calvin observed:

> Again, since God dwells in the land of Canaan, having chosen His abode among the children of
> Israel, his sanctity is also profaned. The sum is, that, in every respect, care should be taken lest
> the land, which is sacred to God, should be contaminated by bloodshed.[596]

5.7. גר and the Practice of Usury

As an introductory note, it is interesting that, although the MT of Ex 22,25 does
not speak about the גר here in the context of usury, Calvin in his commentary
repeatedly introduces the גר in the context of laws on usury. For instance, he
draws a link between usury and its cruel practices, and the hierarchical social
structure that existed in ancient Israel. As was noted earlier, there were two
basic classes: a well-to-do upper class, and an often impoverished lower class.
The rise of the monarchy increased the hierarchical social stratification, since
it resulted in 1) a royal family, 2) a patrician class centered in the cities, and 3)
a peasant class.[597] The rich and upper class drew wealth from the land which in
turn made the state of the lower class even more precarious. It is in the context
of this new socio-economic reality that the laws concerning justice and charity
find their place. Interestingly, a similar social structure could be found in Geneva during Calvin's time. There was the upper class which consisted of mer-
chants, printers, and magistrates, as well as the lower classes largely made up
of incoming refugees and peasants.

Calvin notes that there was a demand for a certain kind of morality when it
came to the practice of usury and the גר and needy: 'Humanity ought to be
very greatly regarded in the matter of loans, especially when a person, being
reduced to extremities, implores a rich man's compassion.'[598] The lending of
money for interest is subject to civil law, but with respect to the poor it is specifically the rule of charity that must predominate:

> A precept is added as to lending without interest, which, although it is a political law, still de-
> pends on the rule of charity; inasmuch as it can scarcely happen but that the poor should be
> entirely drained by the exaction of interest, and that their blood should be almost sucked away
> [...] It is plain that this was a part of the Jewish polity, because it was lawful to lend at interest
> to the Gentiles, which distinction the spiritual law does not admit. The judicial law, however,
> which God prescribed to His ancient people, is only so far abrogated as that what charity dicta-

---

596 CALVIN, *Comm. in Mosis reliq. libr.*, Nu 35,33 (CO 24,641).
597 FRICK, *The City in Ancient Israel*, 205.
598 CALVIN, *Comm. in Mosis reliq. libr.*, Ex 22,25 (CO 24,680).

tes should remain, i.e., that our brethren, who need our assistance, are not to be treated harsh-
ly. Moreover, since the wall of partition, which formerly separated Jew and Gentile, is now
broken down, our condition is now different; and consequently we must spare all without exception, both as regards taking interest, and any other mode of extortion; and equity is to be
observed even towards strangers.[599]

Calvin considers the lending of money for interest evil when practiced among
Israelites; however, he did not condemn the practice strongly when it came to
Gentiles and strangers. Yet according to him, special attention must be paid to
humanity, equality (ratio analogica) between the parties, and in the case of
those who are in a condition of *ignobilitas*, charity must be exercised.[600]

Calvin also notes the serious consequences the use of euphemistic terms
could have for the members of the lower class:

> Thus, when all men detested the word *foenus*, another was substituted, which might avoid un-
> popularity under an honest pretext; for they called it usury, as being a compensation for the
> loss a man had incurred by losing the use of his money. [...] Thus there will be always ground
> for his seeking compensation, since no creditor could ever lend money without loss to himself.
> Thus usury, since the word is equivalent to *foenus*, is but a covering for an odious practice, as if
> such glosses would deliver us in God's judgment, where nothing but absolute integrity can
> avail for our defense. There was almost a similar mode of subterfuge among the Israelites. The
> name *neschec*, which is derived from biting, sounded badly; since then no one chose to be like-
> ned to a hungry dog, who fed himself by biting others, some escape from the reproach was
> sought; and they called whatever gain they received beyond the capital, תרבית, *therbith*, as be-
> ing an increase. But God, in order to prevent such deception, unites the two words, (Lev. 25:36)
> and condemns the increase as well as the biting.[601]

In summary, the poor are to be helped liberally, and should not be burdened
with high levels of interest. Phrases such as 'neither shalt thou lay upon him
usury,' and 'if thy brother be waxen poor,' point to how serious the practice of
usury is, and further demand that help be extended to the poor.

---

599 CALVIN, *Comm. in Mosis reliq. libr.*, Ex 22,25 (CO 24,680–81).

600 Many of the early Western philosophers including Plato, Aristotle, Cato, Cicero, Seneca and
    Plutarch were critics of usury. In the legal reforms (*Lex Genucia*) of the Roman Republic (340
    BC), usury and interest were banned. Calvin himself cited from Plato and Cato who outrightly
    condemned usury. As a matter of fact, Cato compares the practice of usury with that of killing
    a person.

601 CALVIN, *Comm. in Mosis reliq. libr.*, Ex 22,25 (CO 24,681–82): 'Let us now examine the words. In the
    first place, where we have translated the words, "Thou shalt not be to him as a usurer," there
    is some ambiguity in the Hebrew word, *nashac*, for it is sometimes used generally for to lend,
    without any ill meaning; but here it is undoubtedly applied to a usurer, who bites the poor; as
    also in Psalms 109:11, "Let the usurer catch all that he hath."'

5.8. Conclusion

The גֵר is someone who is destitute of protection, subjected to many wrongs, exposed as prey, and above all defenseless on account of his *ignobilitas*.[602] Because of their low social status, they need legal protection from all kinds of abuse and oppression. Calvin groups together different *personae miserae*, as in the triad stranger-widow-orphan. As was shown above, Calvin argued that as a non-Israelite, the גֵר would tend to be barred from many of the privileges and religious practices of the Israelite community through social custom, but that the law everywhere accorded the stranger full participation provided he become part of the community by circumcision and other rites of membership. Although in some cases the גֵר is grouped among other non-Israelites, in general the גֵר stands in a unique situation in Israelite society. Israelites are asked to remember their own sojourn in Egypt in Joseph's time, as well as their later slavery there, as motives to extend kindness to the גֵר who now live in their midst in the land of Canaan.

---

602 Cf. CALVIN, *Praelect. in Jer.* 7,6 (CO 37,675).

6. Conclusions

In his Old Testament commentaries, Calvin always translates the term גר so as to reflect the notion of non-belongingness, of being an outsider or even an enemy. The terms נכר and תושׁב, on the other hand, are translated with different meanings. Both Abraham and David are referred to as תושׁב, but in all other instances the noun is used for uncircumcised foreigners who live in Israel's midst. In his exegetical work on the Psalms and the prophets, Calvin translates the term נכר in such a way as to reflect that this group had a positive relationship with the Israelites, while in his Harmony of the Law commentary the נכר is outside the congregation. However, these two terms נכר and תושׁב do not render a meaning of enemity as of the term זר to indicate non Israelites. The term גר, on the other hand, is always translated so as to refer to one who came from outside of the Israelite community, but became part of it by embracing the Israelite faith as witnessed in circumcision.

It should be noted, however, that Calvin introduces the concept of 'stranger' not only when the term גר comes up explicitly in the Hebrew text. There are times when the word does not appear in the biblical text, and where Calvin nevertheless still introduces the word or concept for contextual reasons. This is true, for example, in the case of Joseph in Egypt, Daniel in Babylon, Jonah in Nineveh, and Amos in Samaria, all of whom Calvin identifies as 'strangers' since they live outside of their native place.

6.1. The גר in Israel

For his translation of the noun גר, Calvin often takes his point of departure in the verbal root גור. For him, such circumstances as war, family dispute, famine, dissatisfaction with one's native land, and all sorts of upheavals, forced both Israelites and non-Israelites to seek a place of refuge outside of their home country. The following general pattern can also be discerned: the verb גור was generally used for those Israelites who went to dwell temporarily abroad, while the noun גר came to designate the legal status of those strangers who, while they lived in Israel's midst, were subjected to its internal laws and regulations.

In Calvin's Harmony of the Law, we see that references to the individual גר can be divided into two groups: 1. laws addressed to the Israelites regarding the protection of the גר; and 2. laws there were addressed to both Israelite and גר, that enjoined certain patterns of behavior intended to preserve the holiness of the community. The first set of laws is given in order to guide the conduct of the Israelites with respect to the גר in view of their corporate lives. According to Calvin, the laws focus on the responsibilities the Israelites have towards the גר who lives in their midst. For that reason, the Israelites are addressed in the second person, while the verbs associated with the גר occur in the third person. Thus Calvin uses the noun גר to characterize a relationship between two persons (cf. Ex 22,20 and Dt 14,28–29). The second set of laws focuses on the responsibilities the Israelites and גר have together for the preservation of holiness in the community in the Promised Land. Calvin argues that in this context the גר is reckoned to be a member of the community. The object of these laws is not the גר, but rather the entire community of both Israelites and the 'strangers.' These laws are largely found in the form of prohibitive commands, where the Israelite community is portrayed as consisting of two factions, whether by inclusive clauses (i.e. גר-אזרח), or such constructions as 'the house of Israel – the גר' or 'the sons of Israel – the גר'.

Calvin's Old Testament commentaries clearly and consistently reveal that he considered the גר to be a non-Israelite, who did not have the opportunity to become an Israelite, although these 'strangers' were still to be shown the same generosity as the Israelite widows and orphans received. This is because the condition of these three categories of people is similar: they are a most alienated people, destitute and deprived of material relief, while poverty and hunger are two facts of their daily existence. In placing the גר alongside the widow and orphan as parties that need the protection of laws for the sake of social justice, Calvin portrays the גר as an economically vulnerable person who is most likely landless. The *ignobilitas* of each of these three groups is the hermeneutical key that allows Calvin to treat these three separate groups as a single group of people who need protection and provision. Their lives depend on the well-to-do land owners. Except in his commentary on sabbath laws, Calvin did not give a clear picture of the life these גר lived in the patriarchal household. Because the strangers gather their own harvest, it seems that they are considered to have their own household, and to feed and clothe themselves.

The laws addressed to both the Israelite and the גר in the Harmony of the Law are understood by Calvin as an attempt to prevent the defilement of the land by protecting the sanctity of the community. The obligations required of the 'stranger' are thus only those that affect the cultic purity of the congregation. The other regulations and ceremonies that do not particularly involve ritual purity were not required of גר. Observance of the laws was the condition for the admission of the stranger into the Israelite community, and for his continued coexistence.

6.2. Israel as גר

When the term גר is used in reference to the Israelites, there is not only a social dimension, but also a religious one. In these instances, where the term גר is also applied in a metaphorical sense, it played a significant role in Israel's understanding of its basic vocation. Calvin explains that the Israelites are told not only to remember that their forefathers lived as גרים, but also to be mindful that they themselves lived in *peregrinatio* as well. Calvin most often refers to the Israelites' own past status as wandering strangers in the 'motive-clauses' joined to commands God gives the Israelites to treat well the strangers who now live in their midst. In this case, the Israelites are the benefactors, and are enjoined to be generous to the strangers now living in their midst because they had themselves lived as גרים in Egypt. However, Calvin portrays the Israelites as beneficiaries when they base their petitions in prayer on the fact that they are גרים. In identifying themselves as גרים, the Israelites place themselves under Yahweh's direct protection, so that they can thereby put their hope in Yahweh instead of in the land. For Calvin, the Israelites' absolute dependence on God enabled them to overcome the uncertainty and sense of estrangement they felt when their land was possessed by foreigners.

6.3. The Motive-Clause

Calvin used the noun גר in two ways (גר as individual, and the nation of Israel as גר) in connection with the historical background. First, Israel's previous experience as גרים in Egypt functions as a sort of archetype for the individual גר; secondly, Israel's status as גר similarly finds its prototype in the experience of the patriarchs as גרים in the land of Canaan.

In the Harmony of Law, one can identify six different motive-clauses used by Calvin: (1) appeal to the past, (2) appeal to humanitarian instincts, (3) promise of divine blessing, (4) appeal to a principle, (5) the connection between a law and its goal, and (6) threat of penalty for disobedience. Levenson describes this rationale as subsuming a community's ethos to its mythos.[603]

The appeal to the past has in view not just Israel's time as גר in Egypt, but also their slavery there. For Calvin, this past experience should exhort the Israelites to identify with and be charitable to the גר, as well as the widow and orphan. Secondly, in appealing to humanitarian concern, Calvin again applies the law for observing the Sabbath rest to the entire household. He also insists that daily wages should be paid to the hired workers as they are poor. Calvin thus insists that human kindness be extended to the גר who live in the midst of the Israelites. Thirdly, the aspect of promise and divine blessing plays a significant role as motive-clause. According to Calvin, the generosity required of the Israelites towards the socially vulnerable גר was preceded by God's generosity to them, evident in the bountiful harvests they gathered in. This type of motive-clause thus promises that obedience will be followed by God's generosity towards those who obey. The fourth motive-clause pertains to the principle of not eating meat from a carcass. It is because of their separateness from other people that the Israelites must not eat as other people eat. Eating an animal found dead may be permitted for other people, but it is not for a people who are separated and set apart to God. The Israelites must therefore give such meat to the גר free of cost. The fifth type of motive-clause relates to the tithe. The tithe has to be kept for the Levites, גר, orphan, and widow, so that they may eat and be satisfied. According to Calvin, the intention of the tithe here is to provide support for the entire community that is landless. The final motive-clause centers on the punishment for disobedience. If the hired servants are not paid their wages, they may cry unto the Lord, and then the Israelites will be held as disobedient. Calvin most often notes that the punishment is a curse from God.

6.4. Biography as Hermeneutical Key

For Calvin, the notion of גר is not just an abstract theological concept; it is reality, a reality that shapes his whole ministry in Geneva. He did not become a citizen of Geneva until merely three years before his death, and was thus a stranger for the greatest part of his life. Calvin also married a woman who was not only a widow, but also a refuge. He served as minister among a congregation filled with strangers from around the world. This reality of being stranger among strangers is evident in his exegetical work on the Old Testament, particularly on passages where the idea of גר occurs.

---

603 LEVENSON, *Theologies of Commandment*, 18–19.

In the commentaries of Psalms, Calvin identified himself with David who considered himself a stranger and foreigner. The Psalmist says that he is a גֵּר among people who reciprocate war for peace, and that although his heart longs for peace. Calvin remarks that David's condition resembles that of some wretched individual who is compelled to live and grow old in exile. Just as David lived as a גֵּר in the midst of his own people, Calvin wrote to Bullinger, he himself sought peace but was rewarded with war by the native Genevans.

In his commentary on Isaiah, we see the influence of Calvin's historical circumstances – i.e. the difficulties he suffered in 1546 at the hands of such Genevans as Pierre Ameaux, Ami Perrin, François Mestrat, and the Libertines who openly rose up against the strangers in Geneva, particularly those who had come from France – in his exegesis of the passage that speaks about the Lord sending strangers (בֶּן־כְּנָר) to re-build the wall.

In the commentary on Genesis, Calvin dwells on the importance of extending hospitality towards strangers when other local inhabitants show themselves inhospitable towards them. At this time, Calvin's own Geneva saw the struggle between the foreigners and the Children of Geneva becoming even more intense, so that the Perrinists/Libertines publicly humiliated the foreigners, slandered them and even resorted to physical violence. These events that were going on around him placed a significant role in his exegesis of Ge 18 and 19 that speak about hospitality to strangers. Calvin thus praises the hospitality Melchizedek showed to Abraham, and Pharaoh to Jacob when the latter came to Egypt.

When it comes to God's promises to Abraham, and to the blessing Jacob received from Isaac, Calvin makes it clear that being a stranger is precondition for inheriting God's promises. To put it another way, to become a גֵּר (terram peregrinationum) is part of the blessings of God. Calvin further also advocates sojournment for faithful believers if they cannot practice the true faith in their home country.

When in 1533 Calvin's appeal to the Geneva city council was overturned, and he was consequently told to leave the city; when in 1553 Ami Perrin was elected as syndic, and the atrocities committed against the strangers increased; when Calvin's other appeals were time and again turned down – he reminded the Genevans of the importance the Old Testament gives to listening to the words of strangers. For Egypt was spared because they heeded the words of the stranger Joseph, the king of Babylon was spared because he regarded the words of the foreigner Daniel, and finally the Lord also spared Nineveh because the inhabitants listened to the words of the prophet Jonah, who was גֵּר, and repented.

In the commentary on the Harmony of law, Calvin repeatedly addresses the difficulties faced by the vulnerable strangers, explaining that the Lord is the defender of the stranger, and that he avenges those who oppress them.

In addition to the commentaries, there are the numerous letters Calvin wrote to kings and princes to urge them to protect the stranger-refugees who were forced to flee on account of their faith. Calvin similarly wrote to encourage different strangers who were suffering in their estranged state, and finally corresponded as well with his friends around the world in order to drum up support for the plight of the strangers.

The events of Calvin's life played a remarkable role in his interpretation of the notion of גֵּר in the Old Testament. For that reason, one must consider the context of his life as a key hermeneutical element to understanding his view of the גֵּר in the Old Testament.

6.5. The Hidden Act

Calvin speaks of God's hidden acts whenever the Israelites left their homeland as גֵּר for various reasons. This secret, hidden grace was with the Israelites during their wanderings. In his commentary on Gn 13,16, where God promises to Abraham that he will make his seed 'as the dust,' Calvin finds there to be a kind of contradiction between the promise of God to Abram, and the latter's actual state. Calvin writes: 'Abram is commanded to look at the dust; but when he turns his eyes upon his own family, what similitude is there between his solitariness and the countless particles of dust.' Calvin finds that between these two poles, Abram is expected to exercise his faith. By exercising faith, Abram could discover for himself God's hidden grace:

> For faith is the beholding of absent things [Hbr 11,1], and it has the word as a mirror, in which it may discover the hidden grace of God. And the condition of the pious, at this day is not dissimilar: for since they are hated by all, are exposed to contempt and reproach, wander without a home, are sometimes driven hither and thither, and suffer from nakedness and poverty, it is nevertheless their duty to lay hold on the inheritance which is promised. Let us therefore walk through the world, as persons debarred from all repose, who have no other resource than the mirror of the word.[604]

And for Calvin, it was this hidden grace that sustains Abram until the fulfillment of the promise of God.

Similarly Calvin finds such hidden acts of God in other instances in Abram's life as גֵּר. It was God's secret power which made him as stranger able to become a party in the covenant with four kings (cf. Gn 14):

---

604 CALVIN, *Comm. in Gen.* 13,16 (CO 23,194).

It appears [...] Abram was freely permitted to enter into covenant and friendship with the princes [...] to regard him as one who was not, by any means, to be despised. Nay, as he had so great a family, he might also have been numbered among kings, if he had not been a stranger and a sojourner. But God purposed thus to provide for his peace, by a covenant relating to temporal things in order that he never might be mingled with those nations. Moreover, that this whole transaction was divinely ordered we may readily conjecture from the fact, that his associates did not hesitate, at great risk, to assail four kings, who (according to the state of the times) were sufficiently strong, and were flushed with the confidence of victory. Surely they would scarcely ever have been thus favorable to a stranger, except by a secret impulse of God.[605]

A third instance where Calvin sees God's hidden hand is in Jacob's sojourn to Mesopotamia, when he left his family behind (cf. Gn 29). As Calvin observes:

the providence of God, which caused Jacob to fall in with the shepherds, by whom he was con-ducted to the home he sought; for this did not happen accidentally, but he was guided by the hidden hand of God to that place; and the shepherds, who were to instruct and confirm him respecting all things, were brought thither at the same time. Therefore, whenever we may wander in uncertainty through intricate windings, we must contemplate, with eyes of faith, the secret providence of God which governs us and our affairs, and leads us to unexpected re-sults.[606]

It is the hidden grace of God, his secret impulse and hidden hand, that protects strangers, lifts them to the level of kings, and guides them in their sojourn-ment.

6.6. Exegetical Tool

Aside from elements of his own life, what was also important in Calvin's exege-tical work on the idea of גר in the Old Testament were the various other exege-tical principles he used. They are the principles of utility, edification, simplici-ty, brevity, natural meaning, *Sitz im Leben*, unity of the Scriptures, *equitas*, and finally, the principle of harmony. From among all of these principles, Calvin's work on the גר appears to suggest that his main concern was to be simple and clear, so that both stranger and native-born would be more powerfully struck by a sense of responsibility and obligation.

6.7. Hospitality

For Calvin, hospitality to the strangers is an important virtue. Calvin praises the conduct of Abraham and Lot as related in Gn 18 and 19, where they show hospitality to unknown strangers in Mamre and Sodom respectively. The major reason for the destruction of Sodom is their 'outrageous appetite to abuse the

---

605 CALVIN, *Comm. in Gen.* 14,13 (CO 23,199).
606 CALVIN, *Comm. in Gen.* 29,1 (CO 23,400).

stranger,' while the main reason for Lot's deliverance is that he extended hospitality to those unknown strangers at the city gate. According to Calvin, strangers are wanderers, exhausted from the continuous and regularly dangerous travels they undertake, and the constant search for shelter and care. Thomas W. Ogletree observes that to offer hospitality to the stranger is to welcome something new, unfamiliar and unknown into our lives. Hospitality requires recognition of the stranger's vulnerability in that social context. Strangers need shelter and substance for their travel, particularly when these travels take place in hostile circumstances.[607]

Because Abraham extended hospitality to the three unknown strangers, they reveal the purpose of their visit to Sodom. Strangers have stories to tell which we have never heard before, which could potentially open our understanding and imagination.[608] Strangers should be recognized, considered as equals because they share our common humanity.[609] Hospitality has relevance to the human assault on oppressive social structures, though its bearing on relations between oppressors and oppressed, or even between beneficiaries and victims of social oppression, is ambiguous. Hospitality has to be extended because strangers are without a home, and are forced to live in a society which denies them their full humanity.[610]

Strangers are a phenomenon that all societies, both ancient and modern, must deal with. The reasons for becoming strangers are common to all these societies: war, famine, family and tribal conflicts, blood-shed, disgust with one's home country, and so forth. The reasons can be political, social, economical or religious in nature. Strangers all over the world, and in all times, live in similar precarious conditions and situations. They are landless wanderers, exposed to violence and oppression. They are poor and suffer hunger, and above all, they are alienated. For that reason, Calvin is so insistent that these strangers be given their human dignity. Equality should be maintained between strangers and natives. As God is the defender of the strangers in their *ignobilitas*, the oppressors will face God's wrath. Strangers must be loved, protected, cared for and helped through generosity. The native born (אזרח) is to extend hospitality to the stranger (גר).

---

607 OGLETREE, *Hospitality to the Stranger*, 2.
608 OGLETREE, *Hospitality to the Stranger*, 3.
609 LEVINAS, *Totality and Infinity*, 75.
610 OGLETREE, *Hospitality to the Stranger*, 4.

Bibliography

Primary Literature

The Bible of John Calvin: Reconstructed from the Text of his Commentaries. Compiled by Richard F. WEVERS. Grand Rapids: Digamma Publication, 1994.

Das Alt Testament dutsch der ursprunglichen Ebreischen waarheyt nach uff das aller truwlichest verdutschet. Zurich: Froschauer, 1524–1529.

Novam Testamentum Graece. Edited by K. ALAND, M. BLACK, C.M. MARTINI, B.M. METZGER, and A. WIKGREN. 26th ed. Rev. Stuttgart: Deutsche Bibelstiftung, 1981.

The Geneva Bible (The Annotated New Testament, 1602 edition). Edited by Gerald T. SHEPPARD, with Introductory Essays by Gerald T. SHAPPARD, Marvin W. ANDERSON, John H. AUGUSTINE, Nicholas W.S. CRANFIELD. New York: Pilgrime Press, 1989.

Selected Works of John Calvin

CALVIN, John. *Ioannis Calvini Opera Quae Supersunt Omnia, 59 vols*, ed. Wilhelm BAUM, Eduard CUNITZ and Eduard REUSS (Brunswick and Berlin, 1863-1900).

CALVIN, John. *Commentaries of John Calvin*. 46 vols. Edinburgh: Calvin Translation Society, 1844-1855. Reprint, Grand Rapids: Baker Book House, 1979.

CALVIN, John. *Institutes of Christian Religion* [1536], Translated and annotated by Ford Lewis BATTLES. Revised edition Grand Rapids: Eerdmans, 1986.

CALVIN, John. *Institutes of Christian Religion*. 2 vols. translated by Henry BEVERIDGE. Edinburgh, 1845. Reprint, Grand Rapids: Eradmans 1994.

CALVIN, John. *Canons and Decrees of the Council of Trent*: with the Antidote, in Selected Works, vol. 3.

CALVIN, John. *Four Letters from the Socinus Calvin Correspondence* (1549), in Italian Reformation Studies in Honor of Laelius Socinua, edited by TEDESCHI (Florence, 1965), pp. 215–230.

CALVIN, John. *Selected Works of John Calvin: Tracts and Letters*. Edited by Henry BEVERIDGE and Jules BONNET. 7 vols. Grand Rapids: Baker Book House, 1983.

CALVIN, John. *Sermons of Maister John Calvin, upon the Book of Job*. Translated by Arthur GOLDING. London: George Bishop, 1574. Reprint, Edinburgh: Banner of Truth, 1993.

CALVIN, John. *The Sermons of M. John Calvin upon the Fifth Booke of Moses called Deuteronomie*. London: Henry Middleton 1583. Reprint, Edinburgh: Banner of Truth, 1987.

CALVIN, John. *Treatises Against the Anabaptists and Against the Libertines*. Translated and edited by Benjamin Wirt FARLEY. Grand Rapids: Baker Book House, 1982.

Other Works

Corpus Reformatorum (Halle, Berlin, Brunswick, Leipzig, and Zurich, 1834).

BASIL: *Letters and Selected Works*. Translated and Edited by Philip SCHAFF, Grand Rapids, MI: Christian Classics Ethereal Library. Edinburgh: T&T Clark, 1895.

AUGUSTINE. *The Literal Meaning of Genesis*. Translated by John HAMMOND Taylor. 2 vols, New York: Newman Press, 1982.

AUGUSTINE. *The Trinity fathers of the church* vol 45, translated by Stephen McKENNA. Washington, D.C.: Catholic University Press 1963.

Gregory I, St. *The Life of Our Most Holy fathers S. Benedict*. Grand Rapids, MI: Christian Classics Ethereal Library. London: Thomas Baker 1898.

ERASMUS, Desiderius. *Inquisitio de fide: a Colloquy (1524)*. Edited with introduction and Commentary by Craig R. THOMPSON. New Haven: Yale University Press, 1950.

ERASMUS, Desiderius. *In Praise of Folly*. Grand Rapids, MI: Christian Classics Ethereal Library. University of Michigan Press [1958].

LUTHER, Martin. *Luther's Works*. 56 vols. Edited by Jaroslav PELIKAN and Helmut LEHMANN. St.Louis: Concordia; Philadelphia: Fortress, 1955–1986.

Secondary Literature

ABBA, R., 'Priests and Levites in Deuteronomy', *VT* XXVII (1977) 257–267.

ALLEN, C.W., 'On the meaning of προσηλυτος in the Septuagint', *The Expositor* 10 (1894) 264–275.

ASHLEY, Clinton Matthew, *John Calvin's Utilization of the Principle of Accommodation and Its Continuing Significance for an Understanding of Biblical Language*, Th.D. diss., Southwestern Baptist Theological Seminary, 1972.

BAMBERGER, B.J., *Proselytism in the Talmudic Period*, (New York: Ktav, 1939).

BARR, James, 'The Literal, the Allegorical and Modern Biblical Scholarship'. *Journal for the Study of the Old Testament* 44 (1989) 3–17.

BARTON, Florence Whitefield, *Calvin and the Duchess*, (Louisville, KY: Westminster/ John Knox Press, 1989).

BATTLES, Ford Lewis, *Interpreting John Calvin*, (ed. Robert BENEDETTO; Grand Rapids, MI: Baker Books, 1996).

BATTLES, Ford Lewis, *The Sources of Calvin's Seneca Commentary, in John Calvin* edited by G.E. Duffield, (Grand Rapids, MI: Eerdmans Publishing Company, 1966).

BAUMGARTEN, J.M., 'Exclusions from the Temple: Proselytes and Aggripa I', *JJS* 33 (1982) 215–225.

BAUMGARTEN, J.M., 'The Exclusion of Netinim and Proselytes in 4Q Florilegium', in: idem, *Studies in Qumran Law*. Leiden 1(977) 75–87.

BENNETT, W.H., 'Stranger and Sojourner', in: *EncB*, IV, London (1903) col. 4814–4818.

BLACKETER, Raymond A., 'Smooth Stones, Teachable Hearts: Calvin's Allegorical Interpretation of Deuteronomy 10:1–2,' *Calvin Theological Journal* 34, no. 1 (1999) 36–63.

BLENKINSOPP, J., 'Are there Traces of the Gibeonite Covenant in Deuteronomy?' *CBQ* 28 (1966) 207–19.

BLENKINSOPP, J., *Gibeon and Israel*, SOTSMS, 2 (Cambridge: Cambridge University Press, 1972).

BLOCK, D.I., 'Sojourner', in: *ISBE*, IV, Michigan (1989) 561–564.

BOMAN,Th., 'Review of *The Semantics of Biblical Language*', by J. Barr, *TLZ* 87 (1962) 262–265.

BOUWSMA, William J., *John Calvin: A Sixteenth Century Portait* (New York: Oxford University Press, 1988).

BREEN, Quirinus, 'John Calvin and the Rhetorical Tradition', in: *Christianity and Humanism Studies in the History of Ideas*, edited by Nelson Peter ROSS (Grand Rapids: Eerdmans Publishing Company, 1968).

BRIGHT, J., 'Jeremiah', *Anc B 21* (New York: Doubleday, 1965).

BROWN, F./DRIVER, S.R./BRIGGS, C.A., *A Hebrew and English Lexicon of the Old Testament*, Seventh printing (Oxford 1980).

BUCCELLATI, G., *The Amorites of the UR III Period* (Naples: 1966).

BUEHRER, Richard Lyle, *John Calvin's Humanistic Approach to Church History'*, Ph.D. diss., University of Washington, 1974.

CHEYNE, K. Thomas, *Introduction to the book of Isaiah, with an appendix containing the undoubted portions of the two chief prophetic writers in a translation*, (London: A and C Black, 1895).

CHILDS, Brevard S., *Old Testament Books for Pastor and Teacher*, (Philadelphia: Westminster   Press, 1977).

CLEMENS, R.E., *Isaiah I - 39*, (Grand Rapids: Eerdmans Publishing Company, 1980).

CLINES, D.J.A. (ed.), *The Dictionary of Classical Hebrew, II:* ר - ב, (Sheffield: Sheffield Academic Press, 1995).

COTTRET, Bernard, *Calvin: A Biography* (Grand Rapids, MI: Eerdmans Publishing Company, 2000).

DAVIES, P.R., 'Who Can Join the 'Damascus Covenant'?', *JJS* 46 (1995) 134–142.

DAVIS, Thomas M., 'The Traditions of Puritan Typology', in: *Typology and Early American Literature*, edited by Sacvan BERCOVITCH (Amherst, Mass.: University of Massachusetts Press, 1972).

DE BOER, Erik A., *Calvin on the Visions of Ezekiel: Studies in His 'Sermons Inédits'. With a Critical Edition of the Sermons on Ezekiel 36-48* (Geneva: University of Geneva – Faculté de théologie, 1999).

DE LONG, Irwin Hoch, 'Calvin as an Interpreter of the Bible', *Reformed Church Review*, fourth series, 13 (1909) 165–82.

DE VAUX, Roland, *Ancient Israel Its Life and Institutions*, trans. John MCHUGH (London: Darton, Longman and Todd, 1961).

DOUGLAS, Jane Dempsey, 'Pastor and Teacher of the Refugees,' in: *Calvin in the Work of Heiko A. Oberman: Papers From the Symposium on His Seventieth Birthday* (Leiden: Brill, 2003) 51–65.

DOWEY, Edward A., Jr., 'The Structure of Calvin's Thought as Influenced by the Two-fold Knowledge of God', in: *Calvinus Ecclesiae Genevensis Custos*, edited by Wilhelm H. NEUSER (Frankfurt: Peter lang, 1984).

DRIVER, S.R., 'Deuteronomy', *ICC*, 3 (New York : C. Scribner's Sons, 1909).

DYKSTRA, Russell, 'A Comparison of Exegesis: John Calvin and Thomas Aquinas', *Protestant Reformed Theological Journal* 35, no. 2 (2002) 15–25; 36 no. 1 (2002) 12–23; 36 no. 2 (2003) 10–22.

EICHRODT, W., *Ezekiel: A Commentary* (trans. C. Quin; Philadelphia: Westminster Press, 1970).

EVANS, G. Rosemary, *The Language and Logic of the Bible: A road to Reformation*, (Cambridge [Cambridgeshire]; New York: Cambridge University Press, 1985).

FALEY, R.J., 'Leviticus', in: *The Jerome Biblical Commentary* (Englewood Cliffs 1968) 67–85.

FARMER Craig S., 'Changing Images of the Samaritan Woman in Early Reformed Commentaries on John', *Church History* 65, no. 3 (1996) 365–75.

FARRAR, Frederic W., 'Calvin as an Expositor', *The Expositor*, Second Series, 7 (1884) 426–44.

FARRAR, Frederic W., *History of Interpretation* (E.P Dutton, 1886. Reprint, Grand Rapids: Baker Book House, 1961).

FEINBERG, John S. (ed.), *Continuity and Discontinuity: Perspectives on the Relationship between the Old and the New Testaments* (Westchester:. Crossway Books, 1988).

FENSHAM, F.C., 'Widow, Orphan and Poor in Ancient Near Eastern Legal and wisdom Literature', *JNES* XXI (1962) 129–139.

FLOOR, Lambertus, 'The Hermeneutics of Calvin', in: *Calvinus Reformator: His Contribution to Theology, Church, and Society*, edited by Wilhelm H. NEUSER, Institute for Reformation Studies, Series F, no. 17 (Potchefstroom, South Africa: Potchefstroom University for Christian Higher Education, 1982).

FLOROVSKY, Georges, 'The Fathers of the church and the Old Testament', in: *the Collected Works of Georges Florousky,* Vol. 4: *Aspects of Church History.* (Belmont, Mass:. Nordland, 1975).

FORSTMAN, *Word and Spirit: Calvin's Doctorine of Biblical Authority* (Stanford: Stanford University Press, 1962).

FRICK, S. Frank, *The City of Ancient Israel,* (Missoula: Scholars Press for the Society of Biblical Literature, c1977).

FRIED, Jerome, *The Most Ancient testimony: Sixteenth Century Christian Hebraica in the age of Renaissance nostalgia* (Athens, Ohio: Ohio University Press, 1983).

FULLERTON, Kemper, *Prophecy and authority; a study in the history of the doctrine and interpretation of Scripture* (New York, The Macmillan company, 1919).

GAMBLE, Craig Richard, 'Brevitas et Facilitas: Toward an Understanding of Calvin's Hermeneutic', *Westminster Theological Journal* 47 (1985) 1–17.

GAMBLE, Craig Richard, 'Calvin's Theologian and Exegete - Is There Anything New?', *Calvin Theological Journal* 23 (1988) 178–94.

GAMBLE, Craig Richard, 'Exposition and Method in Calvin', *Westminster Theological Journal* 49 (1987) 153–65.

GAMBLE, Craig Richard, 'Mercy Ministry in European Cities During the Reformation', *Urban Mission,* Vol. 6, (September 1988) 27–31.

GAMBLE, Craig Richard, 'Sacramental Continuity Among Reformed Refugees: Peter Martyr Vermigli and John Calvin', in: *Peter Martyr Vermigli and the European Reformation,* ed. Frank A. JAMES III (Leiden: Brill, 2004) 97–112.

GAMBLE, Craig Richard, *Calvin and Hermeneutics,* (New York: Garland Publication, 1992).

GAMBLE, Craig Richard, *Mercy Ministry in European Cities during the reformation,* Urban Mission Vol. 6 (September 1988) 27–31.

GANOCZY, Alexandre, *The Young Calvin.* (trans. David FOXGROVER and Wade PROVO: Philadelphia: Westminster Press, 1987).

GEMSER, B., 'The Importance of the Motive Clause in Old Testament Law', in: G.W. ANDERSON e.a. (ed.), *Congress Volume.* Copenhagen 1953, SVT 1, (Leiden, 1953) 50–66.

GERRISH, B.A., 'The Word of God and the Words of Scripture: Luther and Calvin on Biblical Authority', in idem, *The Old Protestantism and the New: Essays on the Reformation Heritage* (Chicago: Chicago Press, 1982).

GESENIUS, W., *Gesenius' Hebrew grammar* / as edited and enlarged by E. KAUTZSCH; rev. in accordance with the 28th German ed. (trans. A.E. COWLEY, 2. Oxford, England: Clarendon Press, 1910 (1985 printing).

GIBSON, J.C.L., *Canaanite Myths and Legends* (Edinburgh: Clark, 1978).

GORMAN, F.H., *The Ideology of Ritual. Space, time and Status in the Priestly Theology, JSOTSS* 91 (Sheffield: Sheffield Academic Press, 1990).

GOTCH, F.W., 'Calvin as a Commentator', *Journal of Sacred Literature* 3 (1849) 222–36.

GOTTWALD K. Norman, *The Hebrew Bible: A Socio-Literary Introduction* (Philadelphia: Fortress Press, 1985).

GOTTWALD K. Norman, *The Tribes of Yahweh. The sociology of the Religion of Liberated Israel 1250–1050 BCE* (Maryknoll, NY: Orbis Books, 1979).

GRAHAM, W. Fred, *The Constructive Revolutionary: John Calvin & his Socio-Economic Impact* [East Lansing] (Michigan State University Press, 1987).

GREEF, W. de, *The Writings of John Calvin: A introductory Guide* (Louisville: Westminster John Knox Press, 2008).

GUNKEL, Hermann, *Introduction to Psalms; The Genres of the Religious lyric of Israel,* trans. James D. NOGELSKI (Macon, GA: Mercer University Press, 1998).

HAIRE, J.L.W., 'John Calvin as an Expositor', *Irish Biblical Studies* 4 (January 1982) 74–88.

HALL, Basil, *Calvin against the Calvinist in John Calvin,* ed. G.E. DUFFIELD (Grand Rapids: Eerdmans, 1966).

HASLER, R.A., 'The Influence of David and the Psalms upon John Calvin's Life and Thought', *Hartford Quarterly* 5 (1965) 7-18.

HAVICE, H.K., *The Concern for the Widow and the Fatherless in the Ancient Near East: A Case Study in Old Testament Ethics* (Yale University diss., 1978).

HEATON, E.W., 'Sojourners in Egypt', *ET* 58 (1946) 80-83.

HIRSCH, E.G., 'Proselyte', in: *JewEnc*, Vol X (NewYork - London 1907), col. 220-224.

HOLLADAY, W.L., *Jeremiah : a fresh reading* (New York: Pilgrim Press, c1990).

HORNER, I.M., 'Changing Concepts of Stranger in the Old Testament', *ATR* 42 (1960) 49-53.

HOUTEN, C. van, *The Alien in Israelite Law,* JSOTSS 107 (Sheffield: Sheffield Academic Press, 1991).

IAIT, M. Ian, 'Calvin's Ministry of Encouragement Presbyterian', *Covenant Seminary Review* Vol. 11, (1985) 43-99.

JENSON, P.P., *Graded Holiness. A Key to the Priestly Conception of the World*, JSOTSS 106 (Sheffield: Sheffield Academic Press, 1992).

JOOSTEN, J., *People and Land in the Holiness Code*, SVT 67 (Leiden e.a. 1996).

KAUFMANN, Y., *The Babylonian Captivity and Deutero-Isaiah* (New York: Union of American Hebrew Congregations, 1970).

KAUFMANN, Y., *The Religion of Israel, from its beginnings to the Babylonian exile*, trans. M. GREENBERG (Chicago: University of Chicago Press 1960).

KELLERMANN, D., גור in *TDOT*, trans. J.I. WILLIS; ed. G.J. BOTTERWECK e.a. (Grand Rapids: Eerdmans, 1975) II, 439-450.

KELLERMANN, D., גור, in: *TWAT* I (Stuttgart e.a. 1970-1973), col. 979-991.

KRAELING, Emil Gottlieb Heinrich, *The Old Testament since the Reformation* (London: Lutterworth Press 1955).

KRAUS, Hans-Joachim, 'Calvin's Exegetical Principles', *Interpretation* 31 (1977) 8-18.

KUGEL, James L., *Early Biblical Interpretation* (Philadelphia: Westminster Press, 1986).

LANE, Anthony N.S., *Calvin: Student of Church Fathers*, (Edinburgh: T&T Clark, 1999).

LEAHY, A., 'Ethnic Diversity in Ancient Egypt', in: *Civilizations of the Ancient Near East*, J.M. SASSON (ed.), Vol. 1 (New York: Scribner, 1995) 225-234.

LEEMANS, W.F., *Foreign Trade in the Old Babylonian Period. As revealed by texts from Southern Mesopotamia* (Leiden: Brill, 1950).

LEITH, John H., 'John Calvin - Theologian of the Bible', *Interpretation* 25 (1971) 329-44.

LEVINE, B., 'Leviticus', *JPS Torah Commentary* (Philadelphia: Jewish Publication Society, 1989).

LEVINE, E., *The Aramaic Versions of the Bible* (Berlin - NewYork: Harper & Brothers 1988).

LIVERANI, M., 'Nationality and Political Identity', in: *ABD*, Vol. 4 (NewYork: Double day, 1992) 1031-1037.

LIVERANI, M., 'Prestige and Interest. International Relations in the Near Eastern ca. 1600 - 1100 B.C.', *History of the Ancient Near/Studies* I (Padova, 1990).

LOEWENSTAMM, S.E., *Thesaurus of the Language of the Bible*, II (Jerusalem: Bible Concordance Press, 1957).

LOHFINK,N., 'Poverty in the Laws of the Ancient Near East and of the Bible', *TS* 52 (1991) 34-50

MAYES, A.D.H., *Deuteronomy*, The New century Bible Commentaries (Grand Rapids: Eerdmans, 1979).

MAYS, James Luther, 'Calvin's Commentary on the Psalms: The Preface as Introduction', in: Calvin Studies IV, edited by W. Stacy JOHNSON (Richmond: Union Theological Seminary in Virginia, 1988).

MBUNGA, Mpindi, *Calvin's hermeneutics of the imprecations on the Psalter* (Ph.D. Diss., Calvin Theological Seminary, 2004).

MCCONVILLE, G.J., *Law and Theology in Deuteronomy* (Sheffield: JSOT Press, 1984).

MCELENY, N.J., 'Conversion, Circumcision and Law', *NTS* 20 (1974) 319-341.

MCKANE, William, 'Calvin as an Old Testament Commentator', *Nederduitse Gereformeerde Teologiese Tydskrif* 25 (1984) 250-59.

MCKANE, William, 'Jeremiah', *ICC* (Edinburgh: T & T Clark, 1986).

MCKEE, Elsie Anne, *Diakonia in the Classical Reformed Tradition and Today* (Grand Rapids: Eerdmans, 1989).

MCKEE, Elsie Anne, *John Calvin on the Diaconate and Liturgical Almsgiving* (Geneve: Droz, 1984).

MEEK, T., 'The translation of Ger in the Hexateuch and its bearing on the Documentary Hypothesis', *JBL* 49 (1930) 172–180.

MICHAEL Parsons, *Luther and Calvin on Old Testament Narratives: Reformation Thought and Narrative Text* (Lewiston: The Edwin Mellen Press, 2004).

MILGROM, J., 'Leviticus 1–16', *AncB* 3, (NewYork: Doubleday, 1991).

MILGROM, J., 'Religious Conversion: the Revolt Model for the Formation of Israel', *JBL* 101/102 (1982) 169–176.

MILGROM, J., 'The Changing Concept of Holiness in the Pentateuchal Codes with Emphasis on Leviticus 19', in: J.F.A. SAWYER (ed.), *Reading Leviticus. A Conversation with Mary Douglas*, JSOTSS 227 (Sheffield: Sheffield Academic Press, 1996) 64–75.

MONTER, William E., 'The Refugee Colonies,' in: *Calvin's Geneva* (New York: Robert E. Krieger Publishing Company, 1975) 165–189.

MOORE, G.F., *Judaism in the first Centuries of the Christian era*, I (Cambridge, MA: Harvard University Press, 1966).

MULLER, Richard A., '*Scimus enim quod lex spiritualis est*: Melanchthon and Calvin on the Interpretation of Romans 7:14–23,' in: *Philip Melanchthon (1497-1560) and the Commentary*, ed. Timothy J. WENGERT and Patrick M. GRAHAM (Sheffield: Sheffield Academic Press, 1997) 216–37.

MULLER, Richard A., 'The Foundation of Calvin's Theology: Scripture as Revealing God's Word', *Duke Divinity School Review* 44 (Winter 1979) 14–23.

MULLER, Richard A., 'The Hermeneutic of Promise and Fulfillment in Calvin's Exegesis of the Old Testament', in: *The Bible in the Sixteenth Century*, edited by David C. STEINMETZ, Duke Monographs in Medieval and Renaissance Studies (Durham, N.C.: Duke University Press, 1990).

MULLER, Richard A., *After Calvin: Studies in the Development of a Theological tradition*, (Oxford; New York: Oxford University Press, 2003).

MULLER, Richard A., and THOMPSON, John L. (eds.), *Biblical interpretation in the era of the Reformation: essays presented to David C. Steinmetz in honor of his sixtieth birthday* (Grand Rapids: Eerdmans, c1996).

MULLER, Richard A., *The unaccommodated Calvin: studies in the foundation of a theological tradition* (New York: Oxford University Press, 2000).

MUNTINGH, L.M., *A Few Social Concepts in the Psalms and their Relationship to the Canaanite Residential Area* (Potchefstroom 1963) 48–57.

MURRAY, John, 'Calvin as Theologian and Expositor', in: *Collected Writings*, Vol. 1, *The Claims of Truth* (Edinburgh: Banner of Truth, 1976).

NAPHY, William G., *Calvin and the consolidation of the Genevan Reformation* (Manchester: Manchester University Press, c1994).

NEUSER, H. Wilhelm, 'Calvin and the Refugees', in: *Calvinus Sacrae Scripturae professor* (Grand Rapids: Eerdmans, 1994).

NEUSER, H. Wilhelm, 'Calvins Stellung zu den Apokryphen des Alten Testaments', in: *Text-Wort-Glaube: Studien zur Uberlieferung, Interpretation und Autorisierung biblischer Text*, edited by Kurt ALAND and Martin BRECHT, Arbeiten zur Kirchengeschichte, no. 50 (Berlin: Walter de Gruyter, 1980).

NEWPORT, J.P., *An Investigation of the Factors Influencing John Calvin's Use of the Linguistic and Historical Principles of Biblical Exegesis* (Ph.D. diss., Edinburgh, 1953).

NICHOLSON, E.W., *Preaching to the Exiles. A Study of the Prose Tradition in the book of Jeremiah*, (Oxford, Blackwell, 1970).

NORWOOD, Frederick Abbott, 'The Strangers Model Churches in Sixteenth Century England', *Reformation Studies*, Essays in honour of Roland H. Bainton (Richmond: John Knox Press, 1962) 181–196.

OBERMAN, Heiko Augustinus, 'Europa afflicta: The Reformation of the Refugees', *Archive for Reformation History*, vol. 83, (1992) 91–111.

OBERMAN, Heiko Augustinus, *Forerunners of the Reformation. The Shape of Late Medieval Thought* (London: Lutterworth 1967).

OBERMAN, Heiko Augustinus, *The Harvest of Medieval Theology* (Grand Rapids: Baker Academic 2000).

OBERMAN, Heiko Augustinus, *The two Reformations : the journey from the last days to the new world*; ed., by Donald Weinstein, (New Haven: Yale University Press, 2003).

OLLER, G.H., 'Messangers and Ambassadores in Ancient Western Asia', in: *Civilizations of the Ancient Near East*, J.M. SASSON (ed.), vol. 1, (New York: Scribner, 1995) 1465–1473.

OLSON, Jeannine, E., *Calvin and Social Welfare, Deacons and the Bourse Francaise*, (Selinsgrove, PA: Susquehanna University Press; London: Associated University Presses, 1988) 278–289.

OPITZ, 'Calvin as Bible Translator: From the Model of the Hebrew Psalter', in: SELDERHUIS, Herman J., *Calvinus sacrarum literarum interpres* (Göttingen 2008) 9–26.

PARKER, T.H.L., 'Calvin the Biblical Expositor', in: *John Calvin: A Collection of Essays*, by Gervase E. DUFFIELD (Grand Rapids: Eerdmans, 1966).

PARKER, T.H.L., 'Calvin the Exegete: Change and Development', in: *Calvinus Ecclesiae Doctor*, edited by Wilhelm H. NEUSER (Kampen: Kok, 1980).

PARKER, T.H.L., *Calvin's New Testament Commentaries* (Louisville: Westminster/John Knox Press, 1993).

PARKER, T.H.L., *Calvin's Old Testaments Commentaries* (Edinburgh: T. & T. Clark, 1986: Louisville, Ky.: Westminster John Knox Press, 1933).

PARKER, T.H.L., *John Calvin: A Biography* (Philadelphia: Westminster Press, 1975).

PATTERSON, R.D., 'The Widow, the Orphane and the Poor in the Old Testament and in the Extra-Biblical Literature', *SB* 139 (1973) 223–234.

PEDERSEN, Johannes, *Israel. Its Life and Culture.* I–II (London: Oxford University Press, 1946).

PETERSEN, David. L., 'Max Weber and the Sociological Study of Ancient Israel', in: *Religious Change and continuity*, ed. H.M. JOHNSON (San Francisco: Jossey-Bass, 1979) 117–50.

PFEIFFER, H. Robert, *Introduction to the Old Testament* (New York – London: Harper & brothers, 1941).

POLMAN, Andries Derk Rietema, 'Calvin on the Inspiration of Scripture', in: *John Calvin Contemporary Prophet*, ed. Jacob T. HOOGSTRA (Grand Rapids: Baker Book House, 1959).

PORTON, G.G., *The Stranger within your gates: Converts and Conversion in Rabbinic Literature* (Chicago: University of Chicago Press, 1994).

PRITCHARD, J.B. (ed.), *Ancient Near Eastern Texts related to the Old Testament, Third Editions with supplement* (Princeton: Princeton University Press, 1969).

Puckett, L. David, *John Calvin's Exegesis of the Old Testament* (Louisville, Kentucky: Westminster John Knox Press, 1995).

REIMER, D.J., 'Concerning Return to Egypt: Deuteronomy 17,16 and 28,68 Reconsidered', in: J.A. EMERTON (ed.), *Studies in the Pentateuch*, SVT 41 (Leiden, 1990) 217–229.

ROBERTSON SMITH, W., *Kinship and Marriage in early Arabia*, 3. Aufl. (London: A & C Black, 1903).

ROBERTSON SMITH, W., *The Religion of the Semites*, 2. Aufl. Re-impression (NewYork: Meridian Books, 1972).

ROBERTSON, A.T., 'Calvin as an Interpreter of Scripture', *Review and Expositor* 6 (1909) 557–78.

ROFE, A., 'The Laws of Warfare in the Book of Deuteronomy', *JSOT* 32 (Sheffield, 1985) 23–44

RUNIA, K., 'The Hermeneutics of the Reformers', in: *Calvin Theological Journal* 17 (Fall 1984) 121–53.

SCAER, David P., 'Reformed Exegesis and Lutheran Sacraments: Worlds in Conflict,' *Concordia Theological Quarterly* 64, no. 1 (2000) 3–20.

SCHAFF, P., 'Calvin as a Commentator.' *Presbyterian and Reformed review* 3 (July 1892) 462–69.

SCHAFF, P., *The History of the Christian Church* (Grand Rapids: Eerdmans, 1949–57 [c1907–10] (v.1, 1955 [c1910]).

SCHLEY, D.G., 'Yahweh will cause you to Egypt in Ships' (Deuteronomy XXVIII68), *VT* 35 (1985) 369–372.

SCHMIDT, K.L. / SCHMIDT, M.A., 'παροικος,' in: *Theological Dictionary of the New* Testament, V, trans. G.W. BROMILEY; ed. G. FREEDRICH (Grand Rapids: Eerdmans, 1967) 840–848.

SCHOLL, Hans, 'The Church and the Poor in the Reformed Tradition', *Ecumenical Review* vol. 32 (1980) 236–56.

SEEBAB, H., בחר, in: *TWNT* I (Stuttgart e.a. 1973), col. 592–608.

SELDERHUIS, Herman J., 'Calvin as an Asylum Seeker', in: *Calvin's Books: Festschrift dedicated to Peter De Klerk on the occasion of his seventieth birthday*, edited by Wilhelm H. NEUSER, Herman J. SELDERHUIS, and Willem VAN'T SPIJKER, 283–300 (Heerenveen: Groen, 1997).

SELDERHUIS, Herman J., *Calvin's Theology of the Psalms* (Grand Rapids 2007).

SETERS, J. van, 'Confessional Reformulation in the Exilic Period', *VT* 22 (1972) 448–459.

SETERS, J. van, *Abraham in History and Tradition* (New Heaven – London: Yale University Press, 1975).

SHOTWELL, Willis A., *A Biblical Exegesis of Justin Martyr* (London: SPCK, 1965).

SIMONETTA BRACCESI, 'Religious Refugees from Lucca in the Sixteenth Century: Political Strategies and Religious Proselytism,' *Archiv fur Reformationsgeschichte* 88 (1997) 338–79.

SMALLEY, Beryl, *The Study of the Bible in the Middle Ages* (Oxford: Basil Balckwell, 1952).

SMITH, D.L., *The Religion of the landless* (Bloomington: Meyer Stone Books, 1989).

SMITH, Donald, 'Calvinist Orthodoxy: Malthus and the Poor', *Passive Obedience and Prophetic Protest* (New York: Peter Lang, 1987) 102–120.

SMITH, M., *Palestinian Parties and Politics that shaped the Old Testament* (New York: Columbia University Press, 1971).

SNAITH, N.H., 'Leviticus and Numbers', *NCBC* (London: Nelson, 1977).

SNIJDERS, L.A., 'The meaning of זר in the OT, an Exegetical Study', *OTS* 10, (1953).

SOKOLOFF, Michael, *A Dictionary of Jewish Palestinian Aramaic of the Byzantine Period,* (Ramat Gan, Israel: Bar Ilan University Press; Baltimore: Johns Hopkins University Press, 2002).

SPENCER, J.R., 'Sojourner', in: *ABD*, Vol. 4 (New York: Doubleday, 1992) 103–104.

SPICER Andrew, *Reformations Old and New: Essays on the Socio-Economic Impact of Religious Change c 1470–1630* (Vermont : Scholar Press, 1996).

SPINA, F.A.,   'Israelites as gerim, 'Sojourners' in Social and Historical Context', in: C.L. MEYERS / M.O. CONNER (ed.), *The word of the Lord shall go forth* (Festschrift D.N. Freedman, Winona Lake 1983).

STEINMETZ, David C., 'Calvin as Interpreter of Genesis', in: *Calvinus Sincerioris Religionis Vindex: Calvin as Protector of the Purer Religion,* ed. Wilhelm H. NEUSER and Brian G. ARMSTRONG, Sixteenth Century Essays & Studies 36 (Kirksville, MO: Sixteenth Century Journal Publishers, 1997) 53–66.

STEINMETZ, David C., 'Luther and Calvin on the Banks of the Jabbok', in: *Luther in Context* (Grand Rapids: Baker, 2002) 156–88.

STEINMETZ, David C., *Calvin in Context* (New York: Oxford University Press, 1995).

STEINMETZ, David C., *Misericordia Dei. The theology of Johannes von Staupitz in its late medieval setting* (Leiden: Brill, 1968).

STEINMETZ, David C., *Reformers in the Wings* (Philadelphia: Fortress Press, 1971).

STEINMETZ, David C., *The Bible in the sixteenth century* (Durham: Duke University Press, 1990).

STROUP, George W., 'Narrative in Calvin's Hermeneutic', in: *Calvin Studies* III (Richmond: Union Theological Seminary in Virginia, 1986).

TCHERIKOVER, G., ''Natives' and 'Foreigners' in Palestine', in: *The Age of the Monarchies: Culture and Society*, A. MALAMAT (ed.), Vol. 4, (Jerusalem: Massada Press, 1979) 87–95.

THOMPSON, John Lee, 'The Endangerment of Lot's Daughters in Sixteenth-Century Exegesis,' in: *Writing the Wrongs: Women of the Old Testament Among Biblical Commentators from Philo Through the Reformation* (Oxford: Oxford University Press, 2001) 214–17.

TIGAY, H. Jeffrey, 'Deuteronomy', *JPS Torah Commentary* (Philadelphia-Jerusalem: Jewish Publication Society, 1996).

TODD, William Newton, *The Function of the Patristic Writings in the Thought of John Calvin* (Th.D. diss., Union Theological Seminary, 1964).

TORRANCE, Thomas F., *The Hermeneutics of John Calvin*, (Edinburgh: Scottish Academic Press, 1988).

TRUEMAN, Carl R., and R. Scott CLARK (eds.), *Protestant Scholasticism: Essays in Reassessment* (Carlisle: Paternoster, 1999).

VAN ROOY, H.F., 'Calvin's Genesis Commentary – Which Bible Text Did He Use?', in: *Our Reformation Studies*, series F, no. 21. (Potchefstroom: Potchefstroom University for Christian Higher Education, 1984).

VAULX, J. DE, 'Refuge', in: *DBS* 9 (Paris 1979) col. 1480–1510.

VAUX, R. DE., *Ancient Israel: Its life and Institutions*, trans. J. MCHUGE (London: Darton, Longman and Todd, 1961).

WALCHENBACH John, *John Calvin as Biblical commentator : an investigation into Calvin's use of John Chrysostom as an exegetical tutor* (Pittsburgh: Univ. of Pittsburgh, 1974).

WEBER, M., *Ancient Judaism*, trans. and ed. H.H. GERTH and D. MARTINDALE (Glencoe: Free Press, 1952).

WEISER, Artur, *Psalms a Commentary*, trans. Herbert HARTWELL (London: SCM Press, 1971).

WELLHAUSEN, J., *Prolegomena to the History of Israel*, trans. J.S. BLACK and A. MENZIES (Gloucester: Peter Smith, 1983).

WILDBERGER, H., 'Israel und sein Land', *EvTh* 16 (1956) 404–422.

WILDBERGER, H., 'בחר bhr erwahlen', in: *THAT* I (Grand Rapids : Eerdmans, 1977), col. 275–300.

WOUDSTRA, Marten, H., 'Calvin Interprets What 'Moses Reports': Observation on Calvin's Commentary on Exodus 1–19', in: *Calvin Theological Journal* 21 (November 1986) 151–74.

WOUDSTRA, Marten, H., 'John Calvin's concern for the Poor,' *The Outlook*, vol. 33 (February 1983) 8–10.

YOON, Kyung Kim, *Hermeneutics and the Law, A Study of Calvin's Commentary and Sermons on Psalm 119* (Th M. Thesis, Calvin Theological Seminary 2000).

ZEITLIN, S., 'Proselytes and Proselytism during the second Commonwealth and Early Tannaitic Period', in: ZEITLIN, S., *Studies in the Early History of Judaism*. Vol II, New York (1974) 407–417.

ZIMMERLI, W., *Ezekiel I*, trans. R.E. CLEMENTS (Philadelphia: Fortress Press, 1979).

ZIMMERLI, W., *Ezekiel II*, trans. J.D. MARTIN (Philadelphia: Fortress Press, 1983).

ZOBEL, H.-J., 'Israel' in Agypten', in: S. KREUTZER / K. LUTHI (Hrsg.), *Zur Aktualitat des Alten Testament, Festschrift G. Sauer Zum 65. Geburtstag* (Frankfurt am Main e.a. 1992) 109–117.

Curriculum vitae

Gopalswamy Jacob (1966) was born in a Hindu family in India. After his conversion to Christianity he studied theology and received his Bachelor of Divinity in 1993 from Serampore College (West Bengal). In 1998, he completed his Master of Theology in the field of Old Testament from United Theological College Bangalore. His Master's thesis was: *The silence of God in the Psalms of Lament*. After serving as lecturer in India Theological Seminary, Karnataka, he moved to pastoral ministry. He was ordained and served as minister in the Reformed Church, Chennai, India. He has translated the *Heidelberg Catechism* and the *Belgic Confession* in Tamil. Further, he translated reformed church liturgies in Tamil for the benefit of the Reformed Churches in India. Gopalswamy Jacob is the founder and chairman of one of the non-profit Christian development organizations which caters 600 children in Tamilnadu. He and his wife Jackie Jessica have two sons, Gerrit and Calvin.

Publicaties van het
Instituut voor Reformatieonderzoek

Editors
Herman J. Selderhuis
William den Boer